The Situated Self

The Situated Self

J. T. ISMAEL

UNIVERSITY PRESS

2007

OXFORD
UNIVERSITY PRESS

Oxford   New York
Auckland   Bangkok   Buenos Aires   Cape Town   Chennai
Dar es Salaam   Delhi   Hong Kong   Istanbul   Karachi   Kolkata
Kuala Lumpur   Madrid   Melbourne   Mexico City   Mumbai   Nairobi
São Paulo   Shanghai   Singapore   Taipei   Tokyo   Toronto

Published by Oxford University Press, Inc.
198 Madison Avenue, New York, New York, 10016

www.oup.com

Oxford is a registered trademark of Oxford University Press.

Library of Congress Cataloging-in-Publication Data

Ismael, Jenann, 1968–
    The situated self / J. T. Ismael.
      p.   cm.
    Includes bibliographical references and index.
    ISBN-13 978-0-19-517436-6
    ISBN 0-19-517436-4
    1. Self (Philosophy)   I. Title.
BD450.I597 2006
126—dc22   2006040061

9 8 7 6 5 4 3 2 1
Printed in the United States of America
on acid-free paper

For Mom
From me and Dad and Shereen

Acknowledgments

Over the years it took me to write this book, I've written acknowledgments in my head more times than I can count, and all I can think to say now, to the small number of very special friends and colleagues who helped in countless ways, is thank you.

Huw Price.

David Chalmers, Richard Healey, John Pollock, Shaughan Lavine, Keith Lehrer.

Ken Taylor. Elijah Millgram.

Recently, Michael Gill, Terry Horgan.

Andy Clark.

Kim Sterelny's comments on an early draft were invaluable.

The students in my seminar in the Spring of 2005, and especially Orlin Vakarelov.

My department head Chris Maloney. My very patient editor Peter Ohlin and my production editor Gwen Colvin for her superhuman forbearance.

Three old debts, dearly held and long in repayment, Paul Benacerraf, Dick Jeffrey, Tyler Burge.

Above all, my parents and my sister.

The manuscript was originally written during a six-month sabbatical spent at the Institut Jean Nicod in Paris, and I am grateful to them, and especially to Joelle Proust, for friendship and hospitality. The most substantial rewriting was done during a year at the National Humanities Center under support of the National Endowment for the Humanities. I am very grateful for their support and I can't imagine a more gracious host. Finally, I'm grateful to my nieces, Aisha and Nadia, for making the summer, the book was finished fun. Paul Teller and his graduate reading group at the University of California, Davis, read the completed manuscript, and their penetrating comments came at just the right time. Many thanks.

Contents

The Situated Self

I

Introduction

There are some problems in philosophy that give you vertigo, and for the type of philosopher that is attracted to these kinds of problems, the question 'What am I?' is irresistible. There is a long tradition in philosophy, supported by powerfully persuasive arguments, that holds that selves resist incorporation into the natural order, i.e., that we cannot be mere things among things. The facts about our reflective view of ourselves that underwrite the philosophical arguments are closely related to the pressures that lead to the instinctive dualism of the man on the Clapham Omnibus. They include the intimacy of reflexive representation and its immunity to error, the privacy and the irreducible quality of our mental lives, the ability to separate oneself in imagination from all of one's properties, and the simplicity and apparent unanalyzability of the notion of a self. This book is an attempt to gain some understanding of these pressures, to isolate them, and to see if they can be resolved. I see them as formal difficulties rooted in the structure of reflexive thought and argue that the obstacles they present to a naturalistic conception of the self are resolved when we adopt an embedded, embodied view of mind. In part I, I introduce the embedded view, taking a model of the mind derived from Frege as foil, and using an adaptation of Putnam's Model-Theoretic Argument to motivate the transition. I argue that the Fregean Model has anomalies that reveal a deeper, supporting structure. In part II, I work through some of the most currently influential arguments for dualism and say where they go wrong. In part III, I turn to issues concerning the identification and individuation of selves, arguing again that the supporting structure that resolves the anomalies of section 1 and undermines the dualist arguments discussed in part II also provides the solution to problems that arise in this connection.

We can introduce the context in which thought about the self arises with a myth of origin that goes something like this.[1] Sometime between the time of the primordial sludge and the present, the world separated itself into little pockets of functionally integrated structure, enclosing them in packages of skin and putting internal subsystems—minds—in control of certain of their gross behaviors. At first, the subsystems were effectively encapsulated information-processing units that served as loci for informational pathways converging from across the landscape. The outer surfaces of the pockets intercepted signals sent from their surroundings, which were fed through a system of internal wiring that brought them to bear on behavior. Eventually, the pockets grew legs. Mobility provided a potential advantage in exploiting resources, but disturbed the natural informational pathways. The pockets no longer bore continuing perceptual links to particular places or properties. Signals carried information about different places on different occasions, and a type of signal that indicated one property in one context indicated something else in another. One solution to this dilemma is to allow systems some mobility, but confine them to an ecological niche within which the properties of interest have relatively stable sensory representations. Another is to have systems construct an internal model of the world, on which their positions and changing sensory states can be plotted and explicitly related to places and properties of interest. The internal model can serve as an effective storehouse for information about places and properties with which the pockets are not in continuous sensory contact, allowing them to track objects across changes in position, and properties across changes in sensory representation.[2] The arrangement succeeds by combining objective representation with a system of self-location that loosens the internal ties between *ideas* and sensory representations to counterbalance the loosening of external ties between *things* and their sensory representations, in a manner orchestrated to preserve

---

1. This sketch is meant to evoke Dennett's story in "The Origin of Selves."

2. It is convenient to generalize the notion of mobility so that it applies not simply to movement across space but movement across kinds of context. Therefore, I will speak of variation in lighting conditions, or the change from an aerobic to an anaerobic environment, as movement whether or not they involve change of spatial location. What we need to know, in order to understand the kinds of internal structure that an agent needs in order to maintain stable links will depend on how mobile it is, in this sense, i.e., how much actual variation there is in the environments to which it is exposed.

continuing links between ideas and things. The pocket whose activity is controlled by an internal model of the environment, unlike more primitive cousins that respond directly to stimuli, is able both to establish and maintain the stable informational links with parts of the external landscape even while those parts are not making a direct impact in the form of experience, and to accommodate changes in the context-dependent informational content of sensory states.

The business of building up an internal image of the landscape is a demanding task, and pockets are hindered by limited energy and information, restricted to what they can glean from a very short history of experience, in a small region of space, across a small number of circumstances. It isn't until a network of informational pathways is set up between pockets by language—prosthetic links supported by agreement among the senders and receivers of the information—that the full potential of the additional structure is realized. The new network makes the informational and cognitive resources of the community of newly interconnected pockets available to each part of it, and allows them to embark on the collective task of building up a communal image of the environment. Information is shared, labor is divided, learning accumulates and gets passed across generations. The collective memory embodied in genes and inherited behaviors is thus supplemented with specific information recorded in plastic media whose effect on behavior is regulated by the agents themselves. It is of fundamental importance in understanding our own minds that most of our information now comes to us through socially and linguistically mediated channels. Instead of navigating a natural environment by the sounds and smells of predator and prey, we navigate environments of our own design by signs and labels that we invent. And the stream of carefully selected information that the world funneled to us through natural channels has become an indiscriminate torrent of news concerning countless different times and places, from sources that bear no fixed connection to the information they carry; information that has been tagged and ripped from its source, and needs to be reassembled after it enters the head.

It's within the rich representational environment of an explicit model of the world that the mind can reflect, raising questions about its own nature and the relations between the properties it exemplifies and those it represents. I will be looking first at the role that reflexive constructions play in guiding the internal course of the information coming into the mind, managing its impact on the internal model of the landscape, and choreographing its effect on behavior. I will then look at the way that reflexive constructions interact with the nonreflexive representations embodied in the model. I'll be arguing that in order to understand that interaction we need an approach to the mind that treats dynamical relations—covariation relative to a range of contexts—as the fundamental relations between mind and world rather than intentional relations—*of* ness or *about*ness—that are treated as fundamental on the Fregean Model. On the dynamical approach, the components of thought are conceived not as abstract objects that bear their intentional properties essentially, but as mental particulars with a role in the internal dynamics of moving agents and only nonintrinsic (causal/informational) relations to their referents. The central notions are representational media and coordination. Representational media are effectively information channels, and to coordinate a medium with its subject matter is to establish and maintain the causal and contextual relations in virtue of which its states carry the information they do across the range of contexts in which they are employed. There are three interacting representational media in the story above: experience, language, and thought. Experience is the medium in which Mother Nature speaks to a subject. The signals sent out by objects in the world are conveyed to the world in the form of patterns of light, color, sound, and so forth. Thought is a representational medium through which information flows from one part of the subject to another. Language is an interpersonal medium that provides the channels through which information flows between subjects. Reflexive constructions do their work in the spaces between media; they play an essential role in mediating the interactions among these media, and between these media and their common subject matter.

Because the vocabulary of coordination and representational media is not a familiar part of the philosophical lexicon, this section requires a bit of new, but simple and intuitive, apparatus. In its favor, I can say that it abstracts from inessential detail, provides a general framework that brings the relations that are important for understanding reflexive constructions into relief, and avoids some of the specific misunderstandings that arise from more familiar vocabulary. We start with a generic notion of information that applies both to natural media and those that involve an element of convention, and we focus on the way that experience, thought, and language interact in the exchange of information. This is an extremely abstract level of description,[3] but it is the one at which the formal relationships I am interested in stand out clearly. Since one needn't hold that all features of thought or language can be reconstructed at this level, philosophers with richer conceptions of mental and linguistic content

---

3. Linguistic interactions that don't involve the exchange of information (e.g., thanking, reassuring, insulting, and so on), for example, simply don't register on this level, just as a good deal goes on in economic interactions that doesn't register in the exchange of goods. The difference between giving something to B and B stealing it, for example, has nothing to do with who got what from whom.

don't make concessions to reductionism by relaxing into it. We learn much if we follow the information, become familiar with the mechanics of transporting it, the formal requirements on media that carry it, and the epistemological demands on recipients. We get used to the idea that all media have contexts of application. And we become sensitive to the lighter demands on media that are applied in restricted contexts, cognizant of the requirements on translating into media with wider contexts, and comfortable with the idea that the information-bearing properties of media are always relativized to their users and contexts of use. All media move information across particular kinds of contextual divide; they provide channels for the propagation of information among more or less vaguely delineated classes of interlocutors. We can state this by saying that media have limited range, if range is understood not in terms of distance but in terms of the transformations of context and interlocutor that a medium can withstand. All of this will help us understand why reflective thought has the properties that it does.

The insight that the notion of information, because it spans the space of both the internal and external goings-on, provides the right conceptual vantage point from which to understand the relations between mind and world is taken from Fred Dretske and others. It allows us to give a unified dynamical description that passes smoothly from the physical transitions that govern the flow of information in the natural environment to the conceptual transitions that govern the flow of information in thought. The element that's missing from the information-theoretic framework up to this point is a clear account of the difference between a system that uses information contained in sensory states to navigate and one that steers by an explicit internal model in which those states are explicitly represented and related to the environment. I zero in on that part of the picture, that is, on the construction of explicit internal self-models, the mechanics of steering by these models, the dynamical advantages that accrue to their employment, and the role of reflexive structures in keeping them centered. But the focus on explicit modeling is adamantly *not* meant to suggest that I hold that all or even most of the interesting activity in the mind involves self-modeling. I take it for granted that the part of the mind that is explicitly engaged in self-modeling is only a small part of the distributed machine that controls behavior, a late addition to a largely self-organizing bureaucracy, with a limited role. Human behavior is the product of a potent combination of emergent organization and directed control. But I do think that something of real cognitive interest happens when a system begins to self-model. It's an empirical question how widespread this internal modeling is, and whether it extends beyond the simple map keeping that has been observed, for example, in mice. I suggest that at least some apparently uniquely human cognitive capacities can be traced to the explicit representation of the intrinsic properties of our informational states and, if that is right, it marks an important discontinuity between humans and other animals. The mind's internal portrait of itself creates the space for reflective thought. It is here that the conundra that lead us to dualism arise. However, it will be one of the recurrent themes throughout the book that the resolution of those conundra requires us to take a wider view, to see the self-representing subsystem in the mind in the context of the larger dynamical system in which it is embedded, and to look beyond or below the self-models at the wiring and connections that keep the information flowing smoothly into it, and then back out again.

I have made opportunistic use of the work of many, in some cases freely adapting views and arguments when it served the argumentative contexts. In other cases, I simply acknowledge a debt and try to build on work without repeating it. John Perry's account of the reflexive structure of indexical expressions has been kicking around in my head for some time, and when his books came out in 2000,[4] I found that he was saying with a different emphasis but more clearly and elegantly much of what I had already written about their role in coordinating perception and action with thought. I took over his terminology and changed my focus to parts of the puzzle that he didn't elaborate. Velleman's Lockean theory of the identity of selves provided the crucial piece of the puzzle in section 3, showing how the causal links that are hidden from the subject could be constitutive of his identity over time, while also providing the springboard for the response to Dennett in the chapter that follows. From Dennett I have plundered unscrupulously, taking much but leaving behind some of what he would regard as precious. A less salient, but more seminal influence is Anscombe, whose paper "The First Person" convinced me that the fundamental dichotomy in thought—the one behind the familiar dualisms of mind and matter, subject and object—was the first-person versus third-person one. It is a lesson that can also be learned from Nagel, who has been persistently, and with great philosophical sensitivity, chronicling the way that the problem of relating the first-person and third-person points of view expresses itself. The image that has always struck me in this connection, one that I return to at end of the book, is that of an Escher picture with the Self providing the ambiguous structure, for example, the corner that has to be interpreted as protruding in the context of one interpretation, receding in the context of the other, or the step that has to be interpreted as leading up in the context of one interpretation, down in the context of the other.

4. See Perry's *Reference and Reflexivity*, and *Knowledge, Possibility, and Consciousness*.

PART I

The Situated Mind

This section introduces and motivates a view of the mind that contrasts with traditional representationalist approaches in treating a dynamical relation—coordination—as the basic mind-world relation. The complex, ongoing business of getting and keeping thought coordinated with the world is examined, with special attention to the role of reflexive structures.

2

Traditional Representationalism

Here is a bit of reconstructive background history painted in broad strokes that will be useful to set the stage philosophically for the view of the mind that I will be recommending. Frege put in place a way of understanding the relationship between language, the mind, and the world that dominated philosophy in the English-speaking world for a century and a half. Frege himself was a mathematician; his primary interest was in thought about mathematical objects, and he was not hesitant to dismiss features of natural language that he regarded as *merely* linguistic.[1] The combination of interest and attitude led to Frege's blindness toward the context sensitivity of thought, for although Frege recognized that languages contain devices whose referents depend on their context of use, he denied that this was in any way revelatory of the structure of thought.[2] The last thirty years of philosophy of language have made us less glib about the ways in which

1. One of the most often cited passages in his work reads: "It is one of the tasks of philosophy to break the domination of the word over the human mind by laying bare the misconceptions that through the use of language almost unavoidably arise concerning the relations between concepts and by freeing thought from that which only the means of expression of ordinary language, constituted as they are, saddle it." See *Begriffsschrift*, in *Frege and Gödel*, ed. J. van Heijenoort, 70.

2. As he says: "To every expression belonging to a complete totality of signs, there should certainly correspond a definite sense; but natural languages often do not satisfy this condition, and one must be content if the same word has the same sense in the same context." Ibid., 58.

representation—both in language and in thought—depends on contextual, nonintentional relations between thinkers and the objects of thought, but the modifications have been mostly conservative and Frege's framework has been largely retained.

The central notion of Frege's model of thought is that of a sense. It is introduced in a famous passage from "On Sense and Reference," in which he writes:

> It is natural, now, to think of there being connected with a sign . . . besides that to which the sign refers, which may be called the reference of the sign, also what I should like to call the sense of the sign, wherein the mode of presentation is contained. . . . The sense . . . is grasped by everybody who is sufficiently familiar with the language or the totality of designations [signs] to which it belongs.[3]

Senses are explicated and invoked in Frege's writings in ways that have generated exegetical dispute.[4] And Frege's followers have rejected elements of his view about which there was no dispute. But most of them shared with Frege the view that the internal character of a thought—the intrinsic nature of its components and the way they are put together—determines what the thought is about. They shared the view, that is to say, that sense determines reference, where senses were conceived as bearing their semantic properties essentially. What a sense refers to was held to be independent of when or where it is deployed and utterly impervious to any facts about the situation of the speaker who deploys it.[5]

I will treat this as the defining thesis of the Fregean Model.[6] The continuing influence of the Fregean Model is witnessed by flipping through almost any textbook in psychology or the philosophy of mind. Here, for example, is the first line in a widely used psychology textbook:

> The study of cognitive development is dominated by the view that concepts are essentially packets of theory-like knowledge . . . though there have been and continue to be many variations and disagreements concerning the character of the associated knowledge. The essence of this family of views is that the knowledge packet

---

3. Ibid., 57–58.

4. For a helpful and historically sensitive discussion, see Burge, "Sinning against Frege."

5. Burge, too, treats this as the defining feature of a Fregean sense. He writes: "A trademark of a Fregean [sense] is that . . . nothing in its expression or in its being thought affects its referential relations. *Its relation to its referent depends purely on its own nature and on the inventory of the world.*" Ibid., 430, my emphasis.

6. To call this a Fregean Model is like calling a stick figure a portrait of George Washington, although Frege's influence and the centrality of the doctrine in his own thought give it a claim to his name.

associated with the concept determines what in the world a given concept refers to or designates—it fixes what the concept is a concept of.[7]

As I mentioned, Frege himself recognized that there are expressions in natural language whose relations to their referents are not determined by an associated sense, but, in part, by contextual properties of tokens. 'I', for example, refers to the person who utters it, and 'here' to the place, and 'now' to the time of utterance. To recognize that there are no individuating senses linguistically associated with these expressions allows that there may always be denoting senses associated with the thoughts they are used to express. One way to resist the implication that we can make identifying reference in thought to objects other than by employing an individuating sense is to hold—as Frege expressly did—that indexicals are specialized linguistic devices that allow us to express thoughts in a psychologically neutral way, although there are no indexical *thoughts*. Thoughts are made up of senses and their senses determine their reference. On the face of it, without any restriction on the kinds of things that can serve as a sense, the thesis can seem hard to dispute. What could it mean, after all, to be thinking about an object or property A (as against B or C) if not that you have something in mind—an idea, a concept, some perhaps attenuated description—that denotes it?[8] In fact, however, there were some important dissenting voices urging the recognition of thoughts whose reference, or subject matter, is not determined by the nature of their components and the way those components are put together. There were voices that urged that there are thoughts whose truth conditions depend directly on who has them, the time and the place at which they are had, or the context in which they occur. Many of the arguments that were given as support presented examples of thoughts that were supposed to have this property, while others had a broadly transcendental character. The latter tended to be inspired by Kant and suggested that non-Fregean thoughts of this kind are needed to ground Fregean thoughts.

2.1   BURGE ON BELIEF DE RE

Burge's discussion in "Belief *de re*" is a landmark in early dissension from the Fregean orthodoxy. *De re* beliefs, for Burge, are beliefs about objects where there are no individuating senses or ideas, nothing in the head at all

---

7. See A. Leslie, "How to Acquire a Representational Theory of Mind," 197.
8. I use 'denote' always in application to concepts, and to mean 'applies to'.

that can serve as a component of thought whose intentional properties pick out the object that the belief is about. The facts in virtue, of which a *de re* belief is about the relevant *res*, are external to the believer and her state, determined immediately by contextual relations between her and the objects of belief. In Burge's words:

> There will often be no term or individual concept in the believer's set of beliefs about the relevant object which *denotes* that object. This is not to deny that the believer always has some mental or se-mantical instrument for picking out the object—a set of concepts, a perceptual image, and a demonstrative. But whatever means the be-liever has often depends for its success partly but irreducibly on fac-tors . . . not part of the mental or linguistic repertoire of the believer.[9]

Burge argues for the existence of such beliefs in the early part of the paper by bringing out the psychological implausibility of holding in par-ticular cases that speakers possess individuating concepts. Arguments of this sort are, by their nature, inconclusive because they require estab-lishing psychological premises (viz., that the speakers in question have no identifying knowledge) that opponents will simply deny. It is always at least arguable that there is something in the head—even an extrinsic description like 'the stuff in Lake Michigan', 'the disease the doctors at Harvard call "arthritis"', or 'the guy logicians call "Godel"'—that picks out the object.

These considerations can be strengthened in an almost decisive way, however, which Burge curiously mentions only in passing. The trick is not to look for cases in which speakers achieve reference in the absence of individuating concepts, but to look for cases in which they possess indi-viduating concepts, although their thoughts are not *about* the objects those concepts denote. The most obvious examples are first-person thoughts by delusional subjects, or cases in which thinkers have mistaken ideas about the time or place at which they entertain a now-thought or here-thought. The literature on indexicals is full of examples like this; there is the case of the deluded Heimson who believes of himself everything that is actually true of Hume. He believes, for example, that he was born in Edinburgh, wrote the *Treatise*, loves backgammon, and so on, so he associates with his use of 'I' a fully individuating sense that, in fact, denotes Hume. Or there is Rip van Winkle who awakens from his long rest with a fully individ-uating but mistaken conception of the date. He believes of the present moment everything that is, in fact, true of the day on which he entered his

9. Burge, "Sinning against Frege," 352.

slumber. If the reference of one's 'I'—and 'now'—thoughts are whatever is denoted by the associated sense, Heimson's I-thoughts ought to be about Hume, and Rip van Winkle's now-thoughts ought to be about times long ago. But they are not. There is no temptation whatsoever to think that the deluded Heimson's I-tokens refer to anybody but Heimson, even though the rich and fully individuating concept he associates with them applies unequivocally to Hume.[10] The contextual elements don't merely supplement the conceptual ones and individuate when there isn't enough information, they *trump*; in at least some cases—paradigmatically, thoughts about oneself, the present moment, and one's own location—it is *contextual* relations between thinkers, or particular temporally situated thinking events, and the world that are unequivocally determinative of reference. That is not the end of the story; enough ink has been spilled about these sorts of cases, in the time since Burge wrote, to fill Lake Michigan. Frege himself notoriously held that every person has a uniquely individuating sense that is not available to others, and that serves as sense in her I-thoughts. The same treatment would have to be extended to 'now' to get the right results in the Rip Van Winkle case. This would require that every subject has a uniquely individuating, infallibly accurate sense associated with every moment in time, that can only be entertained in thoughts occurring at the moment in question. Together these could plausibly yield individuating senses for anything that could be referred to using indexicals. 'Here', for example, would be associated with the sense [the place that I am now located], 'you' would be associated with the sense [the person to whom I am speaking]. The result is clumsy, but it gets the truth conditions right.

Toward the end of the article, Burge suggests, more tentatively, some broadly transcendental considerations for the doctrine that *de re* attitudes are prior to, and necessary for, fully conceptualized thoughts of the sort that the Fregean Model is well suited to describe. I mention them because they are important precursors to what will follow. One is a developmental argument to the effect that language learning would be impossible without indexical thoughts:

> It is hard to imagine how one could learn a language without being exposed to sentences whose truth value changed over relatively short periods of time. If the truth value of certain sentences were not keyed to salient and changeable aspects of the immediate environment, the neophyte would have no means of catching on to the

---

10. The example comes from Kaplan, "Demonstratives."

meaning of the sounds he hears—no means of correlating those sounds with an independently identifiable parameter. Attitudes acquired in the process of understanding such sounds are *de re*.[11]

The other argues that we wouldn't attribute genuine objective thought (i.e., thought about the world) to a being who didn't also have at least some *de re* thoughts, i.e., to a being who couldn't identify contextually presented particulars, in at least some cases, as the extensions of its concepts.

> It would be widely agreed that current machines that are programmed with indexical-free (mathematical) language do not autonomously use or understand language. What is missing? Such machines do nothing to indicate that the symbols *have any semantical, extralinguistic significance.* To indicate this, they should be able, at least sometimes, to recognize and initiate correlations between symbols and what they symbolize.[12]

A being who failed to recognize word-world connections, no matter how adept at manipulating words and relating them to one another, would not be, he is suggesting, regarded as using those words to *refer*. Both of these arguments suggest not only that speakers have *de re* thoughts but also that such thoughts are prior to, and necessary for, Fregean thoughts. They suggest that without the intentionally unmediated connections between *de re* thoughts and their subject matter, there are no intentionally mediated ones, either. Genuinely representational states must be connected in an inferential network that includes conceptually unmediated reference. Aside from gestures at perceptual and demonstrative beliefs, memory, introspective beliefs, and thoughts about oneself, Burge says little about the nature of these intentionally unmediated relations, ending the article with a call for a systematic account.[13]

Although more explicitly responding to Strawson, who was arguing along similar lines,[14] Evans's influential discussion of demonstrative identification in *Varieties of Reference* can be seen as the beginning of an answer to Burge's call. Evans's distinction between identification-dependent and identification-free reference is essentially Burge's distinction between belief *de re* and (purely) *de dicto* belief. Like Burge, Evans argues that perceptual

---

11. "Sinning against Frege," 347.

12. Ibid., 348.

13. "The lead role of *de re* attitudes is sponsored by a contextual, not purely conceptual relation between thinkers and objects. . . . There is no adequate general explication of the appropriate nonconceptual relation(s). . . . Developing such an explication would, I think, help articulate the epistemic notion of intuition in its broadest, least technical sense, and contribute to our understanding of understanding." See "Sinning against Frege," 262.

14. See Strawson, *Individuals*.

and demonstrative reference is identification-free, and that identification-free knowledge is both irreducible and prior to the identification-dependent kind.[15] Evans had a good deal to say in a positive vein, about what these nonintentional relations are. And much of what he said has been absorbed into the information-theoretic picture Dretske, Perry, and others have developed. The picture requires something of a gestalt shift from the Fregean way of conceiving of thought, and I'll introduce it with one of Perry's early discussions.

2.2 PERRY: THOUGHT WITHOUT REPRESENTATION

What is it to be able to think about an object? One way is to have a thought with a Fregean component that denotes it, but Perry's suggestion is that there is another way, which he describes by saying that one can have it as an unarticulated constituent of one's thought. An unarticulated constituent of a thought is an object, event, or property reference to which needs to be made in specification of its truth conditions, but which is not designated by any of its semantically significant components. By way of explication, Perry introduces a population of folks who live in a place called Z-land, and spend a lot of time talking about the weather. We suppose initially that they don't talk to travelers, and have no phones or radios, so that the only place for which they get any information about weather is Z-land, and when they talk (and think) about the weather, they make no explicit reference to Z-land. They say simply 'it is raining', 'tomorrow will be sunny, with high clouds', 'I hope there is snow this winter'. If the weather reports and beliefs of Z-landers are controlled by weather in Z-land, and if these reports and beliefs play the right role in specifically Z-land–directed behavior, then—Perry is suggesting—they are about (or, in his terminology, they *concern*) weather in Z-land, whether or not Z-land is explicitly represented in them, that is, whether Z-landers even have the concept of space or the resources to individuate places conceptually. What makes the Z-landers' weather thoughts thoughts about weather in Z-land is not their internal nature (i.e., what parts they have, how those parts are arranged), on this view, but by Z-landers' situation, (i.e., by how weather thoughts are entered in the heads of Z-landers, in the causal chains running from perception to action).

---

15. "Judgments involving Ideas which give rise to the possibility of identification-free knowledge have an epistemological priority over judgments involving all other Ideas of objects: were there no such judgments or Ideas, no singular knowledge would be possible." See Evans, *Varieties of Reference*, 181. Evans uses 'Idea of an object' in a technical sense to refer to something that provides a basis for identification.

What makes Z-land an unarticulated constituent of Z-lander weather beliefs is the sensitivity of those beliefs, unmediated by any representation of place, to weather in Z-land, and the Z-land–directed behavior to which those reports and the beliefs they express give rise. There are two separable components here: the informational link between weather beliefs and Z-land, on the one hand, and the role of those beliefs about the weather in determination of behavior. Ordinarily, we need to keep track of the places we are getting information about—perceptually, from newspapers, through reports from others, and so on—and relate them explicitly to the places from which we act. Usually it is the weather in Tucson that determines whether I carry an umbrella; if I will be in Vancouver tomorrow, however, I had better check the forecast there. Information about different places bears differentially on behavior in a manner that depends directly on where we are located, and one needs to keep track of both and relate them to each other in order to know how to behave. What is special about the case of the Z-landers is that since all of the weather information they receive concerns Z-land, and all of their activity takes place there as well, the connection between perception and action can be secured directly. There is no practical need for an intervening Z-land proxy.

This early paper of Perry's is tremendously suggestive in encouraging the broad perspective that is partly developed in his own later work, but also, much more explicitly, in the view that is emerging from the parts of AI that have traded in the old computational model of mind as disembodied processor of symbols for one that sees it as a component of an embodied system designed to solve practical rather than theoretical problems—problems about how to get the system to move the way appropriate to its circumstances, whose terms are imposed by all kinds of contextual contingencies, and whose solutions are inveterately local and bound to context. The point of the world-representing structure in the head on this dynamical approach is not to mirror Nature, but to set up the links between elements in a structured internal landscape and the external space that keep the body moving in the right directions. Once one is thinking in these terms, it is easy to see that under certain conditions *representation* isn't the most efficient way to achieve the desired coordination. If all that an agent needs is to know what is going on in her own neighborhood, it suffices to give her a source of information whose states have an implicitly indexical spatial content. The content of the states will vary with her location in a way that keeps her behavior attuned to where she is located, relieving her of the burden of explicitly keeping track. She never mistakenly acts on irrelevant information because she only gets information that is immediately relevant to action. Why, then, do we represent? Our own experience has an implicitly indexical spatial and temporal

informational content, and for the purposes of keeping behavior at <,>
attuned to what is going on at <, >, we could be wired to respond immediately to experience. The answer, again implicit in this early article and
fully developed in Perry's later work, is that we need to register and record
the time and place at which sensory information is acquired if we want to
store it, combine it with information acquired at different places and times,
and bring it to bear on action undertaken at yet other places and times. Our
internal representations of the world serve as a kind of clearinghouse where
information, ripped from the context in which it is acquired, is deposited,
stored, and retrieved on demand. The advantage to the agent is a drastic
increase of the information available for the regulation of behavior. No
longer limited to information contained in her occurrent perceptual states,
an agent can bring all of the information accumulated over a history of
experience to bear on every act.

This conception of ideas, not as Platonic objects, but as mental particulars, located in a nexus of informational connections with the world
is a fundamental reorientation in our way of thinking about the mind.
The emphasis on their practical role in coordinating the behavior of the
embodied, embedded agent is a further, equally important, shift. Perry's
proposal is our first glimpse of the dynamical underbelly of Fregean
thought. Once one begins thinking in these terms, it is a small step to begin
to see increasing amounts of our cognitive activity as a matter of nonconceptual interaction among the brain, the body, and the environment, and
the traditional, hyperintellectualist conception of thought embodied in the
Fregean Model emerges as an accurate image of only a tiny portion of
cognition, most of which is, like the proverbial iceberg, hidden from the
gaze of consciousness. We are systems designed by nature to navigate a
complex and changing environment; the capacity for thought that con-
forms to the Fregean Model is a consequential but relatively recent ecological development, one that is parasitic on, and necessarily embedded in a
context of, nonconceptual, nonintellectual interactions among the brain,
body, and world. Brooks, Clark, Hutchins, Haugeland, and many others in
AI, fueled by research in robotics, complex systems analysis, and cognitive
psychology have made huge steps in elaborating the alternative picture, and
it constitutes a powerful rival to the image of mind embodied in the Fregean
tradition.

3

Confinement

In the last chapter I introduced the Fregean Model of Thought, pointed to mutterings of dissent from it within the Fregean tradition, and discussed an early paper of Perry's that introduced a way of thinking that allowed for departures from its defining thesis. In this section I want to argue more decisively that some non-Fregean form of reference-determination has to be recognized.

3.1   THE MODEL-THEORETIC ARGUMENT

The defining thesis of the Fregean Model of Thought is that sense determines reference. Senses are assumed to be individuating concepts. If you collect together all of your beliefs about an object, A, some subset of those beliefs will jointly constitute the sense that you associate with 'A', and 'A' will refer to that object, whatever it is, denoted by the associated sense. Applied globally, this view about what determines the extensions of concepts is what Lewis refers to as 'global descriptivism', and he interpreted Putnam's Model-Theoretic Argument as showing that it has the consequence that consistency and cardinality are the only alethic constraints on belief. If global descriptivism is true, according to Lewis the only way to form false beliefs is to believe contradictions or mistake the world's cardinality.[1] The only way that the world can genuinely *guide* the formation of belief is if the direction of determination—in at least *some* cases—goes from reference to sense rather than the other way around; there must be some cases in which that in virtue of which 'A' represents what it does is independent of, and prior to, the 'A'-containing beliefs we form. Lewis stated this by saying that there must be external constraints on reference.

Quite aside from the question of whether Lewis's rendering of the argument is correct, his version is certainly valid. The kernel of insight is a recognition of the practical impotence of inner acts of intending that our ideas refer to this or that feature of the landscape for establishing any genuine mind-world connection of a kind that translates into constraints on belief. A complete internal catalogue of referential intentions in the form of a model-theoretic mapping ("[dogs] refers to dogs, [snow] refers to snow, . . .") is at best descriptive of mind-world links; it cannot establish them. I'm going to give an adaptation of the argument, even further removed from Putnam's original formulation and without trying to be faithful to his intentions, that brings out the conclusion of importance for my purposes.[2] Don't think of it as an interpretation of Putnam's argument; think of it as an argument inspired by Lewis's version of Putnam's Model-Theoretic Argument. I'll call it the Argument from Confinement.

The Argument from Confinement

Assume:

1. Confinement: the mind only has representationally unmediated access to its own contents.
2. Voluntarism: what our ideas represent is 'up to us'.
3. Externality: representation is an external relation; it doesn't supervene on the intrinsic properties of its *relata*.

These are all theses drawn from Putnam's presentations of the argument. Apropos of Confinement, he writes:

> The mind never compares an image or word with an object, but only with other images, words, beliefs, judgments, etc. . . . On any theory,

---

1. Putnam alludes also to empirical constraints. I have omitted these because, unless the sense-determines-reference thesis is qualified to allow external constraints on observational vocabulary, empirical constraints are empty.

2. The argument has a fraught history. Lewis's version has had tremendous influence, but it is a contentious question whether Lewis captured Putnam's intentions.

when the child learns the use of the word 'table', what happens is that the word is linked in certain complex ways ('associations') to certain mental phenomena.[3]

Apropos of Voluntarism, he writes:

On any view, the understanding of the language must determine the reference of the terms.[4]

Also,

The world doesn't pick models or interpret languages. *We* interpret our languages or nothing does.[5]

And again,

The idea that the 'non-psychological' fixes reference—i.e., that nature itself determines what our words stand for is totally unintelligible.[6]

Apropos of Externality:

The correspondence C [between ideas, or terms in a mental vocabulary, and the world] being a relation to things which are external and mind-independent, is itself something outside the mind, something 'external'![7]

Now we argue from these premises that there is no way for the world to guide our internal representational activity. The reasoning is as follows. If the way things are in the world is to guide how the mind represents these things as being, the mind has to be able to specify relations between the components of thought and the world independent of which thoughts it decides to have. The way things are arranged in the world, together with the relation between things in the world and the components of thought, has to dictate, or constrain, the formation of thought. If it were in the mind's power to pick out ideas with one hand and parts of the world with the other, this could be done by producing a catalogue of <idea, object> pairs. But if the mind makes use of ideas in picking out objects, what it ends up with is either empty, or presupposes that the very links it was trying to set up are already in place: e.g., {<'dog', referent of 'dog'>, <'cat', referent of 'cat'>...}. Specifying its interpretation in this way would

---

3. See Putnam, *Realism and Reason*, viii.
4. Putnam, "Models and Reality," in ibid., 24.
5. Putnam, Ibid., ix.
6. Ibid., xii.
7. Ibid., 207.

require a view of the mind and its relation to the environment from the outside, and this violates Confinement. Here is how Putnam puts in the introduction to *Realism and Reason*:

> I can't simply pick one particular correspondence C and will (or stipulate) that C is to be the designated correspondence relation, because in order to do that I would need already to be able to think about the correspondence C—and C [is] 'external'![8]

If we are confined to constraining interpretation 'from the inside', there is a familiar way to do it. We construct a model and let it act as an implicit definition of its components. So, for example, we build a map and stipulate that points on the map represent their *relata* under the best-fitting interpretation (characterizing 'best-fitting' in a way that yields a relatively determinate interpretation under plausible assumptions about the size and complexity of the domain). The procedure has been formalized for the linguistic case by the Ramsey-Lewis-Horwich account of the interpretation of theoretical terms.[9] That procedure would need to be extended in the present context to yield an interpretation of all nonlogical vocabulary. The formal presentation of the procedure can make it look arcane, but Lewis illustrates it nicely with the mundane example of a detective theorizing about the unknown perpetrator of a crime. In asserting 'Jack the Ripper did this, that, and the other', the detective partly *hypothesizes* that there is a single culprit at the root of this, that, and the other, and partly *stipulates* that the relevant individual be called 'Jack the Ripper'. To say that 'Jack the Ripper' is just the detective's new name for the bad guy, whoever it might turn out to be, is to say that the detective's Jack-the-Ripper-Theory implicitly defines 'Jack the Ripper'. The theory can be extended indefinitely without altering the basic procedure. The detective could have hypothesized, for instance, that there were a couple of related culprits jointly responsible for the crimes, or perhaps a whole network of underground bandits who characteristically manifest themselves in just such bloody work, identifying them collectively by their joint crimes and individually by their relations to one another and their roles therein, coining names for the group and each of its members.

It makes perfect sense to say that this procedure, generalized, is how ideas get hooked up with external things; we construct a vast internal representation, postulating a set of objects arranged in a system of external

---

8. Ibid.

9. See Lewis, "How to Define Theoretical Terms." Carnap, in the *Aufbau*, seems to have been the only one to have attempted the full reconstruction.

relations and characterized internally by a tangle of related properties, all related to the world by the intention that they refer to whatever bits of the world actually exhibit the network of postulated relations. Our tools for hooking onto the world are fashioned from the inside, and they hook onto whatever bits of itself the world offers up where they fall. The problem with this is that it leaves us without a sense to assign the idea that the way the world is *guides* the construction process. This is what the formal part of Putnam's argument is supposed to demonstrate for the case in which the representation has the form of a first-order theory. If we can't set up relations between the elements in a representational network and the domain of representation *before* we start arranging them into an image of that domain, how we arrange them is unconstrained by the way things stand in the domain. Setting up such relations, however, is precluded by Confinement and Externality, for it would require setting up an external relation between two classes in terms that appeal only to what is intrinsic to one. And since external relations are precisely relations that don't supervene on the intrinsic properties of their *relata*, this would seem ruled out *by definition*, as it were. One might as well try to specify the spatial relationship between the earth and the moon mentioning only the intrinsic properties of the earth.

Putnam is not denying that there are external relations between mental and physical properties and particulars: causal-informational links, for example. The problem is that there are also *schmausal*-informational and *schnausal*-informational links (i.e., the relation a mental state bears to a physical one just in case the ones occurring, respectively, three and four minutes earlier were caused by it) and no way for the mind to single out the causal rather than the schmausal or schnausal ones as determinative of the real world *relata* of its ideas. Framing thoughts like '[cat] represents cats' is idle for purposes of relating [cat] to cats; the most it can do is act as a partial implicit definition of [represents]. In general, if our access to a domain, Y, is mediated by representations in a medium X—that is, if we have no independent access to the Y-domain, and no way of identifying external relations between X and Y elements—it appears that we have no way of setting up the external correspondence that gives the X-representations their internal Y-significance. Nothing about a particular X makes it a representation of *this* Y rather than *that*. And if this is right, it means that if we don't have X-*un*mediated access to the Y-domain, we don't have any X-mediated access either. The Model-Theoretic Argument formalizes the worry for the special case in which internal representation takes the form of a first-order theory, but the intuitive heart of the argument, which is the dilemma posed by the combination of Externality and Confinement, is indifferent to the form of internal representation.[10] To put it informally, we've got the world on the one hand and the internal world-representing structures on the other, and no way to jump outside the head and get our minds directly on the latter, hence no way to hook the two up. The argument is powerful and, even in its intuitive version, worrisome.

Putnam's response is to reject the idea that facts about what ideas, or terms, represent are facts about their relations to the external environment at all. They are, he holds, purely psychological. The position has been elaborately and eloquently developed over three and a half decades. There are two popular classes of alternative response. Both exploit the fact that Putnam's argument falls short of showing that there are no external links between ideas and things. It shows only that such links as there are, are not (or not in their entirety) *set up* by internal acts. The first (defended by David Lewis) holds that facts about the world that are metaphysically independent of thinking/speaking agents play a role in determining what our ideas are about by narrowing down the classes of eligible referents. Only certain sets of objects are metaphysically fit to serve as extensions of ideas, and 'A' represents a just in case 'A' is mapped onto a by the best-fitting interpretation that assigns only the right kind of extension (Lewis's Natural Classes) to basic predicates.[11] The issues raised by these accounts fall outside the scope of the present discussion. Suffice it to say, for our purposes, that it's not enough to add external conditions to an account of the facts in virtue of which 'A' represents what it does. One has to say how those kinds of fact constrain the formation of belief. The reference-determining facts on Lewis's account seem precisely precluded from playing this role by their epistemic inaccessibility. No one, so far as I know, has shown how to fill this gap, and I don't see how it can be filled.

The more popular response to the argument holds that representation is some form of causal-informational connection between ideas and the environment. We don't *will* our ideas out into the world with thoughts of the form "cat" shall represent cats'; they're already connected in the causal order. Mother Nature did the connecting for us. Minds are embedded in bodies, and a well-designed mind acting as a control system for a body is inserted into the perception-to-action pathways and is configured internally to map experience onto action in a way that gets the body moving in ways that promote survival. The mental particulars that act as causal intermediaries between experience and action are selected for their behavioral role by Mother Nature because of the information they typically carry in our

---

10. If the argument works for 'thoughts' and 'things', it also works for any <representation, domain of representation> pair for which the assumptions hold.

11. I use single quotes for names of ideas.

environment. There is infighting among those who hold this view (heretofore, CI theorists) (p.88), but on a CI view, how the contents of the mind are wired into the causal pathways is a matter of design. The mind is a network of internal pathways arranged to funnel information through sensory channels into motor pathways, and it is Mother Nature that decides how our internal states are connected externally in the world. The problem with this arrangement, it would seem, is that it leaves no room for Voluntarism.

Dilemma

So it looks like the argument really presents a dilemma. *Either* representational relations are internal (to say ' "A" represents such and such' is really to say something psychological, something about how 'A' relates to other ideas, images, etc.), in which case our representational activity is unconstrained by the way that the world is *or* representational relations are external, in which case we don't have voluntary control over them. We reject the view that the mind plays a role in setting up links between its contents and the external environment. Confinement, that is to say, looks like it entails either ∼Guidance or ∼Voluntarism. Putnam was uncompromising about retaining Voluntarism: facts about what my ideas represent are facts about what I *intend* them to represent. If those turn out to be purely internal, so be it (in his words "we interpret our language or nothing does"). CI theorists, by contrast, have little patience for Voluntaristic intuitions. Design choices, for the pure CI theorist, belong to Mother Nature.

The Loophole

In fact, however, I don't think CI accounts have to be saddled with the anti-Voluntaristic conclusion in its full strength. There's a loophole in the Argument from Confinement that can be exploited to trace a path between simple acquiescence in the mind-world connections that Mother Nature has prepared, and Putnam's internalism. The challenge that the argument presents is to say how the mind could set up external relations to the environment from a position of confinement. It is answered in two stages. I pointed out above that this was an instance of the problem of establishing external relations between a pair of structured domains, R (for representation) and D (for domain of representation), by appealing only to what is intrinsic to R. And it seemed as though there's as solid a case against that as there could possibly be, since external relations are precisely those that don't supervene on the intrinsic properties of their *relata*.

But in the special case in which R is included, or partially included, in D, any one-one mapping between them will have what the mathematicians call 'fixed points', points that get mapped onto themselves. These can be identified from a position of R-confinement without using any representational relations, and used by R as internal points of reference in calibrating the rest of its contents against D. Think of how we calibrate the Celsius and Fahrenheit scales against each other. We say that they coincide at −40; we identify −40 as a fixed point in the function that maps temperatures in centigrade onto their counterparts on the Fahrenheit scale. If we have a pair of spaces, like the Celsius and Fahrenheit scales, with a measure defined over each and possessing no global symmetries, identification of a single fixed point will single out the only structure preserving mapping between them. In general, however, identification of fixed points will only constrain a mapping. It will provide complete calibration if, and only if, every element in each space can be uniquely characterized by its relations to fixed points.

We can put this formally. Consider a pair of functions: one, g, that takes each point in a space into the point on the map that represents it, and another, h, that takes each point on the map into the point in the space at which it is located. Form the function $f = h.g$, where '.' indicates functional composition. In this case, f is a function from points on the map to points in the space. It is continuous because g and h are continuous. If the map is situated in the space it represents, it has a fixed point, and the fixed point is sure to be unique.[12] So all we need to constrain interpretation from the inside, at least in this special case, is a means of identifying fixed points—a symbol that we can add to a situated representation, whose job is to indicate the local coincidence of sign and signified, or a thought we can form that would do the same—and we will have a way of identifying a mapping onto a (partially) external space from a position of confinement. In other words, fixed points come with a built-in architectural link to what they represent. Since fixed points are internal to R, there is no need either to *represent* them (i.e., to make use of external relations between R and points on the map) or to 'jump outside of R', to identify them.

12. With one exception, viz., in the degenerate case in which the space represents itself. In the case of discrete spaces, we say that there is one point that 'centers on' the point it represents, for, in such cases, there is no point of coincidence. What there *is* is an infinite string of nested representations, each of which *contains* a representation of itself (where 'containment' is a spatial relationship, and here means containment in the space in which the representation is extended), and where the relative sizes of representer and representee approach zero. A close look at the red dot on my map, for instance, will reveal a full reproduction of the map together, of course, with the little red dot at its center; that dot would, in its turn, contain a reproduction of the reproduction of the map, together with the red dot on *it*, which, in its turn ... and so on until we hit the limits of resolution of the map.

The most familiar example of the use of fixed points to establish a conventional interpretation of a situated representation—a representation, that is to say, that is situated in the domain it represents—is the familiar red dots we place on building directories and the like. These dots identify a fixed point in the intended mapping between the map and the external space. They don't represent a first-order feature of the domain; they identify the point of coincidence between sign and signified, if you like. Think of them as devices of semantic descent. They provide a chute that takes you down a semantic level in the way that quotation marks take you up.[13] If you can identify the fixed points on any situated representation, you've got it architecturally anchored in the domain of representation. It's an ingenious sort of trick. It applies both to analog and digital representations; it can be applied to temporally situated representations of time and first-person representations of an impersonal world. It can be applied to coordinate notional networks with structured sets of particulars, or conceptual networks with structured sets of properties. It will be available for any representation, or representation-generating system, that is situated in the space it represents, that is, any representation that falls within its own representational scope.[14] The defining feature of such representations is precisely that one-one mappings onto the space they represent possess fixed points, and once the fixed points are identified, they provide a kind of internal frame of reference that can be used by the system to calibrate its contents against the external environment.

Someone in the grip of Putnam's argument will think that we have simplified but not solved the problem. He may argue as follows: you have said that you identify the intended interpretation by placing the red dot on your internal map, but what about the interpretation of the red dot? How do we know that red dots identify fixed points rather than *schmixed* points, where a schmixed point is one that represents a point that is twenty-five meters due north of itself? Before, we had the problem of interpreting symbols on a map of the world. Haven't we now just got the problem of interpreting symbols on a *meta*-map? The response here is to shift the focus decisively from semantic relations to what I will call below architectural relations. To say that I place a red dot on my internal map is to make a quite complicated statement about how it figures functionally in determining my movements.[15] Don't worry for the moment about the details; picture an

---

13. I am supposing that the red dot does more than identify a point; it has an orientation. It's more like a red vector.

14. Any set of objects arranged in a system of external relations forms a space.

15. Think of how it works with external maps; if I want to use my map to steer myself to B, I have to find the point on the map that represents my present location and the one that represents B, and then point the line that connects them at B itself, and walk in that direction.

opening in the internal functional machinery labeled 'fixed point goes here'.[16] Acts of self-location load a map into the machinery by lining the red dot up with the slot. It's a purely mechanical procedure, no different from lining up the needle on a compass with the arrow marked 'N', sliding a key into a keyhole, or loading a film into a projector. The brain does it for us with little conscious regulation in the case of space, but in other cases, it requires deliberate attention. Without it, there is no forming objective beliefs on the basis of what we see or using objective information about the lay of the land to guide movements.

There is, in this respect, no difference between internal and external maps, and there is no difference between maps and other kinds of representation. Acts of self-representation quite generally situate representations in the causal pathways between perception and response. They determine how experience is fed into the representation, on the one hand, and how its contents bear on behavior, on the other. To self-represent is not (or not just) to be in a certain kind of internal state—for example, to have a sentence of a certain kind in one's belief box. It is to do something that connects the contents of one's belief box to the wider world. The lost traveler who finally places his red dot has loaded the information contained in the map, which was in his hand the whole time, into the pathways that determine motion. Until the red dot is in place, the map and the information contained in it is not incorporated into the causal loop that controls his movements.[17] To 'know where you are' in a sense that contrasts with being lost is to have a map loaded into the internal pathways poised to guide movement. A centered map is not, as some have thought, an uncentered map with an extra bit of very personal, very peculiar, incommunicable content (called variously "reflexive," "indexical," or "self-referential" content). It is one that is incorporated into the navigational activity of a situated agent. It is more informative than an uncentered map not because it contains more information, but because it makes the information in an uncentered map available for navigation. The common mistake of thinking that centered maps have additional content, and hence that there is some feature of the world represented on a centered map that isn't (and *cannot* be) captured by its uncentered cousins—and hence, in its most insidious form, that there are features of the world that don't supervene on what is represented on those

---

16. The label, obviously, is dispensable.

17. There is a difference, of course, between situating a representation of A, and representing the situation of A. Putting a picture of Kurt Gödel on my wall is a way of situating a representation of him. Describing his whereabouts is a way of representing his situation. It is only in the special case of reflexive representation of one's situation that one situates a representation *by* representing his situation.

uncentered cousins, and can't by captured be any objective representation—is one we will see again and again in sections to follow. It is one manifestation of the familiar philosophical error of mistaking pragmatic role for semantic content.

Placing my internal red dot in this sense doesn't *interpret* my map, but by assigning it a place in the causal order, it effects a much more concrete rigging between the two spaces. I'll call this kind of rigging 'coordination' and distinguish it from interpretation.[18] To *interpret* a structure, A, in a structure, B, is to adopt a convention that associates the parts of A and the parts of B. The legend on a map provides a physical interpretation of the map and a Tarskian truth definition for a language provides a real-world interpretation of the language. Interpretation of this sort is a mental act, and it is, as Putnam says, 'up to us' in the sense that the association is purely conventional. The problem with interpreting thought was that we didn't have the right kind of access to the objects of thought to establish a conventional mapping. To *coordinate* A and B, by contrast, is to establish the causal and contextual relations in virtue of which the parts or properties of A carry information about the parts or properties of B. You coordinate the height of mercury in the vial of a thermometer with the temperature *at a particular place* by putting it *at* the place, thereby establishing a causal pathway between the two. And you coordinate the 'on'-switch of a heating device with the height of mercury in the vial of thermometer by hooking them up with each other, again, establishing a causal pathway between the two.

Ramsey, and Dretske following him, referred to representations as 'maps that we steer by' to express an insight about the role they play in mediating perception and action. The lost traveler faces a practical, rather than an intellectual, task; she doesn't need to *interpret* her map (the legend on the side and the names attached to places do that well enough; she knows perfectly which blue blotch represents Lake Havasu, which dotted line represents Moosehead Trail, which square represents the campsite she wants to get to). Her problem is to coordinate the map with the landscape, that is, to get it inserted into the causal pathways running from perception to action in a way that lets her steer by it. And to do that, she needs to self-locate. The task for the situated agent is the same; she has to get mental particulars inserted into the causal pathways running from perception to action so she can steer by them, and to do that she needs to self-represent.

Putnam fretted that there was nothing the mind could *do* that would set up discriminating, conventional relations to elements in the external

---

18. Treat this as a terminological stipulation; we need separate labels.

landscape. There was no purely psychological act that it could perform that would count as setting up the conventional relations that would interpret the former, because there is no way of picking out elements in the latter domain without *using* the very representational relations that our conventions are meant to set up. I responded by pointing out that our representations are connected in the space of things in virtue of playing a role in the determination of behavior, i.e., being situated in a certain way in the causal pathways that lead from perception to behavior, and that we assign them that role in part by voluntary acts of self-location. This was enough to defuse the difficulty, in principle, of establishing any kind of external relation between the two, given the kind of restricted access to the objects of representation Putnam described. But the external relations thereby established are causal rather than intentional ones. The objector above tries to reinstate Putnam's worry by saying: 'we always acknowledged that there were all kinds of nonintentional relations between our representations and the world, that thoughts occur in space and time, and that their components bear causal-informational links and so on, to things in the external landscape. The problem was to specify from the inside which of the indefinitely many such relations we could choose, each of which would map those components onto different features of the landscape, the one that maps them onto their intended referents? What can we do that would count as forming the intention that is the causal-informational rather than the schmausal-informational or links that determine reference?'

On this question, I side with Putnam; there's no such thing as an intended interpretation for thought.[19] His insight that inner acts of intending that our thoughts be interpreted thus and so were empty is important and correct. My recommendation is that we use Putnam's insight to wean ourselves of the hyperintellectualized model of thought that finds expression in the Fregean Model and attend to the mechanics of coordinating thought with the world. If there is something magical about the idea that some inner act could will one's thoughts out into the world,[20] there is nothing magical about coordination. With CI-theorists, then, I share the view that interpretation was the wrong notion all along. When we're talking about the relations between thoughts and things, it's

---

19. This overstates the case. There is room for a view (like, e.g., Davidson's or Brandom's), according to which that intentional notions take shape somehow in the space *between* perceivers; i.e., that they become applicable in a social setting in which there are multiple, communicating perceivers. The real conclusion of the argument should be that if there are intentional relations between thoughts and things, they are derivative of the relations between words in public discourse and ideas. Intentionality, in that case, flows *from* language *to* thought, rather than from thought to language.

20. A common theme also, of course, in late Wittgenstein.

coordination that we're after. Interpreting representations is something thought *does*—one interprets the words of others and maps and texts, for example, by establishing a mapping in thought, between them and one's representation of the world—but thought itself doesn't need to be interpreted.

I'm suggesting we need to extend the CI account in a way that provides an explanation of the measure of voluntary control the mind has over how its contents relate to the external environment. There was something right in Putnam's insistence that what our ideas represent is up to us, if we accept in principle that our minds are not prepared by Mother Nature with a full repertoire of ideas neatly tucked into the pathways between perception and response. We don't come into the world, for example, with ideas of foie gras, Volvos, or entropy. These are our invention and we have to forge the links that connect them with the wider world. If the informational links between mind and world were all natural, that is, if they were established and maintained wholly by physical law and external circumstance, there would be no room for genuinely cognitive activity. Thought would be an extension of experience rather than a distinct medium. What the story about fixed points and self-representation adds is an account of the active role that the mind plays in establishing and maintaining the informational connections between its contents and the world. CI accounts might be the full story when it comes to magnetosomes and maybe even mole rates, but they're not for us.

3.2   ARCHITECTURAL VS. SEMANTIC RELATIONS

It is best, I think, to leave the internal/external distinction behind, because it breaks down at the crucial point, in favor of a distinction between semantic and architectural links. Semantic links are links among elements in a representational medium. They connect words with words in a language, and ideas with ideas in a mind.[21] Architectural links, by contrast, connect elements in a representational medium with their subject matter, or with elements in other media—anything that is not itself integrated into the same semantic web.

---

21. The notion of a representational medium will be introduced more explicitly in chapter 4. Any kind of a link among ideas, for my purposes, will count as a semantic link. There are different kinds of semantic links: rigid ones, those built into the medium, and soft ones that reflect contingencies of the subject matter. For example, 'bachelorhood' is rigidly linked to 'maleness' and only softly linked to 'George Clooney'. Representational media work, in general, by encoding structure that reflects structure in the domain, and should encode rigidly whatever structure is fixed in the domain.

The argument from Confinement brings the need for architectural links into relief and exposes the impotence of intellectual activity to forge them. Representing, or intending, that ideas relate thus and so to the world, the argument goes, establishes semantic links between elements internal to a medium. These links never reach outside the medium to the objects of representation. The CI response shrugged off the worry, pointing to architectural links already in place. The problem was that if we treat representation as a purely architectural relation, it looked like we would have to relinquish any role for intellectual activity in forging representational relations. Mother Nature, on this view, determines how the contents of the mind are entered into the wider world by wiring them into the perceptual and motor pathways of bodies. The way out of the dilemma was to recognize that the mind is not just a sieve through which information passes in a manner dictated by design. The mind has movable parts and plays an active role in moving them. It builds little internal models of self and situation and keeps them wired into the pathways with self-locating acts. The models can have parts of any kind that you please, and self-locating acts establish genuinely architectural links between the parts of the model and the wider world. We'll see in sections to come how this can be generalized and exploited to recover a vigorous voluntarism.

3.3   CONCLUSION

From now on, I'll be focusing on this business of building internal models and the acts of self-location that regulate their position in the internal dynamics. It is the architectural rigging afforded by the continuing role of internal models in the cognitive economy of the agents that produce them that connect them to the world. The expository purpose of preceding sections was both to wean us of the representationalist picture embodied in its purest form in the Fregean Model and to make room in the CI account for an understanding of the active role that the mind plays in regulating its relations to the environment. The shift to dynamical ways of thinking comes with a change of focus. The focus in the representationalist approach was on intellectual activity, the making and breaking of links between ideas. The dynamical approach embeds this activity in a larger system, focusing on the dynamical interfaces between what goes on inside and what goes on outside. It is only through abandoning the intentional vocabulary that we get the right take on relations between thought and world, and it is only through this wide-angle lens that the construction of internal models and the singular role of that very special class of thoughts that employ reflexive or self-referential devices—what I called above devices of semantic *descent*—comes clearly into view. The primary role of these devices is not to carry information about objects but to wire ideas into the architecture. We'll see in part II why it matters to get this right, although in the remainder of part I will be addressing the mechanics of model construction and use.

4

The Dynamical Approach

This section will introduce the central notions. We treat the conscious mind—its introspectively accessible component, which I'll refer to elliptically as 'the mind'[1]—as part of a larger dynamical system and focus on the interfaces with other parts of the system; that is, experience, on the incoming end, and action or volition, on the outgoing end. The fundamental point of contrast with traditional representational approaches is that whereas representational approaches treat intentional relations expressed by model-theoretic mappings as fundamental mind-world relations, the dynamical approach takes relations of covariation relative to specified ranges of contexts as basic and recognizes no mind-world relations that can't be understood in these terms. Formally, representation is a two-place relation between elements in the internal and external landscapes that discriminates between extensional equivalents. Dynamical relations, by contrast, are three-place relations among internal elements, external elements, and ranges of contexts and they don't discriminate among features of the environment that coincide across the relevant range. Many of the approaches that employ representational vocabulary, including many that fall squarely

---

1. This is to avoid clumsy locution. In this section, when I mean to refer to the whole cognitive system, I'll follow Chalmers's terminology and speak of the 'psychological mind'.

in the Fregean tradition, will be reconstructible in dynamical terms, but the translation into dynamical terms will require making the role of context explicit.[2] That is one of the virtues of the approach; where the Fregean approach downplayed the role context plays mediating relations between thoughts and things, the dynamical approach brings it into sharp relief. Another virtue of the approach is that it allows us to bracket ontological questions by giving us a neutral vocabulary that spans the inner and outer landscapes. We can seamlessly describe dynamical relations between the parts of a complex system with physical and mental components.[3]

4.1   THE CENTRAL NOTIONS

The two central notions of the dynamical approach are those of a representational medium and coordination. Coordination is a three-place relation between a pair of quantities and a range of contexts; quantity A is coordinated with quantity B relative to the set of contexts C just in case B covaries with A in C, that is, just in case there is a dynamical process that correlates A-values with B-values in C.[4] There is no restriction on what kinds of contexts C can include; for example, it can include all metaphysically possible contexts, all physically possible ones, or all physically possible ones in which some contingent condition obtains. When B is coordinated with A in C, it can be the bearer of information about A to any system S in C that can discriminate B-values, and in that case we say that B can act as a representation of A for S in C. B can be a simple quantity like the position of the gauge in your car that carries information about the height of gas in the tank, or it can be a complex, multidimensional quantity like the configuration of pixels on a computer screen. The world is governed by laws that bring the states of different systems into coordination with one another under conditions that define contexts. Some coordination occurs naturally, without the deliberate activity of human agents. The processes that coordinate tides with the position of the moon, for example, or the one that coordinates the height of the mercury in the

---

2. Even someone who holds that representation is an irreducible, internal relation between ideas and world will have to recognize a level of purely dynamical description and needn't eschew the apparatus of the dynamical approach.

3. So long as it is assumed that the mental supervenes on the physical, then the physical laws will carry over to the mental realm and we get a smooth dynamics that is indifferent to ontology.

4. I use bold letters for quantities, and I restrict covariation to one-one mappings. Although the mapping is one-one, the relationship is causally and temporally asymmetric. A-values can cause or produce B-values by a more or less attenuated process.

vial of a thermometer with ambient temperature, involve no human hand.[5] In other cases, human activity is an essential part of the coordinating process. Think of the process that coordinates the representational states of a compass with the direction of a landmark in the distance. The physical laws keep the compass needle pointing northward, but it is the action of the user that turns the face of the compass so that the line points at the landmark. When the coordinating process doesn't require human participation, I'll say the medium is a natural one; when it does, I'll say it's conventional.[6]

As I said, the activity of coordinating a medium with its subject matter is different from that of interpreting it, so long as interpretation is understood in model-theoretic terms.[7] To coordinate a medium with its subject matter is to establish a dynamical relation between the two. To coordinate the position of the pointer on front of a measuring device with the states of a measured system, for example, is a matter of creating the controlled conditions inside the device—laying the wiring and setting up the connections—that keep them evolving in sync. Interpreting a medium is an intellectual rather than a practical act; you interpret a medium by producing a representation of its relation to its subject matter. The legend on a map interprets the map by representing the relations between symbols on the map and the landmarks that they represent. A Tarskian truth definition for a language interprets it by representing the relations between its terms and their extensions. Interpretations are always given *in* a medium, and providing interpretations is a way of achieving coordination, if and only if the medium in which the interpretation is given is already coordinated with both the object medium and its subject matter. If there are any media that are coordinated with their subject matter by interpretation, there must be some that are coordinated by other means.

Putnam's argument undermines the kind of representationalism that mistakes a relation between two structures—for example, a representation on the one hand, and what is represented, on the other—with something internal to one. No map—internal or external—*has* representative significance unless it is linked by a coordinating chain that reaches outside of it into the space it represents; nothing in my head carries information about the external landscape unless it is linked by a chain that reaches right out

---

5. We build the thermometer, of course, but we don't play an active, continuing role in the dynamical process that keeps the thermometer and ambient temperature in sync.

6. This distinction is heuristic. There is a spectrum of degrees of involvement rather than a dichotomy. The terminology is not meant to suggest any view about the nature of convention.

7. I will omit this qualifying phrase from now on.

into the world, to the objects I see, smell, wrap my arms around, and interact with in ways that aren't representationally mediated. The non-conceptual, dynamical relations are basic, ineliminable, and irreducible. If these links aren't in place, as Putnam saw quite clearly, no inner activity will put them there. If they are, as CI theorists and other externalists saw equally clearly, no inner activity is needed. Talk of interpretation is appropriate in two contexts. It is properly applied to media such as languages and maps, which are coordinated with the world by an external medium, and which can be used, when interpreted, as additional links in the chain coordinating thoughts with things. It also applies to description of purely internal connections, for example, when I formulate the thought "cats" represents cats', part of what I do is link the idea 'cats' to a motley bag of associated impressions and ideas (e.g., lumps of warm fur, a characteristic smell, the memory of a special Christmas, an old nursery rhyme, a favorite aunt). The idea simultaneously unites the impressions and integrates them into the conceptual network. Similarly, when I formulate the thought ' "bachelor" represents unmarried males' I connect the idea of bachelors to the ideas of marriage and maleness. Coordination, however, is a more fundamental notion, and when it comes to describing relations between the internal and external world, it is the only one that applies. We should replace Putnam's "we interpret our languages or nothing does" with "we interpret our *thought* or nothing does" and accept the second disjunct.

4.2 COORDINATING MEDIA WITH ONE ANOTHER

We say that a pair of media are coordinated with each other just in case there is a dynamical process that maps states of the one onto states of the other. When a pair of media are coordinated with each other, the two then form a chain that acts as a single medium leading back to the subject matter of the first.[8] Here is a nice description taken from Hutchins's *Cognition in the Wild,* of the complex chain of coordinated media that carries information about the spatial relation of a ship to some cited landmark to the ship's log:

> First, the space in which the ship and the landmark lie is a macro-space. We would like to measure the directional relationship of the ship to the landmark in this space. To do that, we must reproduce that directional relationship in a second space: the microspace of the

8. Whether we say that the second medium inherits the subject matter of the first or takes the states of that medium that feeds it as its subject matter will depend on our interests.

alidade. When the alidade is aimed and the hairline falls on the image of the landmark in the sight, the directional relationship of the ship to the landmark is reproduced in the directional relationship of the alidade eyepiece to the hairline. The physical structure of the alidade guarantees that the directional relationship of the eyepiece to the hairline will, in turn, be reproduced in the directional relationship of the center of the gyrocompass card to the point on the edge of the gyrocompass card over which the hairline falls. Thus the directional relationship of the ship to the landmark is reproduced in a third space: the microspace of the gyrocompass card. . . .

The printed scale on the gyrocompass card permits the analog angular state of the alidade to be converted to a digital representation. This digital representation may have intermediate external representations . . . [but it] appears without fail as a written number in the column labeled with the name of the landmark in the bearing record log.[9]

The ship serves as a model for the processing that goes on in the mind; our phenomenal states are representational media that carry information about the relatively local space outside our bodies. The process—partly conscious, partly unconscious—that transforms these first into spontaneous perceptual beliefs "wrung from us by experience,"[10] and then into the full considered products of conscious reflection, is from a dynamical perspective no different from the long line of representation and re-representation inside the ship that transforms the visual cues received by the watchman into the final plotted position on a central map. Ideas are linked to the external landscape—concepts to properties and notions to objects—not by special meaning-giving mental performances ('*intending*'), but by chains of coordinated media both inside and outside of the head, kept in sync by a motley collection of processes, some purely natural, some involving deliberate activity. Mother Nature manages the connections between phenomenal states and the signals intercepted by the retina, but we play a significant role in arranging things, both inside and outside the head, to establish and maintain channels that carry information into the mind. There has been a lot of excellent work on our role in designing the external environment that fits quite nicely into this picture.[11] I'll be focusing on the other components: the role of the agent in organizing the internal landscape, and the interaction between the external and internal components of the coordinating chains.

9. Hutchins, *Cognition in the Wild*, 123.

10. The phrase is Sellars's.

11. See, especially, Clark, *Being There*, also, though with more emphasis on the role of the environment in aiding practical interaction with the world, *Natural-Born Cyborgs*.

Whatever transformations the signals sent out by the colored surfaces, chiming bells, and smelly cheeses undergo as they travel the ambient space, through the sensory pathways, and make their way into the mind, and whatever conscious processing they undergo after we become aware of them but before we arrive at our fully considered beliefs, the whole process is a long chain of coordination among different representational media, maintained only in the last stages by conscious intellectual activity. These transformations are heavily dependent on contingent features of the local environment, and only somewhat reliable, but they do manage to keep our behavior subtly attuned to our typical environments. They can be broken into relatively natural subprocesses. There is the passage of the signals from object to the sensory surfaces; the passage from the sensory surfaces to the brain, where the translation into experience is made; the transformation into perceptual belief, and finally cogitation, inference, and self-conscious theorizing. The detailed description of the stages up to cogitation is the business of the sciences; physics, biology, cognitive science, and psychology all make contributions to this part of the story. Philosophy has traditionally focused on the conscious formation of explicit beliefs, ignoring the role of the body and its immediate environment in mediating the relations between thought and the world. I'll be paying more attention to how thought fits into the bigger picture, how it interfaces with other media, and what it adds, in purely dynamical terms to the coordinating chains leading into the head and back out through the motor pathways.

Some Important Points about Coordination

There are five points to be made about coordination.

1. It doesn't matter how attenuated the coordinating process is, i.e., how long or complex the line of representation and representation is,[12] one can *use* the information contained in any medium to which one has access, whether or not one has a theoretical understanding of the process itself, so long as one remains within its context of use. I can use my thermometer to get information about temperature without any understanding of chemistry; the biologist can use her microscope to get information about cells without knowing the physics of the instrument; and I can use my eyes, ears, and nose to get information about my environment without an understanding of the complicated physical interactions in virtue of which they carry information.

---

12. If a pair of media are coordinated by a natural process, or by a process that can be characterized in purely mechanical terms, then translation between them is, so to speak, automated; one can hook up a machine to do it, or teach someone to do it without knowing what either of the media represent.

2. The coordinating relation between a medium and the object system is an external one, which means that it places no constraints on the internal relations between states of the medium and their subject matter. The pricking of my thumbs doesn't resemble wickedness, nor does the weather report delivered by the radio announcer resemble a sunny day.

3. Coordination is always relative to a range of contexts. It can be vague and we may or may not have a way of explicitly characterizing the relevant range. We may know it only, for example, as 'ordinary conditions' or 'conditions like *these*'. It may not even be explicitly characterizable because there may be an endless string of potential defeasibility conditions, an ineliminable *ceteris paribus* clause.

4. The reliability of a coordinating process is a matter of degree.[13] Most of the processes we actually use to get information about the environment are only more or less reliable, under conditions we don't quite know how to specify.

5. Coordination is not causation. Coordination is a physically well-defined, explicitly context-dependent relation with no intrinsic direction. Causation is a much richer, asymmetric relation whose roots in the physics are unclear.[14]

These definitions tell us the dynamical conditions under which a quantity can act as a representational medium: to say that quantity A can act as a medium carrying information about quantity B from one to another context in C just in case A covaries with B in C tells us, for example, what is required of a medium that carries information about the world from one subject to another over time and across space. What it can't do is tell us in what capacity A is acting in a given situation. The problem is that every quantity pertaining to every system is associated with a whole manifold of media, each with its own context of use. It's only in the context of an ongoing practice—the role of A in the life of a community, or in the intrinsic dynamics of an A-sensing system—that we can say whether A *is* acting as a representational medium and which medium it is acting as, that is, what its context is, and what information it carries. That will depend on pragmatic factors—who is using it, how it is being used— and a general understanding of these matters is needed before the notion of representational medium becomes generally applicable in describing instances of information exchange.[15] Fortunately, since I will be talking

---

13. The notion of reliability requires an independent specification of subject matter. We can think of P as merely a somewhat reliable process for gauging temperature only if we have some independent means of identifying temperature as the target of measurement.

14. This is important apropos of the remark that the difference between events and their epiphenomenal effects is invisible to a dynamical perspective.

15. For a promising beginning toward such an account, see Haaken, *Information and Self-Organization*.

about media with deep, natural boundaries—that is, thought conceived as an intrasubjective medium structured by the requirements of coordinating across a spatial and temporal divide, and language conceived as an intersubjective medium structured by the requirements of coordinating across a personal divide—we'll be able to proceed without any attempt to develop a general pragmatics.

4.3 CONCLUSION

As I said, I'll be focusing on a tiny part of the whole complex machine; the internal models constructed by world-representing agents and how they interface with incoming and outgoing media. To zero in on it, I'll simplify a good deal, leaving everything around it schematic in representation, and bracket complications that can be bracketed. There is one especially notable omission; I will say a lot about the role of the natural environment in coordinating thought with the world but little about the social context. The social context raises very difficult issues that demand separate treatment.[16]

16. But see Sterelny, *Thought in a Hostile World.*

5

Self-Description

Now we have the dynamical approach in place and we have seen how situated acts of self-location, under the right conditions, work to coordinate points on a map with space. I've said nothing yet about the dynamics, but of that, more later. The next step in elaborating the picture is to introduce the descriptive analogue of self-location. For these purposes, we trade maps for languages.[1] I will suggest if a language contains predicates that apply to the properties it exemplifies, and it contains reflexive expressions that identify those properties, we have the makings of self-describing sentences that do for its descriptive vocabulary what self-locating acts do for spatial vocabulary. These sentences bring the descriptive apparatus

---

1. Although the properties of a map do often have representative significance (the color of a state might, for example, represent its political affiliation), they don't often fall under their own descriptive scope and they are typically interpreted by a legend written in the margin in English or some other natural language. We could, however, invent a descriptive analogue of a red dot on a map, and we can use a special symbol—a purple star, say—to identify fixed points if there are any. If we are given a page covered with hundred French color predicates each written in the hundred different colors of ink, for example, and we attached a purple dot to predicates that exemplify the colors they describe, this would allow us to coordinate predicates with properties without a legend or dictionary. Suppose you and a friend want to invent a new vocabulary for musical notes, but you have no old vocabulary you can use to interpret your new terms. You can coordinate the new vocabulary with notes by singing the new names in the pitch that exemplifies them and employing a verbal marker in place of the purple star to indicate each is a fixed point.

of the language into alignment with the properties it exemplifies (and by extension, with other properties connected in the same causal web) in just the way that the sentence "Here is <,>" brings its spatial vocabulary into alignment with points of space where '<,>' is a generic set of co-ordinates. This will take a little unpacking. Later I will suggest that we use the same reflexive devices to bring the descriptive apparatus of thought into alignment with an internally exemplified palette of properties: colors, tastes, smells, sounds, feelings, and so forth.

5.1 EXEMPLIFICATION

First, some generalities about exemplification. We say that when A has the property p, then A *exemplifies* p. A piece of red fabric exemplifies redness, Xanthippe, after Socrates' death, exemplified widowhood. Representational media not only represent properties, they also exemplify them: utterances exemplify decibel levels, inscriptions exemplify shapes and colors. And the properties they represent can interact with the properties they exemplify. A perspectival drawing of a cube represents a three-dimensional figure but exemplifies two-dimensionality, an inscription of the word 'red' in black ink represents redness but exemplifies blackness, my utterance '. . . was said by Plato' represents the property of being said by Plato, but exemplifies that of being said by me. One way of representing properties is by reflexively identifying properties exemplified. A novel, for example, might contain the sentence 'The ink with which these words are written is the very color of her hair, and her skin, the color of these pages'. A story told by a first-person narrator might begin 'My voice on that night is as you are hearing it'. Again, the reflexive expressions are functioning as devices of semantic descent; providing chutes that take us from representations of properties right to properties.

Let's say that expressions or thoughts that reflexively identify the properties they exemplify are self-presenting. Self-presenting expressions don't travel well; like indexicals, they represent different things in different contexts, where the context is supplied in this case, not by location in time or space, but by the medium in which it occurs.[2] In the example of the reflexively presented quality of voice, if the same words are written instead of spoken, or spoken in a different voice, they have a different

2. There is some benign circularity here. Media will be individuated by the intrinsic properties of their informational states, but which properties are informationally significant will depend on which properties are identified by exemplification.

semantic significance, different truth conditions. In the example of the reflexively presented color, if the same words are penned in a different shade, they have a different extension. To get ways of referring to properties that aren't tied to the medium, in the sense that their representational content is invariant under transformations of medium, we need to join reflexively presented properties with descriptions. This parallels the fact that in order to get ways of referring to particulars that aren't tied to a spatiotemporal context, we need to join indexically identified particulars with singular terms. Here's an example of a property presented reflexively and described: 'My voice on that night is as you hear it. The children called it 'growly'.' Now we have a way of referring to the quality (the expression 'growly') that can be transported outside the medium; anybody can use it, it can be expressed in script or speech, or in arbitrary languages. Let's say a sentence that describes a reflexively presented property is self-describing. Self-description is the descriptive analogue of self-location, the process by which we trade in indexical identification of a particular for a representation. In both cases, we start with an expression that can only be used to identify its extension from a particular context for one whose link to its extension survives transformation of context. We need only to generalize the notion of a context to apply to media, where media are individuated in part by the intrinsic properties of their informational states.

So if the properties exemplified by a medium fall within its own descriptive scope, then for every property exemplified by the medium, there's going to be an expression that applies to it, and self-describing expressions will establish architectural links between the descriptive vocabulary of the medium and its subject matter. And just as in the spatiotemporal case, the fixed points provide an internal frame that comes with built-in architectural relations to the subject matter, and can be used to align the medium with its descriptive domain. Combining the two, we have a medium whose singular vocabulary is coordinated with space by self-locating acts and whose descriptive vocabulary is coordinated with the properties of things by acts of self-description.

When we formulate thoughts that describe properties exemplified in experience—thoughts of the form 'this is what salt tastes like', 'this is what pain feels like', 'this is what it's like to see red'—that is what we are doing. In dynamical terms, the effect of these thoughts is to incorporate phenomenal profiles into the conceptual network, and in so doing, establish indirect dynamical relations to nodes in the network that can be related to them conceptually. The result is a single web in which concepts are linked to properties by chains passing through phenomenal properties, the internal components of which are semantic and the external components of which are architectural. The concept 'salt', for example, is linked semantically to salty taste, which is in its turn linked causally to the chemical compound NaCl. There is detail that will need to be worked out to fill this in. But let's push on and take a closer look at the resulting relationship between thought and experience.

5.2   THOUGHT AND EXPERIENCE

I'll distinguish representation in a natural medium from representation in a conventional medium, calling them respectively N-representation and C-representation. The difference between natural and conventional media, recall, is that natural media are coordinated with their subject matter by natural law, whereas the coordination of conventional media requires deliberate human support.[3] An element e* in a natural medium N-represents p under conditions c*, just in case it indicates p, when c* obtains. The examples I used earlier to illustrate exemplification (e.g., 'black' written in black ink, 'gruff' said in a gruff voice. . .) involved conventional media, but natural representational media also both exemplify and represent properties. Every natural property, of course, both exemplifies and N-represents itself, but the properties of a natural medium can also N-represent properties they don't exemplify, relative to a restricted set of conditions c*, so long as the natural laws entail that they carry information about such properties in c*; bruises on skin, for example, exemplify blueness and ordinarily (that is to say, under ordinary conditions) N-represent tissue damage; the smell of rotting fruit exemplifies acridness and ordinarily N-represents fermentation.

We often use the properties exemplified by a natural medium to convey information they don't naturally carry by assigning them a conventional status. So, for instance, audiences in game shows hold up differently colored cards to represent positive and negative answers to questions; we use the color and size of coins to represent their value; and strings of shapes and sounds in language to represent everything from color to chemical composition. But we can also take a natural medium and assign the properties it exemplifies a role in conventional system intended to express their natural content. In this case, instead of using the medium to convey independent information, we exploit its natural connections to the world to let Mother Nature speak to us *through* it. This is what we do with measuring instruments when we attach labels to the positions of

---

3. The distinction here is intuitive and heuristic. Nothing important rests on it.

their pointers; we translate the natural content of their informational states into our own language, expressing it in a form that lets us feed it directly into thought.

The better the fit between the natural and conventional content of the states of such an instrument—that is, the closer the labels come to expressing their natural content, or the more invariant the extensional coincidence of natural and conventional content—the better the job we have done of translating the natural signals it receives. We have done a perfect job just in case the properties of the medium C-represent what they N-represent in all possible contexts. More generally, we will be successful relative to the context defined by conditions c* just in case the properties in question C-represent what they N-represent in c*, and the process increased the portability of the information contained in N-states. Of course, if we want to *use* the information contained in such states to govern dynamical behavior, labels are an unnecessary intermediary. We can, as I mentioned earlier, use the information contained in the states of a thermometer to govern the behavior of a heating device, by establishing an architectural connection. We simply hook them up to each other, bypassing the need for explicit symbolic representation.

Now turn to the relationship between thought and experience. Experience is a natural medium, and from a dynamical perspective the purpose of the network of ideas erected overtop of it is to assign it a role that expresses its natural content in a form that allows it be communicated across contexts and control dynamical behavior at a spatial and temporal distance. For these purposes we need to attach labels to phenomenal profiles whose content is invariant under transformations of context and coincides with their informational content (at least, coincides well enough that under the circumstances to which we are *actually* exposed, looseness of fit doesn't lead to practical disaster). This is the same theoretical undertaking that we face in attaching labels to the positions of the pointer observable on a measuring instrument. If we restrict attention to measurements of unobservable properties, the parallel is exact. Just as we don't have any access to such properties that is not mediated by causal impact on positions of pointer observables on instruments, we don't have any access to external properties that is not mediated by causal impact on properties exemplified in experience. Indeed, the latter is just a special case of the former, with experience acting as pointer. The body is, effectively, the mind's measuring instrument; the mind renders the information fleetingly registered on its sensory surfaces in an invariant form, combines it with old information from the same source, and keeps the whole accumulated stock poised to guide action.

There are two important qualifications. First, we shouldn't view the process of attaching labels too literally; experience bears conceptual content not in the way pointer positions bear labels, but in the way that words bear meanings (or perhaps in the way that a gesture bears tenderness or laughter bears joy). Phenomenal profiles don't get associated with something distinct from them that *has* conventional representational significance; we stop the regress before it gets started by saying that they acquire significance by getting caught up in the representational net. They literally *become* ideas. Thought arises gradually out of experience, with the distinction between properties presented and properties *re*presented emerging by degree as a product of the process of articulation in a manner that I'll sketch in the next chapter. We don't start with a fully articulated language of thought and have to wire it into the perceptual network, nor do we start with raw experience and go individually through the steps of articulation. Innate structure interacts with early experience and deliberate instruction in an interplay that developmental psychologists teach us is both exceedingly complex and highly individual. We learn quickly in the course of things to parse experience and use it to navigate, but the distinction between the medium and the message emerges in a gradual process of decoupling that becomes increasingly pronounced and self-conscious as we mature.

Second, I want to caution against thinking of phenomenal profiles as *objects* of perception. They are nothing more than self-presenting internal states. Like the reflexively presented ink in "the ink in which this sentence is written" or the quality of voice in an utterance of "the sound of my voice," they are bearers of both natural and conventional content they can be described in acts that establish internal connections between their natural and conventional content. We don't make much representational use in language of the qualitative properties of the medium, and self-presentation and self-description in written and spoken speech is uncommon. But thought makes heavy representational use of the self-presenting properties of phenomenal states. They are the points at which natural and conventional content meet. Natural information flows through the links they provide into the representational apparatus where it is channeled over the web of ideas by the semantic connections among ideas. If everything works as it should, information flows from the world, through experience, into the representational network of thought, whereafter it is fed into the machinery that governs locomotion in a way that gets our bodies moving in a manner that is at once fine-tuned to the present situation and informed by an accumulated history of experience from different parts of space. The properties exemplified in experience—not just simple qualities associated with a single modality (e.g., the taste of sugar, or the look of red), but the complex cross-modal patterns I've called phenomenal pro-files—patterns that we can reidentify and respond to—get promoted to the status of representations. It's not a status they have naturally, or intrinsically, but one they acquire by getting caught up in thought. And the content they acquire is conventional in the sense that it is at least partially 'up to us'. We get to say in how *this* profile gets integrated into our ideas, the role it plays in the deliberative machinery, how it guides behavior, and so on. That is something that varies from person to person and changes over time in the life of an individual as she becomes increasingly adept at reading the signals coming in from the environment. Each of us has to learn to decide questions of the form: Is that a sign of friendship or ag-gression? Is this the look of something to eat or something to avoid? Is that the sound of water, and is that the smell of fire? These sights and sounds and smells bridge the gap between concepts and properties in the way that −40 bridges the gap between Celsius and Fahrenheit scales, in the way the word *bureaucrat* bridges the gap between French and English, and in the way that my sister bridges the gap between my family and that of her in-laws. They are fixed points, positioned at the interface between the space of causes and the space of concepts.

5.3   GENERAL THEMES

I hope that we're beginning to get a sense of the dynamical problem to which self-representation—which I use as shorthand for the construction of internal models and the regulation of their dynamical role by acts of self-location and self-description—is a solution. The mechanisms that control behavior for mobile beings have to be either sensitive only to the imme-diate environment or very different from the mechanisms that control the behavior of immobile systems, because mobility disturbs natural connec-tions to the environment that would otherwise be provided by experience. In computational terms, unconstrained motion means that the situation of the agent—not only position in space, but all contextual parameters that affect the informational content of internal states—has to be treated as a free variable. When situation is treated as a free variable and the infor-mational content of internal states depends on situation, and dynamical role depends on informational content, one has a very difficult design problem. The solution—quite ingenious as a piece of engineering—is self-representation. The system constructs internal models of the world that are fitted into the pathways between experience and action with adjustable hinges regulated by self-locating and reflexively self-describing acts. This provides the degrees of internal freedom needed to counteract the effects of movement and maintain continuing links with particular features of the landscape. The position of the models varies directly with the external situation of the body in a way calculated to preserve coordinating links that would otherwise be disturbed by motion.

How does the calculation work? This is an empirical question, of course. The spatial case has been a focal point of research in cognitive psychology. Alignment seems to be maintained through largely unconscious computation that may involve application of a difference-minimizing procedure. On this hypothesis the brain effectively solves simultaneous equations for changes in the landscape and changes in the body's position in the landscape (i.e., changes in perceptual content and changes in perceptual perspective) in ways that minimize overall difference. Evans's Simple Theory of Perception introduced the process in a rudimentary form into the philosophical literature. You start with a centered map, take new readings, and, assuming continuity of change and motion, make the most minimal changes along two dimensions—your position *in*, and your spatial perspective *on*, the landscape. So, for example, a ship navigating by a map might explain changes in current reading partly by the water moving faster and partly by changes in the ship's speed. Changes in distance from a mobile landmark might be explained partly by changes in the position of the landmark and changes in the position of the ship.

It is important not to confuse the processing that attaches self-locating contents to visual experience with the conscious computation that uses that self-locating information to regulate behavior. The mind uses sensory information to re-self-locate on an internal model, and what is presented to the conscious mind is a content that is already factored into an objective and reflexive component. The content of experience is self-locating. Visual experience presents itself to the conscious mind as a perspectival view of a spatially ordered landscape, a view of the space from a certain location in it. The objective component of these self-locating contents is used to revise one's model (if you self-locate at Rillito River and notice that the riverbed is dry, you add that information to your map), and the reflexive component is used as input to a computational cycle that I'll refer to heretofore as a *self-representational loop*.[4] I'll say more about the form of the self-representational loop in part 3, but for now think of it

4. By its position in the internal pathways, I mean how it is modified by perception and how it modifies behavior.

as the self-conscious deliberative process that mediates self-location and action. It takes the self-locating contents of perceptual states as input and generates prescriptions for action.

There are some important differences between the tasks of keeping notions and concepts coordinated with the world. Keeping track of places across variation in location is so practically essential that it requires no instruction and little conscious regulation. We are wired to think spatially, and cognitive scientists have been trying to work out the complex combination of conscious and unconscious processing involved in spatial navigation. Learning to keep concepts coordinated with properties across variation in spatial context is less essential, much slower, and less systematic. On the side of concepts, invariance is only partial, and is achieved in increments. Before turning attention to how this works in the next chapter, I want to pull back and recap briefly the central points.

5.4 INTERNAL WORLD-MODELS AND SELF-REPRESENTATIONAL LOOPS

We have been viewing thought, experience, and action as representational media and have been focusing on the interfaces between them. Experience feeds into the mind, is translated into thought, and is fed back again out to action. We've looked at the complicated dance of self-location and self-description by which thought is brought into, and kept in, alignment with the spatial and temporal landscape using indexicals, and the role of the self-presenting properties of experience in aligning the descriptive apparatus of thought with the world.

Experience is a natural medium, and from a dynamical perspective the purpose of the network of ideas erected overtop of it is to assign it a role that expresses its natural content in a relatively invariant form, one that allows it to be communicated across contexts and control dynamical behavior at a distance. The mind takes information coming through different sensory pathways and acquired at different times and places, renders it in an invariant form—one that allows it to be combined and stored—and keeps the whole accumulated stock poised to guide action at any place in the spatial and temporal landscape.

Information flows into the natural pathways, through phenomenal properties, and into the representational apparatus where it is channeled over the web of ideas by the internal, semantic connections that link idea to idea. If everything works as it should, it is fed thereafter into the machinery that governs locomotion in a way that gets our bodies moving in a manner that is at once fine-tuned to the occurrent situation and in-formed by a whole accumulated body experience.

I have used the notion of information, but that is only because a purely dynamical description would have been too complicated. Ulti-mately, it is all just wiring and connections keeping the states of different media covarying relative to a range of contexts. The relativity to a range of contexts is ineliminable. Choose your contexts differently, and you will get different patterns of covariation. But there is a (roughly delineated) range of contexts that corresponds to the biological niche of a system (the range of contexts it needs to navigate to survive). Those are the contexts covar-iation with respect to which Mother Nature selects for, and they're the ones in which we are, for the most part, interested.

Covariation of this sort may or may not be robust enough to support intentional content, but it needn't be the whole story. I suspect that notions rich enough to support many of our intuitions about content will depend on (i) how much structure gets added up-top, not only with self-representation, but with the iterated hierarchy of self-evaluation and self-control, and (ii) the interaction of thought with language, where language is an essentially social medium. It's arguable, for example, that we need multiple perceivers exchanging information about a common environment, before we have anything constrained enough to count as representation. And its arguable that we need the back and forth of argument and the practice of giving and taking reasons before we have the normativity that many have argued is essential to intentionality. All of this can be added to an account in which the fundamental mind-world relations are the relations of covariation.

Our representations of the world have moving parts, and we can talk about how the parts change and move with features of the world. The unique semantic property of reflexive representation (that it *is* what it represents) is what allows it to place real constraints on dynamical relations between ideas and things. This is clearest with singular vocabulary, when one is attaching a set of coordinates to a place, or a name to a face, but the generalization to descriptive vocabulary is straightforward. A concept is linked to a phe-nomenal profile with a thought of the form 'this is what red things look like (under conditions like these)'. So long as phenomenal properties are con-nected by not merely semantic, but real dynamical links to properties in the external landscape what we need to do to wire the whole descriptive network into the world dynamically is to establish semantic links between phe-nomenal profiles and terms in the network, in exactly the way that we interpret a coordinate representation of space by establishing semantic links between coordinates and points that we can ostend. There's a lot of com-plexity in the case of self-description that has no analogy for self-location, as well as some important differences. These will get sorted out in stages.

The mind operates with an internal model of the world that has a great deal more than merely spatiotemporal structure. There are qualitative dimensions of representation; we build up something more like an internal *picture*, where this captures the use made of the qualitative properties of the medium. And the picture has causal written into it. We represent the landscape as a richly structured network of causally interacting parts. Our models capture both the way things are and the way they hang together under change. We elaborate them as we go, keeping track of the position of the body and all of the features of the environment that make a difference to the informational content of our phenomenal states and putting that information to use. To put it in terms that get rid of the middleman, the mind represents itself as a nexus of incoming and outgoing causal pathways, centered on a body. It keeps track of its own states on the incoming and outgoing ends, and it uses the former to regulate the latter. The continuous process of self-location and self-description allows the mind to exploit the context-dependent informational content of its phenomenal states to fullest advantage in regulating behavior.

When it comes to self-description, the task is to bring a palette of internally exemplified properties into alignment with descriptive concepts by acts of self-description such as like "the properties here exemplified are such and such," or "such and such is the property exemplified here." The process will be successful just in case some internal states exemplify properties that are nomologically connected in the wider world.[5]

In chapter 6, we will see in more detail that internally exemplified properties carry information that depends on their position in the landscape, and explicit representation adds the degrees of freedom between phenomenal state and concept that are needed to establish robust connections. Once the links are in place—the internal model and the representation of the links between concepts and properties can become as complicated as you please—we can coin concepts to refer to anything that we can connect to a phenomenal profile by a link as contingent, attenuated, and context-dependent as can be. We can coin concepts for any property that can be implicitly defined by its phenomenal profile, anything whose presence we can gauge perceptually, under circumstances we can recognize.[6] We coin a concept for X by forming a thought of the form "X is a

---

5. Notice that it doesn't matter for these purposes whether phenomenal states are brain states or epiphenomenal effects of brain states. They're still connected in the nomological net on the incoming end in a manner that makes them bearers of information.

6. Measurement contexts in science are highly regimented versions of this. We can have concepts of electric charge and quark color because we can set up conditions under which they covary with phenomenal states by a very long and fragile link starting with the pointer observable on a measuring apparatus, and leading into the microscopic realm.

property tracked by this kind of phenomenal state under such and such conditions or the property that manifests itself thus and so in this kind of context." The internal component of the chain connecting the concept to the property is made up of semantic connections between the concept and the phenomenal state the external component is made up of context-dependent nomological relations between phenomenal state and property.

The power of this additional freedom is hard to overestimate. You can always do by design what I am suggesting is done by self-representation (we could build machines that adapt to certain changes in the environment, or process sensory or transducer states in a manner that is sensitive to certain changes in position), but as we will see in chapter 7, building a self-representational loop into a system gives it a way of reorganizing its own internal architecture in response to external exigencies, with a speed and flexibility that is otherwise impossible.

It's important, in all of this, to appreciate the *practical* nature of acts of self-location. Within the context of a dynamical system steering by a map, acts of self-location don't[7] add any new information to the map; rather, they coordinate the map with the environment by aligning it in the perception to action pathways. We saw already with Putnam one knot that an overly representationalist understanding of self-locating acts can get you tied into. This is one of the most insidious mistakes that one can make in metaphysics; Fallacious arguments based on such an understanding can seem utterly persuasive. Section 2 will be devoted to exposing particular instances of it.

5.5   PHYSICAL AND PHENOMENAL CONCEPTS

This section is for aficionados. It concerns questions that will be of primary interest to those with a specialized focus, and that can remain unresolved, I believe, for the larger picture. We have to be careful not to be misled by our external perspective on the media that served as examples above into too simplistic a picture of the relationship between physical and phenomenal properties. Reflexive identification of properties works by exhibiting an exemplar and employing a similarity relation; when you say 'this type of event', you say 'events like this', where the kind of 'likeness' in question is phenomenal similarity. Phenomenal similarity is defined over internal events. Internal events have an intrinsic phenomenology; events that fall in the same presentational domain can be related to one another phenomenally. External events have an extrinsic phenomenology in virtue

---

7. Or don't necessarily, for the map can be as complete as can be. I'll return to this.

of causing internal events, but they have no intrinsic phenomenology; they don't bear one another phenomenal relations and there are no phenomenal relations between internal and external events. Phenomenal types, for this reason, are restricted to what we might call 'presentational domains', sets of properties that can be simultaneously presented. Each mind constitutes its own presentational domain, and an inner demonstration of the form 'events (phenomenally) like this' cannot extend beyond the boundaries of a single mind, and cannot, for that reason, be identified with physical types, which span presentational domains.

Inner demonstrations together with a relation of phenomenal similarity identify phenomenal types with extensions restricted to presentational domains.[8] Physical concepts are defined over the domain as a whole and span presentational domains. So we don't really pick out physical properties with these internal acts of self-description, and the relationship between physical and phenomenal properties has to be more complex than simple type-type identity. But the difficulties are conceptual rather than ontological in nature. What we have here is a dualism of concept without a dualism of property.[9] Physical and phenomenal concepts are concepts drawn from incommensurate representational schemes, rather like spatial coordinates defined relative to different frames of reference. We know there can be points of extensional contact between such schemes, but we don't have a well-developed vocabulary for describing their conceptual relations.

8. It doesn't matter what representational scheme you employ the everyday world of enduring objects arranged in space, or the more articulated spatiotemporal manifold of physics, there has to be enough of a systematic relationship between phenomenal and physical types that phenomenal states can provide the epistemological basis for recognizing physical types. The general requirement is that physical events have to be implicitly definable in phenomenal terms.

9. There are geometric analogues. Consider the property 'having length of 1 m' defined by provision of an exemplar (the standard meter) and specifying a procedure for determining sameness of length. If the operational definition of sameness of length is well defined only relative to a state of motion, or within certain restricted domains, then the concept 'having length of 1 m' is an analogue of a phenomenal concept.

6

Context and Coordination

We turn now from the day-to-day business of coordinating thought with experience (and action; more, later, on this) to what we might call 'conceptual evolution' and to the role of the environment in maintaining an invariant link between thought and the world. I'll show how coordination breaks down when one moves into unaccustomed circumstances and describe a general technique for decoupling thought from context, by developing an increasingly articulated representation of the causal fabric in which phenomenal states are embedded.[1] Then I'll use the story to recommend a generalization of Perry's vocabulary of unarticulated constituents, introduced earlier with the example of the Z-landers. Finally, I'll bring the discussion back around and incorporate this into the general story of how the mind turns the fragile, fleeting links provided by experience into reliable, continuing connections that reach far into the spatial landscape and deeply into the circle of causes.

---

1. I've been focusing on the epistemic side, but on the practical side, we fine-tune control by developing an articulated conception of the causal relations on the outgoing end as well.

Sellars's discussion of John and his tie shop will serve as the central illustrative example. Sellars writes:

> A young man, whom I shall call John, works in a necktie shop. He has learned the use of color words in the usual way... As he examines his stock every evening before closing up shop, he says, "This is red," "That is green," "This is purple," etc., and such of his linguistic peers as happen to be present nod their heads approvingly....
>
> Let us suppose, now, that at this point in the story, electric lighting in invented.... Just after it has been installed in [John's] shop, one of his neighbors, Jim, comes in to buy a necktie.
>
> "Here is a handsome green one," says John.
>
> "But it *isn't* green," says Jim, and takes John outside.
>
> "Well," says John, "it was green in there, but now it is blue."
>
> "No," says Jim, "you know that neckties don't change their color merely as a result of being taken from place to place."
>
> "But perhaps electricity changes their color and they change back again in daylight?"
>
> "That would be a queer kind of change, wouldn't it?" says Jim.
>
> "I suppose so," says a bewildered John. "But we *saw* that it was green *in there.*"
>
> "No, we didn't see that it was green in there, because it wasn't green, and you can't see what isn't so!"[2]

Concepts, recall, are ideas of properties. By 'phenomenal profiles' I mean reidentifiable patterns of light, color, sound, and so on, that serve as a basis for recognition of properties.[3] I use 'properties' in a noncommittal extensional sense. For convenience, I'm going to call the concepts and profiles under discussion 'color concepts' and 'color profiles', but these are just labels. It is not supposed that they bear anything but external relations— that is, causal-informational links—to colors or to each other.

Here is how I want to describe what's going on with John. He has concepts, with fixed phenomenal profiles, that apply to ties. Faced with changes in profile as ties are carried across the threshold of his newly lit shop, John ventures a couple of causal hypotheses to account for intrinsic

---

2. See Sellars, "Empiricism and the Philosophy of Mind," 37.

3. Phenomenal profiles will typically be complex, cross-modal patterns, and there is no assumption that we can characterize them otherwise than by reference to the properties for which they serve as the recognitional basis. I may know the look of a smiling face when I see it, or recognize the sound of laughter when I hear it, without being able to describe either in terms other than, precisely, the look of a smiling face or the sound of laughter.

changes in ties. When these are rejected by Jim, John recognizes, as I will put it, a 'joint' in the relations between colors (conceived by John, as intrinsic properties of ties) and their profiles, treating the latter—that is, the way colors *look*, the type of experience they produce—now, newly, partly as a relation to ambient lighting.[4] The story continues:

> We return to the shop after an interval, and we find that when John is asked "What is the color of this necktie?" he makes such statements as "It looks green, but take it outside and see." . . . As [he] becomes more and more sophisticated about his own and other people's visual experiences, he learns under what conditions it is as though one were seeing a necktie to be of one color when in fact it is of another.[5]

What John does, in becoming more sophisticated, is precisely learn what conjunctions of circumstances and properties yield the phenomenal profiles he originally associated directly with his color concepts, the profiles that his early linguistic training, which occurred in the context of fixed lighting conditions, taught him warranted application of color predicates. He learns, that is to say, what conjunctions of circumstances and properties yield the greenish and reddish looks that serve as color profiles, learns about the joints in the relation that keep those looks coordinated with the properties they ordinarily indicate. Knowledge of this sort is not a practical necessity so long as John is never confronted with circumstances in which those conditions don't obtain, or, at least, so long as he has no need to judge colors across contexts in which they are allowed to vary. Two things happen to John's color concepts in this process: (1) they get connected in a much richer network of concepts; they become *articulated* in ways in which they hadn't been previously, and (2) the domain in which he can correctly apply color concepts widens. John was always a good judge of colors in the sun, but now he can pass seamlessly from electric light to sunlight without losing track of colors, or running into the kind of confusion he showed in the episode with Jim; he can coordinate the colors of ties in his shop with their colors outside. The more he learns about color, the less reliant he is on particular conditions to judge the colors of things; the more robust his color-detecting ability is across changes in context.

Formally, we can put what John learns thus; a greenish look doesn't by itself indicate an intrinsic property of surfaces. It indicates such a property

---

4. In one way, color is a particularly bad case, because the terminology is so confused and disputed. In another way, it is a particularly good case because the confusions and ambiguities themselves are instructive. They're ambiguous in just the ways that they need to be to let us move seamlessly from phenomenal profiles to nonrelational concepts and then to relational concepts with multiple arguments.

5. Sellars, "Empiricism and the Philosophy of Mind," 43.

only relative to fixed lighting conditions, which is to say that it indicates a relation between the colors of things and ambient conditions: a complex property which is the product of a *pair* of parameters,[6] that can be used when one of those parameters takes a fixed, 'standard' value, to track the other. John learns that what color profiles tell him about the colors of things depends quite generally on the value of a contextual parameter that varies independently. Conceptual articulation manifests itself not just in the ability to apply concepts in a wider range of contexts, but in inference and in sensitivity to defeating conditions. To be able to talk about the way things *look* without committing oneself to their *being* one way or another (which is, in Sellars's terms, a part of the *logic* of looks talk), or to recognize the defeasibility of the inference from 'that tie looks green' to 'that tie is green', is to recognize a hidden complexity in the relations between colors and their profiles, one that isn't reflected in the intrinsic character of the latter, and that needn't be appreciated to apply them under fixed conditions.

6.1   THE GENERAL DYNAMIC

Let's give a general, schematic characterization of this process. Let **X** be a quantity (i.e., a mutually exclusive, jointly exhaustive family of properties that characterize systems of a certain kind), and let's say that I am a good **X**-detector just in case I can reliably judge **X**-values when presented with systems of the kind to which it pertains, under conditions c_I, where c_I is one value of a parameter **C** that takes a range of values. Note that c_I-conditions can be conditions that are 'standard' or 'normal' for organisms like me, or they can be carefully prepared and highly contrived. John was a good color detector under direct sunlight, but the conditions in his shop had him misjudging colors; I am a good detector of the presence of cilantro in objects placed in my mouth, unless I've just brushed my teeth; and most of us are good detectors of radiation and electric charge only when we have the right instruments handy. The difference between these cases lies not in their independence of environmental conditions, but in how special those conditions are relative to our natural ones.[7] We are no more immediately sensitive to the colors of things than we are to their

---

6. It's actually, of course, much more complicated, and that is a part of what *we've* learned as science has uncovered the complex physical process that mediates green surfaces and greenish looks.

7. We need to distinguish *ordinary* conditions from conditions that are *normal*, in the biological sense. Ordinary conditions have a special status because they are the conditions under which we ordinarily learn and apply concepts; normal conditions have a distinguished status because if one is looking for a biological notion of proper function to characterize perceptual contents, she will appeal to normal conditions in saying what our perceptual systems were designed by evolutionary pressures to detect.

electrical or chemical properties. Being a good **X**-detector, then, is a relation to a context, or, better, a set of contextual parameters, and it is a matter of degree.[8] If I am a good **X** detector only under, or *relative to,* c_1-conditions, my **X**-detecting capabilities do not truly belong to me; they are a relation I bear to c_1-conditions. I do not carry them with me when I move outside those conditions; I am only part of a larger **X**-detecting system that includes a c_1-environment.

The process that John went through after the episode with Jim is the characteristic way we win independence from c_1-conditions; we create an internal surrogate of the context that plays the role c_1 played in coordinating phenomenal profiles with **X**-values. In short, we explicitly represent **C** and relate **X**-values to **C**-values. In doing so, we are not making explicit a relationality that was already in place. Our **X**-concepts change; they *acquire* articulation they didn't have before, and that articulation is manifested both in the practical ability to apply them more widely and in their logic (i.e., in recognition of conditions that defeat the inference from 'looks red', or 'is showing a red profile' and 'is red').[9]

As for **C**, explicit characterization and knowledge of how **X**'s vary with **C** can, and typically does, come in stages. We can suppose John began by recognizing the relativity of his **X**-detecting abilities to conditions he could only characterize in indexical terms ("conditions like these, in whatever sense of 'like' turns out to be relevant"), and learned about light and the way the profiles vary with light, only by degree and perhaps never fully. His color-detecting ability becomes more finely tuned to colors across wider ranges of contexts at each step. Graphically, in general terms, letting $\mathbf{X} = \{x_1, x_2 \ldots\}$ be phenomenal profiles, $\mathbf{Y} = \{y_1, y_2 \ldots\}$ be properties of interest, and $\mathbf{C} = \{c_1, c_2 \ldots\}$ be contexts, we can represent things as follows:

$c_1$maps $x_1$into y_1, $x_2$into y_2, $x_3$into y_3, ...
$c_2$maps $x_1$into y_2, $x_2$into y_3, $x_3$into y_4, ...
$c_3$maps $x_1$into y_3, $x_2$into y_4, $x_3$into y_5, ...
$c_4$maps $x_1$into y_4, $x_2$into y_5, $x_3$into y_6, ...
and so on.

There is no problem about coordinating **X** and **Y** values relative to one or another fixed value for **C**, but if we want to coordinate things across contexts in which **C** is allowed to vary, we need something in the head that varies with it. That is what I meant earlier when I said that we had to

8. The degrees are introduced by reliability, which is something that, under the right conditions, we can get a good quantitative measure of.

9. It's not just that John can say to himself 'the inference is defeasible, I know not how'. He has an understanding of the kinds of conditions that would defeat it.

recognize a joint in the relation that coordinates the extensions of concepts with their phenomenal profiles.[10] We need something in the head, that is to say, that varies with the actual C-conditions in a way that keeps **A** and **B** stably coordinated, when we move from one kind of C-environment to another; something that corrects for changes in **C** in a manner that allows us to maintain an invariant connection between **A** and **B**. Here is a way to state it that brings out what the structures in question are doing: We want our judgments about redness to be coordinated with the intrinsic properties of surfaces. But we find that the coordination between color experience and the intrinsic properties of colored surfaces depends on standard conditions. We find out, that is to say, that the relation between red appearances and the redness of surfaces is secured by standard conditions, so we coordinate our color judgments with the intrinsic properties of colored surfaces by letting the relationship between red appearances and our judgments about the redness of surfaces be mediated by *representations* of standard conditions.

There is no practical need to represent fixed features of the environment; no need, for instance, to represent the connections on this side of the skin that connect my sensory surfaces to my brain, so long as they remain intact. I don't have to know anything about how my sensory apparatus works in order to use it to track features of my environment, so long as I don't move outside of the context. Representation gets its practical point with variation and mobility. I need as much and only as much structure in the head as is necessary to coordinate phenomenal profiles with features of the environment that I have an interest in tracking, i.c., the external landmarks that are benchmarks in the determination of behavior. How much that *is* will depend on how mobile I am, and how much my environment varies around me. There are a few things to pay attention to. First, there is the coordinating role that representation plays—a hint of which we saw in Perry's earlier discussion—the contextual parameter introduced to reinstate coordination takes over the role that the context was playing in fixing the connections between properties and their phenomenal profiles. Second, there is the fact that features of context that the agent himself may not be aware of—indeed, may not even have the conceptual resources to represent—can play a crucial role in coordinating

---

10. There are two possibilities: It might be that C has two values, one of which represents standard conditions, and when conditions are nonstandard, the A's don't vary systematically with the B's, and all bets are off. Or it might be, as in the case of colors, that C takes a range of values, and the A's vary systematically with the B's for all of them, but in different ways. If the latter, it is possible to read B-values off of A under any external conditions, so long as we know the value of C.

his ideas with the world. Third, there is the direction of conceptual development, which is toward increasing articulation. The articulation takes the form of creating an internal surrogate for features of context that play a role in coordinating profiles with the world, features that are partly determinative of (i.e., whose variation makes a difference to) the informational content of experience. This kind of bootstrapping redesign is our way of fine-tuning the extensional relationship between ideas and the world, i.e., forming robust (in the specific sense of invariant under changes of context) informational links to features of the environment. Finally, the freedom from context that is won by this technique is a matter of degree, and (something that was important to Sellars) it can be attained in increments. We can be more or less dependent on more or less esoteric external circumstances, and we can measure our dependence along two dimensions: by how disastrously we go wrong when we move outside those circumstances, and how ubiquitous those circumstances are.

6.2   MECHANICAL METAPHOR

There is a mechanical metaphor that I find helpful. We start out with concepts, like John's immature concept of color, concepts that we learn in the nursery, by ostension, in a process of exhibition of instance and foil. These concepts are initially tied directly to phenomenal profiles, so that when the link between properties and profiles is broken by movement into a nonstandard environment (i.e., an environment in which the value of the contextual parameter that coordinates profiles with the property takes an unaccustomed value, a context that changes the profiles of colors), the link between concept and property is broken as well. We gradually develop internal structure, (conceptual joints in the *semantic* chain linking concepts to phenomenal profiles) that mirrors external structure, (architectural joints in the causal chain linking properties to their phenomenal profiles) in a way that allows us freedom to change context without breaking the link between concept and property. We make semantic adjustments on the inside that accommodate architectural changes on the outside, occasioned by shift of context.

Phenomenal profiles—coordinated with the external landscape by Mother Nature and with the internal network of ideas by us—are the interface between the internal and external landscape. The goal for the situated, concept-mongering agent is to be able to accommodate as much external movement as nature will allow without breaking the connection between concept and property, where 'movement' is understood in a very wide sense to include not only motion in the spatial sense but any physically possible transformation of context. And that would require nothing less than internal reproduction of the external links between properties and profiles, down to the lowest level of discernible detail. We want to break all of the contextual constraints that we can on the applicability of our concepts; we want to make the links between concepts and properties invariant under transformations to any kind of context to which we might be exposed, and we do it by adding links to the chain coordinating concepts and experience corresponding to variable links in the causal chain that coordinate experience with the world outside the head. The more we represent, the less cognitively bound we are to context, and the freer we are to roam in search of food and mates. As more of the external links in the coordinating chain between experience and landmarks in the external landscape are mirrored on the inside, more of the world becomes our cognitive home. Although we can loosen the connections to context, they cannot be severed. The cautionary lesson of the Argument from Confinement was that the ties to context can be as flexible and attenuated as you please, but they have to remain intact. If ideas are to be coordinated with the world, if they are to continue to bear information about it, the causal pathways through experience have to remain in place.

6.3   IMPOSING VS. REVEALING ARTICULATION

I have insisted, and Sellars did as well, that this be viewed as the process by which those concepts *become* articulated, not a process in which some implicit relationality is revealed. Parameters are articulated as the practical requirements of coordination demand, that is, as exposure to new contexts requires explicit representation of features of the environment to maintain invariant links between them and elements in the representational apparatus. I emphasized earlier that coordination is a purely extensional notion; one's concepts are coordinated not with fine-grained properties, but with extensionally equivalent classes of properties. Semantic fine-tuning and articulation à la John is a way of making the extensional relations more discriminating. Notice also that it is only because we do have exposure to a wide range of contexts that we can get ideas finely tuned to the landscape; the more limited the range of exposure, the less room there is for extensional discrimination.

I called the concepts John associates with color predicates 'color concepts', but that is only for convenience. My official view is that there was no fact of the matter about whether they were ideas of *color,* rather than any extensionally equivalent property, relative to the range of circumstances across which John has standing dispositions to apply the term (even if those dispositions are vague, tacit dispositions to let the communities as one's own guide, provided only that there are facts—again, of whatever sort there may be—about dispositions on the level of the community).[11] However ill defined and tenuous those links are, once they have been cataloged, there are no *further* facts about the relations between Jim's ideas and colors. You can choose a stage at which to begin calling them ideas *of color;* I won't make such choices. These choices do need to be made at some level, to the extent that we need normative constraints on linguistic and conceptual competence (how well coordinated with the conventional linguistic meanings of terms do a speaker's ideas have to be to count as competent? how much deference and vagueness and context dependence is allowed before we stop according a speaker that status, with all of the rights and obligations it confers?). But we needn't make them here. The personal task for John is to get ideas that bear definite, robust, mobile links to the landscape, ideas that are well enough coordinated that he can use them to steer by.

There is a real, separate question, however, about whether John's concepts were *coordinated* with colors before the episode with Jim. I think the answer there should be yes, but more tenuously by his standing disposition to let his application of color terms be guided by the linguistic community. One's concepts are coordinated by variously attenuated links, largely unknown, mostly unrepresented internally, and John's concept was coordinated tenuously by deference to the community. This sort of deference is quite global and can be more or less discriminating. The insight of the various forms of externalism that have been a staple of the philosophical literature in the last half century was to appreciate that this sort of reliance on external links to the environment (physical, social, linguistic) to keep our ideas coordinated with the world is our native position. Whatever measure of autonomy we have is achieved in the kind of process for which John provides a good model, one that involves representing internally the external component of the chain coordinating phenomenal profiles with the external landscape. We *internalize* as much of the coordinating chain as we can. What this requires will depend obviously, and in very specific ways, on how we are embedded in the world and our particular form of embodiment.

---

11. It can not only be indeterminate; it can be indeterminate whether it is determinate. Does the community have dispositions? Not definitely yes; not definitely no.

6.4 UNARTICULATED CONSTITUENTS

I want to recall the vocabulary introduced in the discussion of the Z-landers, and generalize it in a way that will let us use it to describe this process. Perry defined an unarticulated constituent of a sentence as an object, or property that is not represented by any semantically significant constituent, but reference to which needs to be made in specifying its truth conditions. I want to widen the notion so that it applies to the representational states of any medium, including natural media—for example, experience—for which informational content provides the analogue of truth conditions. An *unarticulated constituent* of a representational state is one that is not reflected in the intrinsic nature of the state, but to which reference has to be made in specifying its content, where 'content' is understood, as earlier, to mean informational content in the case of natural media, and conventional content in the case of conventional media.[12] What is meant by "not reflected in the intrinsic nature of the state" is that intrinsic character of the state can be held fixed and its informational content varied simply by changing its situation with respect to the relevant object, condition, or property. The content of the state varies directly, immediately with the disposition of, or its relation to, the object (or condition or property) in question.

Greenish experiences in and of themselves, really indicate nothing; they have virtually no intrinsic informational content.[13] In the context of a given set of ambient conditions, for an agent with a working set of eyes, however, they can be tremendously informative. The contextual parameters whose values have to be specified to express their informational content are unarticulated constituents of (the natural content of) greenish experiences. The parameters needn't be articulated so long as their values don't vary across the contexts to which an agent is exposed, or at least across those in which he will be forming judgments on the basis of greenish experiences. We can, as John did while he confined his color judgments to the context of his shop, connect the profile directly to the property it indicates under the fixed conditions, but they must be recognized and specified to coordinate across contexts in which they vary.

---

12. There are questions about identifying and individuating unarticulated constituents (e.g., Do the proper parts of unarticulated constituents count as unarticulated constituents? Can unarticulated constituents be disjunctive properties or complex mereological objects?) that are solved by taking the notion of an unarticulated parameter as basic. C is an unarticulated parameter of P just in case one has to know (exactly) which value of C obtains to express the informational content of P. A property is an unarticulated constituent of P just in case it is the value of an unarticulated parameter. And a particular a is an unarticulated constituent of P just in case C is an unarticulated parameter, there is some fixed relation R, such that $C = R(x)$, and $C = R(a)$. This is a bit of complexity that we can mostly suppress.

13. Except the degenerate content that every phenomenal profile has, representing itself.

If we take a broad view and look at the role representations in choreographing action, in keeping fleeing behavior, for instance, synchronized with the presence of danger, it is clear that only a small part of the chain linking the source of danger (the tiger in the distance) to the proximal cause of fleeing behavior (the thought "Tiger! Run!") is in my *head*, and only a smaller, and even more selective part is consciously accessible. For the purposes of coordination, none of the fixed connections need to be represented internally. I needn't *know* anything about the link between the local determinants of behavior and its cause, I needn't have any internal representation of that link insofar as it is invariant. And, for purposes of coordination, it doesn't matter much what the local determinants of behavior are intrinsically *like*; a tinny taste in the mouth or pricking thumbs connected in the right way to lion presences, on the one hand, and fleeing behavior, on the other, would do just as well as a lionish shape in the distance in getting me to run when I need to run. So long as the external link is in place and invariant across the contexts in which it matters (those in which I need it to steer by), there is no need to reproduce an image of it in the mind, and, conversely, no amount of picturing it in the head will effect the needed coordination. But it will play a crucial role in keeping my behavior appropriately attuned to the world. If I begin venturing regularly into contexts that break the external connections I will get into trouble.

The more we represent, the more unarticulated contextual parameters are made explicit, i.e., the less bound we are, practically and cognitively, to particular contexts or types of context, i.e., the freer we are to travel, the more able to make our concepts communicate across a contextual divide. The more of the external links in the coordinating chain between our ideas and the external landmarks that we steer by (the salient features that have important and relatively fixed roles in governing behavior), the more cognitively mobile we become. The process of decoupling is natural, and familiar, in a kind of unself-conscious way, and it is part and parcel of conceptual maturation. We start out (both on the level of the individual and as a community) with quite parochial ideas that are rendered increasingly objective, less tied to the contingencies of our particular situation in the world, by explicit representation of, and relation to, the conditions that define our situation. Compare what Nagel says:

> The development [of the scientific conception of objective reality]
> goes in stages, each of which gives a more objective picture than the
> one before. The first step is to see that our perceptions are caused
> by the action of things on us, through their effects on our bodies,
> which are themselves parts of the physical world. The next step is to
> realize that since the same physical properties that cause perception
> in us through our bodies also produce different effects on other

physical things and can exist without causing any perceptions at all, their true nature must be detachable from their perceptual appearance and need not resemble it. The third step is to try to form a conception of that true nature independent of its appearance either to us or to other types of perceivers.[14]

6.5   COORDINATING NOTIONS WITH PARTICULARS: SPACE AND TIME

This business of articulating unarticulated parameters in experience to coordinate across a contextual divide is something we do naturally, as a matter of course, and on a grander scale in the case of spatial and temporal notions. The language in which Mother Nature speaks to us has no names for times or places. Just as we register the place about which a thermometer provides information not in the content of its informational states (the height of the mercury in the vial), but in the place at which it is located, Mother Nature registers the time and place about which an experience contains information in the time and place at which it is received. If we didn't need to pass information forward in time or if we were rooted to a spatial location so that all of our thought occurred in a fixed spatial and temporal context, there would be no need to represent space or time.[15] It is only because we need to get our experiences to communicate with one another across a spatial and temporal divide that we need parameters that keep track of time and place. The fact of mobility means that we have to take connections that could otherwise be built into our environment onboard. The fixed environment of thought for the human is a human body, whatever limitations that imposes on where we can wander and what we can sense. The time and place of acquisition are unarticulated constituents of every experience. Making spatiotemporal parameters explicit is the first and most crucial step in the gradual process of decoupling.[16]

This concludes the introduction to the process of articulating unarticulated parameters and the role of the representational apparatus erected overtop of experience in allowing us to maintain informational links to

---

14. Nagel, *The View from Nowhere*, 14.

15. Ignoring, for the moment, communication with other subjects.

16. I sometimes speak as though spatiotemporal vocabulary is equivalent to all singular vocabulary, and hence if one's spatial and temporal ideas are coordinated with the world, one's whole notional network, i.e., all of one's ideas of material particulars, is coordinated with the world as well. That's not right; moving bodies are independent degrees of dynamical freedom.

landmarks in the external landscape across changes in context that disrupt the links provided by experience. On the side of particulars, explicit representation of spatial and temporal parameters permits coordination over time and across space. On the side of properties, explicit representation of variable conditions that support covariation between properties and phenomenal profiles permits coordination across changes in context that disturb those links, by transforming with them in a way that keeps the informational connection intact (think of them as changes in frequency needed to keep an open channel). It is important to note that it is characteristic of unarticulated constituents to have to be *discovered*. What makes them unarticulated is precisely that there is nothing to suggest them in the intrinsic character of experience. If they weren't exposed by difficulties coordinating across contexts, we would be unaware of them entirely. We don't typically initially have the conceptual resources to represent them; articulation is introduced to reinstate coordination. The picture that I hope is emerging is this: ideas are connected to the world by a long chain of representation and re-representation, all kept in coordination by a combination of physical law and (more or less) loose and local regularities. Some of the links are ordinary physical interactions among naturally occurring systems, some are interactions between artificially designed systems, some involve interactions with other people or the interaction of people with physical systems, and some involve interactions with other ideas. Your body is just a physical system in interaction with all these others, a kind of mobile measuring device, with your phenomenal states playing the role of pointer observables. To unpack their informational content you need to express unarticulated constituents, and arrange things on the inside in a way that keeps information flowing smoothly from the world, through experience, over the representational apparatus, and, ultimately, into the functional machinery that determines behavior. You need to get yourself equipped with a good internal map, and get labels attached to your phenomenal profiles that come as close as possible to expressing their natural content, learn how to use those labels to locate your self on the map, and get the map wired into the deliberative machinery all in a manner that gets you moving in the right directions, and reacting appropriately to your circumstances.

Putting aside the problem of locating yourself in space and time and focusing on the business of attaching concepts to phenomenal states as a kind of internal calibration, it is clear that being well calibrated is a matter of degree. If concepts attached to your profiles only represent what those positions indicate *more or less, some of the time,* or *under certain conditions* (i.e., if the part of the chain coordinating action with circumstances that passes *through* those profiles isn't perfectly tight), your behavior will only be *more or less* attuned to your environment, *some of the time, under certain conditions.*[17] If evolution tells the right story of how we got to be hardwired the way we are, and our profiles either come with built-in labels or with rules for constructing labels under pressure from inputs, we can count on natural selection to have us reasonably well-attuned to the environments in which we were, as a species, raised, but it is bound to have exploited whatever local regularities it could find in doing so. The difference between perfect, universal, law-like correspondence, and good enough local coordination to keep us well fed and reproducing is not one that Mother Nature minds. She is, as Dennett says:

> A stingy, opportunistic engineer who takes advantage of rough cor-respondences whenever they are good enough for the organism's purposes, given its budget.... It is *because of what a structure happens to indicate* that it is "selected for" or "reinforced in" a further causal role in the economy of control of the organism, but it will be selected for, or reinforced in, this role *whenever* it is 'close enough for government work' as the engineers say.[18]

We would *like* to develop maps that *perfectly* reflect the structure of the environment in *all* of its relevant detail[19] and get ourselves calibrated so well that we can locate ourselves on them spontaneously and with perfect reliability. Barring that, we can just bend our energies on improving on Mother Nature's design, tightening links she left a little loose. Natural information is everywhere, every part of space and time is chock-full of information about other times and places; there are light waves, footsteps in the sand, scars on bodies, rings in trees. The trick, for opportunistic, information-hungry, mobile systems like us, is to learn how to read the information and put it to use. I'll have more to say about this process of bootstrapping self-design in sections to come.

6.6 CONCLUSION

The information we get from experience is situated. Its content depends on when and where it is received and the values of the relevant contextual

---

17. Thus Dretske, *Explaining Behavior,* 57: "Sometimes ... the dependency between a natural sign and its meaning derives, at least in part, from other sources. It is partly the fact, presumably not itself a physical law, that animals do not regularly depress door buttons while forging for food that makes a ringing doorbell *mean* that some *person* is at the door. In many cases of biological interest, a sign—some internal indicator on which an animal relies to locate and identify, say, food—will only have local validity. It will, that is, be a reliable indicator only in the animals natural habitat."

18. See Dennett, "Ways of Establishing Harmony," in *Dretske and His Critics,* edited by McLaughlin, 122. Italics mine.

19. That is, in all of the ways that make a difference to successful and unsuccessful action.

parameters. We can express it in a form that is portable across time, space, and all kinds of context so that there are no insurmountable natural barriers to limit our mobility. But in doing so, we can't just compile the descriptions of our experiential histories in a big folder; we have to preserve the information presently embodied in the way those states are distributed. This is just an instance of the general point that when we trade in a situated information-carrying device for a portable one, we have to insert something into the *content* of its states that reflects the information currently embodied in the relevant features of its *location*. We have to insert something that indicates its place in time, in space, or in the history of a certain body.[20] The informational state of the portable device, precisely because it breaks the contextual ties on the bearing of information, will always have more structure than the situated one. So, just as when we pool the information from different files in a cabinet we have to label the information with the name of the file it came from, when we combine in thought the signals coming in over time from experience, we have to label them with the time and place at which they were received. When we pool our own information with that of different subjects, we have to label it with something that reflects its source. This is why our sensory states *are*, but our descriptions of them are *not*, as Anscombe and Wittgenstein emphasized, subjectless. The description of experience—if the crucial information embodied in its context, that is, in its being the experience *at a particular point in the history of a particular subject*—is not to be lost, has to contain more structure than experience itself. It has to have spatial, temporal, and personal parameters.

Those, then, are my dual answers to what's good about unarticulated constituents, and what's bad about them. Why are they good things? They don't reify structure beyond practical necessity. They are Mother Nature's way of saving herself from endless repetition. This is a lesson that the embedded, embodied movement in cognitive science has taught us. Why are they bad things? They place contextual constraints on the propagation of information. That is a lesson that the movement has sometimes forgotten. It explains why there is so much structure reified between the ears i.e., why we build world models and carry them around with us.

20. Again, where the relevant sort of location is always location in the space in which the information is distributed, and portability is portability from one point in that space to another.

7

Self-Representation, Objectivity, and Intentionality

We have been looking at how the distinction between experience and the objects of experience emerges with the erection of the representational apparatus over experience in the kind of process that Jim went through. The ties between experience and ideas are gradually loosened until the representational network becomes sufficiently articulated to give ideas a life of their own, breaking constitutive connections to particular phenomenal profiles. Ideas can then be identified and individuated by their internal roles and a substantive story, full of metaphysical and nomological contingencies, given to explain connections between ideas and phenomenal profiles (e.g., between Bill Clinton and the *look* of Bill Clinton to various observers under various conditions, or between redness and the *look* of red things to various observers under various conditions). Phenomenal profiles are treated as information-bearing intermediaries with intrinsic properties of their own, and external relations to their extensions. We saw that self-description plays a crucial role in this process, and I want to suggest here that the formal requirements on self-describing media shed light on two elusive questions in philosophy of mind. The first is a question that Dretske raised in *Naturalizing the Mind*. Why do we have conscious access to the intrinsic properties of experience? In his terms, what is experience for? The second is a question that has hounded philosophy of mind since Brentano. In what sense, if any, is thought *intrinsically* intentional? What is the property that some states have of pointing, or purporting to point, beyond themselves?[1] After addressing these questions, I'll close part 1 by making explicit the answer to the question of why we self-represent, and what advantage self-representation gives us in the fight for survival.

It would be good to get a somewhat broader perspective than we took in the last chapter. Dynamical vocabulary is well suited to bring the semantic framework into contact with the psychological literature on sit-uated cog-nition because it is designed to talk about relationships between re-presentational media. Particularly apropos here is work by Cosmides and Tooby on the cognitive and biological underpinnings of the character-istically human capacity to couple temporarily with a wide range of cog-nitive environments. We have seen how to view the mind as part of the dynamical machinery of the body charged with the task of transforming perception into action in a way that gets the body moving in the right way in the presence of predator, prey, and mating opportunities. Only the last leg of the chain of causes leading from the distal features of the environment to behavior is inside the brain. A brain that is organized internally to complete the chain effectively in one environment will not, in general, do so in environments in which the external segment of the chain differs in relevant ways. If we characterize a brain by its dynamical organization and look at the roles played by signals, we can say that a brain works well in a context c just in case signals that indicate **A** in c lead to **A**-appropriate behavior. It's easy to see that a brain that works well in c will not work well in other contexts. In an environment in which the same signals have a different informational content, behavior will be ill suited to circumstance.

It takes a long history of adaptation to get brains biologically attuned to environments, to get the deer running from the lion, magnetosomes swimming towards anaerobic environments, and frog tongues darting out at passing flies. A good fit between the external and internal components of the chain that lead from the distal environment to behavior, between the internal behavior-producing states and the distal causes toward which behavior is directed, takes a good bit of fine-tuning. A brain is not an autonomous system, but a highly structured part of a large natural ma-chine that fits into its environment like a key into a lock. Movement into environments in which the external component of the chain is different requires internal reorganization to maintain fit. This observation leads to what Cosmides and Tooby have called the Dilemma of General Intel-ligence. If signals have fixed roles, there seem to be two options. Mother

---

1. I use 'intrinsic intentionality' and 'objective purport' interchangeably.

Nature can produce brains that are well attuned only to a wide range of circumstances but, because they can only act on signals with an invariant significance, have a limited behavioral repertoire. Or she can make brains that act on a wide range of signals but are behaviorally well attuned to a narrow range of circumstances.[2] She can, that is to say, either make brains that fit like a key into a higly specific cognitive environment, tailored so that the internal wiring is the image of the external links between sensory surface and distal cause, that is, so that the built-in causal pathways lead from the sensory signs of lions to lion-appropriate behavior (and in general, from the sensory signs of **A** in c to **A**-appropriate behavior) *in c*, nevermind that the same signs have a different significance outside c. Or she can make all-purpose brains that react in ways whose appropriateness doesn't depend on particularities of situation; brains that act only on signals that have the same significance always and everywhere, with input-output functions that read like general policies, insensitive to the situations in which they are implemented. The way out of the dilemma is to find a way of letting the functional roles of sensory or transducer states vary with context, allowing them to be regulated somehow by the content-relevant contextual parameters. And that is what self-representation does.

That was quite abstract. Let me repeat it in a slightly different way. The brain is not an autonomous system, but a collection of potentials. It plugs into a structured environment and makes more or less effective use of the informational opportunities presented to it.[3] What those opportunities are depends on what causal chains are in place and how they feed into the sensory pathways; it depends on where the chain of causes that produces this particular pattern of activation over the sensory surfaces leads in *this* context, under *these* particular conditions. This dependence on the environment leads to instability in the significance of experience across contexts. This has to be corrected for, otherwise the system will be confined, by explicit representation and relativization of cognitive role to context. John, for example, relativized the cognitive roles of color profiles

---

2. "General-purpose problem-solving architectures [where 'problem-solving' is to be understood as including practical, not merely theoretical, problems] are very weak, but broad in application, whereas special-purpose problem-solving designs are very efficient and inferentially powerful, but limited in their domain of application. Thus, on first inspection, there appear to be only two biologically possible choices for evolved minds: either general ineptitude or narrow competences." See Cosmides and Tooby, "Consider the Source," in *Metarepresentations*, edited by Sperber, 55.

3. Of course, the most immediate part of that environment is the body, but since the connections between skin and skull are relatively fixed, they don't present the same problems of adaptation as the changing landscape outside the body. For discussion of the role of the body see Clark "Pressing the Flesh."

(which we can take here to be roughly equivalent to the beliefs about tie colors to which they gave rise) to ambient lighting conditions.

Contextual parameters can be suppressed for purposes of intracontextual communication. We can exploit the fact that the parameter has a fixed local value in gleaning formation from the states of c-situated systems (John, for example, needn't make constant reference to lighting conditions in sorting or exchanging information about colors while in the context of his shop), but it has to be articulated for storage, integration into the web of belief, and coordination outside c. This ability to 'speak with the natives' in any context, moving seamlessly across contexts in which similar signals have a different significance, adapting cognitively to accommodate the changing significance, has an obvious selective advantage. As Cosmides and Tooby note:

> Most species are locked in co-evolutionary, antagonistic relationships with prey, rivals, parasites, and predators, in which move and countermove take place slowly, over evolutionary time. Improvisation puts humans at a great advantage: instead of being constrained to innovate only in phylogenetic time, they engage in ontogenetic ambushes against their antagonists—innovations that are too rapid with respect to evolutionary time for their antagonists to evolve defenses by natural selection.[4]

My suggestion here is that the level of explicit representation furnished by self-representation is what adds the degrees of dynamical freedom that permit the dynamical role of signals to transform with context in a way that reflects their changing informational content, keeping behavior in sync with circumstance. The kind of learning that shapes the architecture of the brain takes generations and binds agents to the contexts for which it is tailored. The soft structure that encodes knowledge and belief, by contrast, can be transformed in an instant in response to an unlimited array of signals and chosen to fit the context. A mind that explicitly represents the signals coming in from the environment before acting on them is able to adapt flexibly to changes in their significance.

7.1   DRETSKE'S QUESTION

Now we can turn to Dretske's question: What is the *point* of experience? Why do we have conscious access to the intrinsic properties of experience? Why isn't sensory information used to generate contents that simply show

4. Cosmides and Tooby, "Consider the Source," 54.

up in our belief boxes ready to be fed into the inferential and practical machinery leading to behavior? In Dretske's words:

> It isn't what you see that is important in the struggle for survival, it is what you know about what you see.... It is the conclusions, the beliefs, the knowledge that is important, not the experiences that normally give rise to such knowledge. So why do we have experience?... Why aren't we all, in each sense modality, the equivalent of blindsighters who (it seems) get information about nearby objects... needed to determine appropriate action without experiencing (seeing) them?[5]

Another way of asking the question is, since it's the contents that matter for regulation of behavior, why are the intrinsic properties of the vehicles themselves visible to the mind? It is as though the mind couldn't *use* its representational states without simultaneously *mentioning* them.[6] Dretske's own answer was classic: There is a lot that beings with conscious access to experience can do that generalized blindsight subjects cannot. This is unhelpful without a more precise diagnosis, and that's what we are in a position to give. The answer is straightforward, the quality of a self-describing state is part of its content, since they have self-presenting properties as constituents, and self-describing states are essential to self-regulation. They are necessary to permit the kind of reinterpretation needed for adjusting the dynamical role of phenomenal states to their changing informational content.

Phenomenal states are treated by thought as information-bearing intermediaries whose significance changes with context. They are interpreted and reinterpreted in different contexts by self-describing thoughts of the form '*this* is what such and such looks like under conditions like these', for example, 'this is what red looks like in direct sunlight', 'this is what spinach tastes like when flavored by cumin'. Thoughts of this form are possible only because phenomenal states are visible to thought. They are possible only because thought can take the quality of those states reflexively as intentional objects. Self-presentation gives us the independent grip on the vehicles of content that provides a foothold for dynamical freedom between vehicle and content. Another example of this is that only a language that can both mention and use its own expressions can form sentences that suspend, alter, or relativize their content to context; the wife entering a

---

5. *Naturalizing the Mind*, 119.

6. The distinction between use and mention is one that philosophers learned to make in connection with language. To use an expression is to employ it with its ordinary semantic content; to mention it is to refer to the expression itself. I use the word 'dog' when I say 'the dog is in the yard'; I mention it when I say '"dog" has three letters'.

dinner party whispers to her husband "when i say 'armadillo' inside, that means I want to leave," a spy says to an interlocuter "once we cross the border 'Pepsi' means nuclear waste, 'water' means currency'."

Most of the time, we look transparently *through* experience *at* the world. In this mode, experience is a translucent channel for information about its intentional objects. But when we need to, we can pull the intrinsic properties of the sensory field into the foreground, making them the focus of attention and forming thoughts about them. Think of the difference between tasting in the mode of 'Is that coriander? And do I detect a bit of lemon grass?' and tasting in the mode of 'Yum. That was lovely'. Or think of the difference between looking in the ordinary mode, where the focus is on what you are seeing, and looking of the sort that the eye doctor asks you to do when he places lenses over your eyes and asks you to report on the sharpness of the image. The opacity of experience (to thought) explains something of its psychologically equivocal status.

7.2   OBJECTIVE PURPORT

We turn now to objective purport. Since the space around our bodies is not *inside* us, although the causes of movement have to be inside, Mother Nature equips us with ideas, i.e., internal proxies (images, tactual sensations, smells, sounds, and so on) coordinated with objects in space by more or less robust causal connections and entered to the functional machinery that controls behavior. This is her way of letting movement be guided by the disposition of the space through which one moves. There are no lions and cupcakes in the mind, only images of lions and cupcakes that act as cues for lion- and cupcake-appropriate movements. The same is true of the visual impressions that cause frogs to unfurl their tongues at passing flies, and the internal states that cause sunflowers to move with the sun as it crosses the sky. In all of these cases, it is usually held that what lends a state objective purport, or makes it an *intentional* state, is its role in a larger cognitive economy.[7] What makes the frog's visual impression an impression *of* something, what lends it an intentional sig-

---

7. One might wonder "Doesn't my own thought provide the external perspective on that of others that distinguishes their experience from its intentional objects, and can't I apply the distinction, by analogy, to my own?" The response is that that gets the order of conceptualization wrong. The very idea that others have experience is not suggested by experience; it is a product of the articulation that distinguishes one's own experience from what it is (purportedly) *of*.

nificance, is its role as an information-bearing intermediary between flies (or perhaps some more coarse-grained or generic object) and behavior selected for its appropriateness in the presence of flies. Intentionality, from this point of view, is an extrinsic property. The idea of a state that somehow *intrinsically* purports to point beyond itself can seem to border on incoherence. It is we, who see both frog and fly, who distinguish the information-bearing states of the frog from the fly they carry information about. It is we who are in a position to relate one to the other.[8] It is only from an external perspective that that distinction, and the notion of objective purport that rests on it, makes sense. For these reasons, attempts to characterize intentionality in naturalistic terms have tended to reject the intuition that intentional purport is intrinsic to thought.

I want to suggest that the intuition needn't be entirely dismissed. There is a formal property of thought that is closely tied to its self-transformative capacities that captures a sense in which intentionality can be said to be *intrinsic* to thought, but only *extrinsic* to the information-bearing media that govern the behavior of frogs and sunflowers. Let's start with the observation that the objective purport of frog experience is visible from the perspective of an external medium relative to which it is opaque. The external medium provides a metaperspective from which the frog's own states can be both distinguished from, and related to, their contents. Since frog experience is transparent to itself—the frog has a visual image of the fly but no visual image *of* the visual image—it follows that the intentional purport of frog experience is extrinsic to frog experience. Now let's generalize this. We say that the objective purport of the states of an arbitrary representational medium is visible only from the perspective of media to which it is opaque (that is to say, that has ways of representing its vehicles of content) and which have the resources to represent the relations between those vehicles and their intentional objects. So, for example, we say that the objective purport of a language like English, or some formal computer language, is visible to any language in which its intended interpretation can be expressed. Human thought, as we have seen, is opaque to itself and has the resources to represent the relations between its own vehicles and their intentional objects.[9] It incorporates the metaperspective from which the intentional purport of its own states is visible. This is just a fancy way of saying that thought has the reflexive resources to take its own states as

8. Imagine, for simplicity, that we actually see the frog's visual image.

9. There are some very difficult questions that I'm deliberately leaving unanswered. Are thoughts cognitive roles? How are they individuated? Do all thoughts have a phenomenology? What are the vehicles of thought?

intentional objects. We have thoughts about our own thoughts and we can distinguish them from, and relate them to, what those thoughts are about.[10]

I propose that we interpret intrinsic intentionality, or objective purport, as a property not in the first instance of representational states, but of representational media, and a property that a medium has just in case it incorporates the external perspective from which vehicle can be distinguished from content. This connects the notion of intrinsic intentionality to the self-transforming properties of thought. It also importantly has ties to a conception of objectivity with roots in Kant that gives it a claim to capturing something quite central. A medium that has this property can distinguish 'seems' from 'is.' Here Strawson states it in one of the most searching examinations of the notion of objectivity in the last half century:

> I earlier introduced the word 'objective' by giving it . . . a sense in terms of the distinction between oneself and one's states on the one hand, and anything on the other hand which is not either oneself or a state of oneself, but of which one has, or might have, experience . . . I shall mean by a non-solipsistic consciousness, the consciousness of a being who has a use for the distinction between himself and his states on the one hand, and something not himself or a state of himself, of which he has experience, on the other.[11]

There is more to be said; vastly more than can be said here. Naturalists have mostly rejected the rationalist tradition that treats objective purport as the distinguishing, definitive feature of human thought, partly on the grounds that the only way to understand it is as a magical sort of intrinsic quality. The proposal here is unmysterious, easily incorporated into a naturalistic account, and it captures the valid core of the intuition that thought wears its objective purport on its sleeve. It has some other nice features. As remarked, it provides a purely formal criterion for intrinsic intentionality. It has the consequence that thought is the primary source of intentionality, it connects self-representation to intrinsic intentionality, and it locates the roots of intentionality in more phylogenetically primitive self-transforming capacities of the sort that Cosmides and Tooby describe.

Together with the lessons learned in earlier chapters, this suggests a pair of slogans to locate thought in the natural order: (1) objective significance flows from the bottom up; information flows from the world up through the chain of coordinated media. If any of the media in a coordinated chain that ends with thought has external significance, there has to be one at

---

10. Indeed, they have two ways of representing their own states, reflexively and nonreflexively, and I've been making a lot of hay out of the fact that these two ways of representing their own states are what get conjoined in self-describing thoughts.

11. Strawson, *Individuals*, 69.

the bottom of the heap that reaches outside the mind; and (2) objective purport trickles from the top down. If any of the media in the chain have derived intentionality, there has to be one at the top of the heap that has it intrinsically. Thought stands at the receiving end of objective significance and is the source of objective purport.

7.3   WHY DO WE SELF-REPRESENT?

Turning, again, to the big question.[12] What is the dynamical point of self-representation? Isn't all of this business about building internal world models a retrograde maneuver, reinstating the outmoded view of the mind as mirror of nature? Didn't the movement toward embodied cognition teach us that we don't need internal models, that the world is its own best model? Why do we reify structure that is present in the environment between the ears? Aren't the little worlds between the ears of the billions of featherless bipeds that litter the landscape a profligate waste of structure?

To begin, recall how self-representation works. Instead of being fed directly into the motor pathways, experience is passed to the mind where in creatures like us it is used to modify an internal model of self and situation.[13] The model serves as a central clearinghouse where information acquired over a history of interaction with the world—separated from the context of acquisition and expressed in an invariant form—is collected so that it can be brought to bear on behavior. The model has two components and there are two corresponding dimensions of change. There is an objective component that represents the world in an invariant way and develops in the same way that a painting develops under the brush of the painter or a story develops under the hand of an author.[14] And there is a reflexive component (the generalization of the red dot on a map) that tracks the system's own location. The bearing of the information embodied in the objective component on behavior is regulated by the reflexive component. Think of a cartographer moving through partially charted terrain, simultaneously tracking his own location and adding information acquired in the course of travel. The effect, from a dynamical perspective, is behavior coupled not directly to a relatively informationally impoverished stimulus,

12. This is a design question, better put, perhaps, as: Why are there self-representers? What advantage does self-representation hold that explains its selection?

13. There is no suggestion that the subsystem has to be localized in a part of the brain. Experience is just the form in which the stimulus makes an impact on the map-keeping subsystem. Information present in the stimulus that isn't registered consciously does not enter the deliberative loop.

14. Objectivity is a pragmatic matter and one of degree; it is measured by the size and importance of the invariance class.

but to a real-time evolving model of the world as a whole, one whose bearing on behavior is sensitive to the system's own position in the landscape.[15]

It is important that we can't get the benefits of storing information without paying the price of self-representation. If we're allowing information about times and places other than the here and now to accumulate in the internal pathways, it's bearing on behavior needs to be sensitive to our current situation, and it is this sensitivity to current situation that self-representation is needed to secure.[16] If I am storing information about the availability of Krispy Kreme donuts in the faculty lounge between 3:00 and 5:00 PM on Tuesday, how it affects my movements had better depend on where the here-now is located relative to that event. The higher the resolution of the model, and the more narrowly we self-locate, the more finely tuned responses can be to parts of the spatial and temporal landscape that lie outside of the current sensory horizon. The distinguishing dynamical property of a self-representing system is the extra degrees of freedom between stimulus and response corresponding to self-locating parameters that gives the system the flexibility it needs in order to put stored information to use.

A bit of regimentation will make this precise. Consider a system S. By S's *first-order dynamics*, I'll mean its momentary conditional dispositions to behave thus and so when presented with a stimulus. We can represent the first-order dynamics with a function—what I will call a *response function*—that maps stimuli onto responses.[17] The first-order dynamics of a non-self-representing system are unmediated dispositions to respond to potential stimuli.

A system that doesn't self-represent can exhibit variation in response function over time. It can, for example, break down or wear out, but aside from this, its response function can be reshaped through conditioning.[18] This kind of adaptive change is familiar, but it requires a learning period in which there is sustained pressure from the environment, and it doesn't carry any real increase in the dynamical complexity of the system in the sense gauged by the number of terms in its response function. One set of dispositions replaces another, but there is no greater variety of responses available to the system from one moment to the next.

<hr/>

15. Notice that the agent's own action feeds back into the deliberative loop; it's one of the variables that affects perception.

16. The dynamically relevant situation of a system is defined by parameters articulated in the self-representational loop.

17. If $F_t(x)$ is the response function that pertains to a system S at t, $F_t(s) = b$ means that S is disposed to respond with b if subjected to stimulus s. I remain neutral on the nature of dispositions aside from a presumption that they are grounded in the intrinsic properties of the system.

18. From now on, I ignore nonadaptive change in response function due to accident, malfunction, or simple wearing out of parts.

Where adaptive systems have a slowly evolving body of unmediated dispositions to respond to stimuli, self-representing systems have a rich body of simultaneous dispositions that permit differential response to the same stimulus depending on the values of self-locating parameters. They are best thought of as dispositions to respond to something much richer than a stimulus: broad situations, represented by a partially specified centered world. Stimuli evoke broad situations, and it's the broad situations that govern responses. What's going on is that in a local setting, the stimulus is the only dynamically relevant part of the environment; it screens off the effect of the rest of the world. A self-representing agent is effectively reconstructing the broad environment inside and setting up causal and informational relations that reach into parts of the landscape that it is not in continuing perceptual contact with.

If we were to put a black box around the internal dynamics and look just at the dynamical relations between stimulus and response, the difference shows up in the speed and agility with which a system responds to changes in situation. In adaptive systems, we see some slow evolution in responses to stimuli over time. In self-representing systems we see spontaneous adjustment in response to the changing values of contextual parameters. Where conditioning allows *adaptation*, we might say, self-representation supports genuinely *flexible* response that adjusts spontaneously, in real time, to the changing values of self-locating parameters.[19] See table 7.1.

Nonadaptive systems are easy to come by; tables, rocks, and shoes all provide examples. Examples of adaptive systems include Birkenstocks, neural nets, and pets. As for self-representing systems, there are cars that are steered by means of a global positioning system, ships that navigate by maps, and centrally controlled armies. The advantages of self-representation are power and speed. The mark of self-representation is responses that vary spontaneously along multiple dimensions independently of stimulus.[20]

19. Again, it's not just the *behavior* that adjusts, but dispositions for behaviors embodied in the system's response function.

20. Self-representing systems do respond when stimulated, of course, but for reasons we'll see, there is no systematic dynamical relationship between stimulus and response. You could write down the response function for the brain, starting with an initial configuration of neurons and applying the physical laws in calculating how the network will respond to pulses, but there, again, the response function will change with every application of stimulus, and over time, there will not be any systematic relationship between stimulus and response. That is the rule rather than the exception with open systems. You only have a dynamically interesting system if there is enough internal stability that the system as a whole has a compact dynamics, i.e., if there are constraints on configurations that result in a configuration-space that is a reduction of the product space of its components. What is the difference between a living body and an arbitrary mereological sum of similar components? What is it that makes the body an interesting dynamical unit? The parts of the body are tied into a relatively fixed configuration, they don't move independently of one another, and they constitute a functional unit; their states affect and constrain one another in

TABLE 7.1

	Stimulus-response machine	Adaptive system that responds to conditioning	Self-presenter
First-order dynamics; counterfactual dependence of stimulus on response	Fixed	Varies slowly under sustained, specific pressure from the outside	Varies in real time
Behavior as a function of stimulus over time	Behavior varies directly with stimulus; it is under environmental control.	Behavior still under environmental control, with an added metadynamical element. The environment is not only controlling behavior but inducing slow change in first-order dynamics.	Behavior is no longer under environmental control, but regulated by an internal map-keeping subsystem that adds degrees of dynamical freedom not present in the stimulus. The system exhibits highly individual responses to the same stimulus from one occasion to the next.

Because self-representation allows the system to take onboard information whose bearing on behavior has to be adjusted with movement, from a dynamical perspective, it is an entirely natural development.

7.4   HOW IS THIS POSSIBLE?

There is a real question about where the additional degrees of freedom come from. Doesn't the behavior of any open system in a local, deterministic setting have to be a function of external input? The answer is that the wiring and connections that mediate stimulus and response in self-representing agents are soft. They are not hard-wired. They are the networks of connections among neurons that encode information in the brain in the form of belief and they change at light speed. The brain is *designed* quite precisely to support this quick uptake of information and to use the information flexibly in coordinating behavior. It does it by making

---

highly regular ways. In the case of self-representing systems, we don't have the kind of internal stability that gives us a dynamics as simple as a stimulus-response machine or a non-self-representing adaptor, but we still have a dynamically interesting unit. I've just given a very compact description of the metadynamical principles that govern the evolution of the response function.

and breaking the wiring and connections inside the system—the net-works of pulsing neurons that link stimulus and response—as quickly as the system can move from here to there. If the processes that mediate stimulus and response are deterministic, then the output of a system (how it behaves) is a function of the input, so we have a counterfactual dependence of stimulus on response. But all we need to get variation along the temporal dimension is rapid change in the dynamically relevant features of the system. It's not pipes or veins, but networks of neurons that provide conduits for the information going from stimulus to response.

The kinds of minds that we have are minds equipped with a central self-representing subsystem, charged not only with representing the world but chronicling personal history. The arrangement underwrites real-time adaptation, foresight, planning... all the trappings of intentionality. It does require centralization of processing and control at a high level; the kind of Central Command or Oval Office in the mind—a place where information is gathered and from which orders are issued—that smacks to some of a Cartesian Theatre. And that, I unabashedly embrace. It's not Descartes' version—or at least not the version of the naive Cartesian, including, I think, the man on the Clapham omnibus. It has learned the lessons of the embodied, embedded view of cognition; its perfectly compatible with a fully decentralized understanding of lower-level pro-cessing.

7.5   LOOSE ENDS

Some odd remarks that are worth making in this connection. It's an empirical question just how widespread self-representation is. There is discussion in the psychological literature of modularized map-keeping among rats and bees, but it seems to be restricted to self-location.[21] There isn't any unequivocal evidence of self-description. One might wonder why, given the benefits. The answer is that self-description requires more ex-pensive machinery, and is more practically dispensable than self-location. A well-designed system confined to its cognitive niche can do without the

21. See Carruthers, "On Being Simple-Minded." The full benefits of the self-representational loop require a much higher degree of centralization on the level of the individual, and the availability of enough information to actually get the process of model-building off the ground. One suspects that the latter requirement is met only where there is sharing of information. There must be a complex story to be told about the coevolution of language and world-modeling, a part of the complex story of the emergence of culture.

extra machinery; it is only when systems need to roam without constraint that the benefits of self-description show up.

The self-representational loop explains why, when it comes to prediction and control, persons are wild cards. They are effectively free variables in the dynamical order. When you send a signal into a self-representational loop, what emerges out the other end is so highly and holistically dependent on idiosyncrasies of personal history—all of the accumulated baggage of a lifetime stored in a medium with a much higher bandwidth than the conditional dispositions of an adaptive system—that it is as good as flipping a coin. Coin flips are perfectly deterministic processes,[22] but the outcome is so highly sensitive to so many conditions that if you insert a coin flip between two links in any dynamical process, you effectively randomize the outcome. The same is true of a self-representational loop. You know pretty much how any old car or toaster will behave if you feed it an input, and so long as things are functioning properly, it will respond in the same way to the same input from one moment to the next. But you never know how an arbitrary person will behave in response to a stimulus. The self-representational loop brings a whole accumulated body of experience to bear on the here and now, making the outcome dependent on factors that not only distinguish one person from another but also one moment in a personal history from the next.[23]

Nature is rife with examples of systems that mimic flexible behavior, navigating complicated terrains and behaving in ways that look as though they were guided by a central map-keeping subsystem, but in which the behavior is really the product of interaction between a set of autonomous or semiautonomous components each doing its own thing. Systems that fall into this class belong to the broad category of what are known as self-organizing systems. Brooksian robots, insect colonies, slime molds, schools of fish, and free-market economies all belong here. There is no settled agreement about whether there is a characterization that will cover all cases, and so it's hard to make general claims about their dynamical properties. But the cases that we do understand turn out to be as inflexible in their responses to stimuli as ordinary adaptive systems, and I suspect strongly that if we found (or designed) a system whose behavior was flexible, we would find that the global dynamics of the system included a self-representational loop. Because the issues are complex and specialized and occur at a level of technical detail that is out of place here, I have relegated discussion to a subsidiary paper, but for those with the patience to soldier through, it is in

22. Again, ignoring quantum effects.
23. See my "Freedom and Determinism."

the contrast with self-organizing systems that the notion of flexibility gets sharpened.[24] The comparison of self-representing with self-organizing systems also provides the basis for comparison with Dennett's views about the self, which we will return to in the final chapter.[25] I hold fast to the claim that there is a real difference between a Brooksian robot and a missile being steered by a GPS, a Dennettian self-less pseudo-person and a real human being, or a self-organizing colony of ants and one whose movements are choreographed by a map-keeping general, a difference in the internal dynamics that shows up on the outside in how flexibly it responds to external influence.

A final remark for a different kind of expert. If we adopt Dretske's account of the role of reasons in explaining behavior, we can give a nice account of the difference between *as-if* and *real* teleological behavior. On Dretske's account, reasons are design explainers. A reason-citing explanation for behavior goes like this: S was caused to X because of stimulus s, but the *reason* that s caused S to X was that it carries the information that p. For example, I was caused to open the door by the ringing of the bell, but the *reason* that bell ringings cause door openings[26] is that doorbell ringings ordinarily carry the information that someone is waiting to be let in. It's a little more complicated, but not in ways that should make a difference here. Reasons, on Dretske's account, are available from an external perspective and explain behavior by explaining design. Self-representers are a special class of Dretske intentional systems that can answer why-questions on their own behalf. They come equipped with an internal self-representing spokes-system that can furnish the reasons for their design. Indeed, we can say of self-representing systems, as we can't say of systems where reasons are available only to an external perspective, that they are *moved* by reasons, in the straightforward sense that representations of Dretske reasons are causally implicated in the production of behavior. In such systems, it's not only that the causes of action are internal to the system, or that the system can report the reasons for its causal organization; it's that the connection between the causes and their effects is under the system's *control*.

The embodied cognition movement had the clear insight that the native position of the brain-body system is that of constant, complex, coupled interactions with the environment, and that adaptive behavior is an emergent property of the whole, that is, it is the interaction between the three components that keeps the whole system running, gets the organism moving in the right ways and doing all of the things it needs to do to

---

24. See my "Self-governance; the limits of self-organization."
25. For discussion of Dennett's views, see my "Saving the Baby."
26. That is, bell ringings like *that* cause door openings by *me*.

maintain the delicate balance that allows it to survive. In the words of two representatives of the embodied cognition movement:

> Adaptive behavior is the result of the continuous interaction between the nervous system, the body and the environment...one cannot assign credit for adaptive behavior to any one piece of this coupled system.[27]

What self-representation adds to this setting is a way of decoupling the body from the environment, allowing the agent to take on an increasing burden of responsibility for adaptation by making corrective judgments on the side of the body for differences in the environment. The result is a much more robust balance. The self-representational loop adds degrees of internal freedom that are simply not present in non-self-representing systems, degrees of freedom that allow the system to adjust spontaneously to changes of situation.

7.6   CONCLUSION

I have been focusing on the local process, treating the mind as a component of a complex dynamical system. So far I have been discussing systems that self-represent in the thin sense that they keep track of their occurrent situation in an internally represented landscape. In section 3, we will look at self-representing systems that keep full-blown, running autobiographies of potentially Proustian complexity, systems that have continuing mental lives more recognizably like our own. First, however, I want to apply the apparatus of this section to some ongoing discussions in the contemporary literature in the philosophy of mind and metaphysics.

---

27. Chiel and Beer, quoted in Clark, *Mindware*, 128.

PART 2

Understanding Arguments for Dualism

The important lessons of this section are negative. Don't mistake problems of coordination as evidence of missing conceptual links (chapter 8). Don't mistake the real and irresoluble inability to communicate phenomenal information through intermediaries as evidence of dualism (chapter 9). Don't get sucked in by grammatical illusions generated by abuses of notation (chapter 10). Together, these lessons remove some of the most powerful philosophical and psychological obstacles to integrating the self into the natural order.

8

Jackson's Mary

I have capitulated and now see the interesting issue as being
where the arguments from the intuitions against physicalism—
the arguments that seem so compelling—go wrong.

—Frank Jackson, "Mind as Illusion," p. 1.

One of the most important arguments for dualism was formulated by
Frank Jackson in 1982. Short, elegant, and powerfully persuasive, the argument runs as follows:

> Mary is a brilliant scientist who is, for whatever reason, forced to
> investigate the world from a black and white room via a black and
> white television monitor. She specializes in the neurophysiology of
> vision and acquires, let us suppose, all the physical information there
> is to obtain about what goes on when we see ripe tomatoes, or the
> sky, and use terms like 'red', 'blue', and so on. She discovers, for
> example, just which wavelength combinations from the sky stimulate
> the retina, and exactly how this produces via the central nervous
> system the contraction of the vocal chords and expulsion of air from
> the lungs that results in the uttering of the sentence 'The sky is blue'.

One day Mary is allowed out of her laboratory and, when shown a
tomato for the first time, she exclaims "Ah, so this is what it is like to
see red." Jackson's claim is that the exclamation expresses a piece of
knowledge that she did not possess when she was in the room. Since she
was by hypothesis already apprised of all of the facts about physical properties and their relations to one another, what she learns cannot be a fact
about relations to physical properties. So it must be a fact about something else. Ergo, physics is incomplete. Physicalism is false.

An important exchange between Jackson and Churchland clarified the
argument in two ways. First, it separated the question of whether Mary
learns something upon her release from questions about her imaginative

capabilities. Churchland challenged the claim that Mary could not imagine while she was in the room what red experience would be like, and argued (rightly) that it was, in any case, an empirical question. To which Jackson replied:

> The knowledge argument does not rest on the dubious claim that logically you cannot imagine what sensing red is like unless you have sensed red. . . . The contention about Mary is not that, despite her fantastic grasp of neurophysiology and everything else physical, she could not imagine, what it is like to sense red; it is that, as a matter of fact, she would not know.[1]

And second, it made it clear that the issue is deeper than the question of whether our current physical knowledge is complete, that is, whether current physics is, with respect to phenomenal properties (that is, properties of the sort that Mary identifies when she thinks 'this-here property', the one exemplified by this experience, the one whose connection to red things is revealed to her when she sees the tomato) in the same position as prequantum physics with respect to black-body radiation. It comes down to the question of whether any communicable body of knowledge could be complete. This should have been clear all along, but it was made explicit in Jackson's response to Churchland's contention that the argument is as successful against the dualist as it is against the physicalist. Jackson retorted that there is no reason to think that everything there is to know about the mind according to the dualist could be learned by Mary while she is in the room, but since no restrictions were placed on what Mary was told or on what went into her books, anything that couldn't be learned by Mary while she was in the room couldn't be communicated by either of those means. And that means that any body of knowledge that was not susceptible to the argument would have to have some incommunicable content.

The argument really presents a dilemma. It doesn't matter for its antiphysicalist force, what fact precisely Mary is supposed to learn when she leaves the room (i.e., whether it is some fact about other people [what it has been like for them when they were seeing red], a fact about her own dispositions [what she is disposed to see if presented with something red], or a counterfactual fact about herself [what it would have been like for her to be seeing red]). If she does learn something and if the fact that she learns something establishes the incompleteness of the knowledge she had while she was in the room, in order for physical theory to complete itself, by these standards, it must be rendered incommunicable. If Mary really

---

1. Jackson, "What Mary Didn't Know," 180.

knows her neuroscience (and we assume she could pass any written exam, and that nobody can tell from the papers she publishes in leading journals that her experience is impoverished in any way), and if she really learns something new when she has the encounter with the tomato—if, that is to say, there is a truth of which she becomes thus newly apprised, expressed by her declaration "Ah, so this is what it is like to see red"—it is evidently not something that could, in principle, be imparted in writing. So, it seems we have a dilemma; either physics remains incomplete or we complete it by adding some inexpressible content. No theory that can be learned while Mary is in the room can teach her what she learns when she leaves.

8.1   WHAT MARY LEARNS

Let's see what Mary learns. Jackson already allowed Mary imaginative acquaintance with a full palette of colors to separate questions about what she knows (in virtue of her physical knowledge, before she is released from her colorless exile) from those about what she can imagine,[2] but we can go farther without precluding her surprise in the encounter with the tomato and give her as much actual prior color experience as we like, so long as we make sure she has no way of figuring out what the colors she is experiencing are called. This, too, was made clear in a paper by Nida-Rumelin, though it, too, should have been clear all along. We can imagine that there is an adjacent room with a full color spectrum painted on the wall, so long as we also suppose that Mary doesn't carry measuring instruments in to determine, for instance, the wavelength of reflected light, or bring any colored matter out, without affecting the argument's conclusion.[3]

While Mary is still in the room, before her encounter with the tomato, she knows that tomatoes have a certain physical structure and she knows what brain state she will be in if she is looking at a thing with that physical structure under any set of specified conditions.[4] She knows, moreover, that things that reflect light in the way tomatoes do are called 'red', so she knows

2. That is, whether she can imagine experience and, in particular, qualitatively simple experiences like red, that she has not *had*: interesting questions, to be sure, but different ones.

3. And so long as Mary is not allowed to determine the state of her brain while she is looking at the colors. The reason for the ban on determining her brain state is that if Mary can determine her brain state, and she can make some assumptions about the ambient conditions, she can use her physical theory to figure out what color she is looking at. This is the reverse of a point that will be important below: if she can determine what color she is looking at, and make some assumptions about ambient conditions, she can use her theory to figure out what brain state she is in.

4. Unless otherwise indicated, conditions are assumed to be standard, and reference to them, suppressed.

what brain state she will be in if she is looking at a red thing. She also knows as much as any of us, objectively, about experience. She has lots of her own. She knows that they bear systematic relations to brain states; and she has read, and even, refereed papers for journals concerning research into the neural bases of various kinds of experience. And so she knows, when she sees the tomato, she is going to have what she and her colleagues call a 'reddish experience', meaning 'the type of experience that ordinary perceivers have when they are looking at red things under standard conditions.'[5] And still there is nothing in all of this that could have led her to expect the kind of experience she has when she finally sees the tomato. That's what Jackson claims, and I agree. To put it a little differently—letting 'b' denote the brain state she will be in under those conditions, which she knows beforehand that she will be in—nothing in the physical description of b could have led her to expect that it has this particular phenomenal profile.

We are supposing, however, that Mary has been in b before, namely, while looking at the spectrum in the adjacent room, so it is a little worse than misleading to say that what she learns when she finally sees the tomato is what it's like to see red things, for that suggests that what she learns is something intrinsic to the experience, and that isn't right. In the modified scenario, different from the original only in respects that were acknowledged as inessential, the experience is not of an unfamiliar kind. Mary knows what it's like to see red things (what its like, that is to say, to be in b) because she's been in it. What she doesn't know (and what she learns upon her release) is what b is called. She doesn't know that *it* is the state that other people know as 'seeing red' or 'having a red experience' and she knows as 'b', and so she doesn't know to expect *it* if she is told that she is about to be shown a red thing.

This suggests that what Mary takes away from the encounter with the tomato is not intrinsic knowledge of a new kind of property, but a new relation between an old, familiar one and an old, familiar description. She

5. Jackson also contends, in the early articles, that nothing could have led Mary to expect to have any experience at all. But why? Even without the extension of the Nida-Rumellin room, there is no reason her books and teachers could not have told her about the experience of seeing red. And in any case, we can allow her as much casual wisdom and scientific knowledge about experience as you please, and also as much actual experience of her own, without alleviating her surprise when she sees the tomato. I agree with Jackson up to this point, that nothing in either the knowledge he allows Mary, or any that I have added to it, could have led her to expect the kind of experience she has when she sees a red thing.

Perry makes the same point: "As I imagine Mary, she is in the Jackson room, reading, perhaps writing, books about the physics and biology of color vision. She knows that people have experiences when they see things (as she does) and these experiences have subjective characters (as hers do) . . . [ignorance] of the fact that other people have color experiences (as opposed to simply failing to know what it's like to have them) was not part of the original setup and is not necessary to feel the problem of Mary's new knowledge" (*Knowledge, Possibility, and Consciousness*, 98).

gets her phenomenal state aligned with the descriptive vocabulary of her theory. What is established in the episode is an architectural relation between a bit of descriptive vocabulary and a property. Another way to bring this out is to notice that it is crucial to her taking something away from the episode that she know that tomatoes are red and that what she is looking at is a tomato. She has to know that 'red' applies to the thing she is looking at, so that she can peel the label off, so to speak, and attach it to her own state. Otherwise, she just says, using Jackson's phrase, 'ho hum'.[6] The description of her own state that she takes away is an extrinsic one, to be sure (viz., 'the state perceivers like me are in under conditions like this, when they are looking at red things'), but it can be, with the right back-ground knowledge (explicit knowledge of knowledge of the kind of context in question and some physics and neurophysiology[7]) translated into an intrinsic description of her brain state. The connection between the ex-trinsic and intrinsic description is an in-house relationship between se-mantically related items, the kind of connection that is established by knowledge. Her physical theory will tell her that under those conditions she will be in b, she needs just to get herself into that situation to attach to the label 'b', once and for all, to the state that pops up.[8] Label 'b' is a more precise description given in intrinsic terms of a state that is described vaguely and extrinsically as the one that perceivers such as Mary, under conditions such as those, are in when looking at red things.

6. Likewise, if she has the general ability to describe the state she is in, she can use her immediate knowledge of her state to generate descriptions of the objects that cause them. Compare: if I have the general ability to describe the place I am at, I can use the spatial relations between the spot and others to generate descriptions of all other, extrinsic descriptions, in terms of their relations to me. I'll need to know somewhat more to translate the description into a direct one, but all I need in order to get my referential hooks into the whole web of spatially connected locations is a representationally unmediated grasp of a place I can describe. Likewise, all I need in order to get my referential hooks into the web of causally connected properties that appear in physical descriptions is a representationally unmediated grasp of a property I can describe.

7. Of course, neither she nor the conditions need to be standard. She needs only an explicit physical characterization of both to use her theory to work out her own brain state.

8. *This* is the state that perceivers such as me are in under conditions such as this, when they are looking at red things. An explicit and precise characterization of ordinary circumstances is something we achieve, if at all, only with theory. If our theories are correct, what states like this really indicate are relations between circumstances and reflectance properties of surfaces [or, holding fixed circumstances and reflectance properties of surfaces, facts about our sensory psychology]. The path to an explicit characterization of ordinary circumstances (the terms of the relation that we can ignore until we venture outside typical contexts) is the one that Jones sets out on in Sellars's Myth. If this is the state I am ordinarily in when I am looking at something red, that means when I am in a state *like this*, and if things are ordinary and I am looking at something red, I can use knowledge of my state to attach color labels to things I'm looking at. The point of doing so—of attaching color labels to things, or, more generally, *describing* the objects of experience, characterizing them in the terms borrowed from a theory—is that those labels are rich with inferential implications that are extrinsic to the experience.

The direction of development for Mary is very different from the ordinary one, the one that we saw Sellars's John go through in chapter 6. Ordinarily, people start with coarse-grained concepts, crudely coordinated with the environment in a context-dependent way, and refine. The process of refinement takes the form of a broadly scientific education: learning how phenomenal states vary not only with the features of the world we ordinarily use them to track but with circumstance and ambient conditions, and learning how to recognize those conditions and correct for changes. At any point in the process, there are some predicates that are tied directly to phenomenal profiles. In John's case, before the episode with Jim, the predicates were color terms conceived as referring to intrinsic properties of surfaces. Later, when John's scientific education is completed, he will attach phenomenal profiles directly to brain states and regard them as providing information only indirectly about anything outside the brain, from retinal cones to the distal surfaces that are the ordinary focus of attention. Mary, by contrast, is starting with a fully articulated scientific understanding and connecting phenomenal terms straight to their physical correlates. Her physical theory tells her how, why, and under what conditions brain states can be used to track colors by phenomenal profile, but the point of direct contact, the place where, as Sellars put it, 'looks'-talk doesn't get a hold, for Mary, will be, from the get-go, brain states. Phenomenal states feed into descriptive vocabulary for Mary, through links with brain states.

So, because Mary knows her neuroscience, she has a fully articulated conception of color states both before and after the tomato encounter. We are supposing she is acquainted with the phenomenal profiles of colors ('color profiles') on both sides of the encounter. She has had red experiences and knows what they are like from the inside. What she learns from the episode is how to coordinate color profiles with descriptive vocabulary. That is what the encounter with the tomato tells her, and that, together with a way of gauging ambient conditions well enough that she can at least recognize standard conditions, is what she needs to be able to call colors by sight. Before the episode, color profiles couldn't serve for Mary as the basis of physical judgments because they made no contact with her physical vocabulary. As soon as she can pull them under a concept, attach a description to them (and it doesn't matter how indirect the description is), she can begin to use them to track physical properties.[9]

9. What makes all of this noncircular is that Mary's reference to her phenomenal states is not representationally mediated. Those states themselves are positioned to serve as constituents of thoughts.

A couple of clarifications: First, it is crucial to understand that to say that 'looks'-talk doesn't have a grip when it comes to brain states for Mary is not to say that Mary cannot imagine or conceive of conceptual developments that would lead her to say 'I know it looks, or seems, like I'm in brain state b, but am I really?' It means that Mary has not made conceptual room for the gap between brain states and phenomenal states in a way that would allow her to assign 'It seems as though I am in b, but really I am not' a definite sense. There is no contingency whose possibility she is entertaining when she asks the question; she doesn't have some specific possibility in mind. Second, there is no reason to think, from the way the case was described, that Mary's concept of red, or even her concept of reddish experience, isn't coordinated with the world before the tomato encounter. If she can carry out measurements to ascertain reflectance properties that are the conditions of 'red'-ascriptions, and she knows that those are the conditions of 'red'-ascriptions, she can apply the predicate as surely as anybody else. And if she can carry out measurements to ascertain the brain states of observers that are the conditions of 'having a reddish experience'-ascriptions, she can apply that predicate too, given the right instruments. The point is that before the episode with the tomato, the coordinating links between these concepts and their extensions didn't pass through red profiles. Before the episode with the tomato, her red profiles were unconnected internally to any concepts.[10]

So, to sum up, it is agreed all around that the post-tomato Mary has an ability that the pre-tomato Mary lacks. She is newly able to apply 'red' spontaneously without inference and without the use of instrumentation. She can apply it without any kind of conceptual or representational mediation. The disputed question, and the one that matters for the anti-physicalist force of the argument, is whether this ability requires knowledge of a fact left out of Mary's textbooks and, more curiously, why no addition to her textbooks can redress the omission. Is there some piece of information that Mary needs to have in order to call colors by sight that is not already included in, and cannot be added to, the story in her textbooks? There are three familiar ways to resist the conclusion. One is to say that the encounter with the tomato is a kind of training.[11] It leaves Mary with a new ability, but no new information. Another is to say that it leaves Mary with old information in a new guise.[12] John Perry simply recognizes a new kind

10. The terminology is notoriously confusing. When I say 'red', I mean to refer to an intrinsic property of surfaces, and when I say 'reddish', I mean to refer to the phenomenal profile associated with that property by standard perceivers, under standard conditions.

11. Lewis and Nemirow adopt this view.

12. Horgan, Churchland, Tye, Lycan, Loar, Pereboom, Bigelow and Pargetter, van Gulick, McMullen, Papineau, and Teller, as I understand them, all advocate versions of this view.

of information, information carried by reflexive content, that can't be included in a theory or conveyed by book.

My response is different. Mary doesn't acquire new information; she establishes a semantic-level-bridging architectural relationship between a concept and a property. The relationships are clearer if we introduce a reflexive property designator—*this-here*—that functions as the descriptive analogue of an indexical, referring reflexively to a property exemplified by the medium in which it occurs. An utterance of '*this-here* sound' refers to the sound exemplified by the utterance, an inscription of 'this-here color' refers to the color exemplified by the inscription, a thought of the form '*this-here* smell or taste or visual quality' has the taste or smell or quality as a semantic constituent. We can also introduce a mental demonstrative to refer to past or future exemplifications. Finishing a meal, one thinks '*that-there* taste was lovely'; getting into a dentist chair, one thinks '*that-there* pain will be immense'. When Mary has thought of the form '*this-here* is such and such', the concept on the right is bound to the property establishing an architectural relationship that, once in place, allows information to flow from phenomenal properties into the conceptual apparatus, in precisely the way that attaching a label to a pointer on a measuring device establishes the architectural relationship that allows information to flow through a measuring device into the conceptual apparatus of a theory. Imagine a more systematic process. Instead of being shown a tomato, Mary establishes bridging links between the physical map of her brain and self-presenting internal states by having lab assistants cause electrical stimulation in areas of her brain. She hooks herself up to the machine, tells her assistants to induce brain-states that she has theoretical knowledge about, and forms self-describing thoughts like 'ah, so this-here is a c-fibre firing, and this-one-here is a d-fibre firing, and now this-one-here is a g-fibre firing,' gradually charting the phenomenal character of classes of physical events.[13] Once Mary has the bridging links in place, she reads her brain states off of her phenomenal states as easily and fluidly as someone who is adept with a map reads her objective coordinates off of the local landmarks. When she's in pain, she thinks to herself 'there go my c-fibres', and treats them in ways that she knows c-fibres respond to. She can now use her physical knowledge to induce states she finds phenomenally pleasant, and so on. What the semantic-level-bridging identities do—both the loose, context-dependent identities that connect phenomenal profiles with tomatoes, and the more precise counterparts that Mary has—is bring phenomenal profiles into

13. If physical and phenomenal concepts were drawn from incommensurable schemes, c-fibre firings in my brain would form a phenomenally motley crew of events. Phenomenal descriptions of physical similarity classes would be no more compressible than a list of their members.

alignment with concepts. Unlike the relationships between indexicals and singular terms, and unlike the loose, extrinsic links between phenomenal profiles and tomatoes, the links that Mary establishes will be, if her theory is correct, context-independent. She can bind the phenomenal state to its physical description with permanent glue.

What Mary needs in order to be able to call colors by sight, and what she acquires when she is shown the tomato, are architectural links between phenomenal profiles and concepts. The reason verbal instruction will not establish them is familiar by now. It is the same reason no amount of staring at a map will connect a point on the map with the ground under one's feet, and the same reason a chronicle of her day's activities will not tell a reader engaged in a repetitive activity which moment is now. Here is a handy representation of the various pieces of Mary's knowledge; those she has while she is in the room, those she acquires in the tomato episode, and those she uses thereafter in calling colors by sight:

1. coordinating descriptions with phenomenal profiles; fixing labels to phenomenal states
    (a) Red things $=_{def}$ the distal causal source of reddish experiences in standard perceivers under standard conditions;
    (b) I am a standard perceiver and conditions are standard;
    (c) I am now looking at a thing of the kind called 'red';
    (d) This-here must be a reddish experience;
2. calling colors by sight
    (e) This-here is a reddish experience;
    (f) Conditions are standard and I am a standard perceiver
    (g) The thing I'm looking at must be red.

Mary knows (a), and (b), while she is in the room.[14] The description in (c) comes from an external source (the fellow who shows her the tomato), and it is the crucial link needed to coordinate phenomenal states and descriptive vocabulary allowing her to draw the conclusion (d). Once Mary knows the facts in (a) through (d), provided she has at least tacit knowledge of statements like (f),[15] she is in a position to draw (g)-conclusions.[16] The missing link is an architectural one that bridges the gap between

---

14. Label (a) is a definition, and (b) is an empirical fact that we can suppose that Mary knows (it is not the *kind* of knowledge that Jackson thinks is inaccessible to the pre-tomato Mary).

15. Provided, that is to say, that she has the ability to distinguish standard from nonstandard conditions and refrains from drawing (g)-conclusions in the latter.

16. Knowledge represented in II is not meant to describe any conscious reasoning, but to make explicit the conditions of perceptual competence with colors: a well-trained perceiver will learn to draw conclusions like (g) when (e) and (f) obtain.

reflexively identified properties and descriptions of them, and it is established by getting oneself into a position in which one has independent knowledge that the concept, or description, applies and seeing what pops up.

Fixing Labels to Phenomenal States

Mary passes through three distinguishable stages: first, she fixes labels to color profiles; then, she uses those profiles to call colors by sight; and later, if she is interested, she sharpens up the extrinsic description and translates it into an intrinsic one. This last transition is easy for Mary. It's an in-house relationship between terms of her theory, just the kind of gap that is bridged by theoretical knowledge. Mary's predicament has nothing to do with whether her theory is correct or complete. It's a coordination problem. The quandary, remedied in the episode with the tomato, is that her color profiles—though they may be described as completely and accurately as you please by her theory—weren't wired directly into the representational network. There were no internal, architectural links between color profiles and concepts.

Let's reiterate some of Jackson's assumptions, together with the ones that we saw we could add without alleviating Mary's suspense about what it will be like for her when she sees the tomato. We assumed that her theory was correct and complete. The sentences in her belief box constitute a complete compendium of all objective truths about the world. If it's not complete without the addition of the casual wisdom that talks explicitly of reddish experiences, add the casual wisdom. We assumed all the vocabulary that appears in her theory is coordinated with the world, both the vocabulary that makes reference to brain states and that which talks of reddish experiences. She knows how to carry out measurements with brain-o-meters and she has procedures that allow her, by carrying out measurements on observers' brain states, to determine whether any observer (herself included) is having a reddish experience. She also has herself, through visits to the Nida-Rumelin room, been exposed to the full spectrum of color experiences. And still, with all of this, so long as she has never been in the position of self-ascribing a brain state or reddish experience, she will not know what to expect when she sees the tomato. Before the episode, Mary was like someone who has been given a paint-by-numbers set and paint but lost the legend that coordinates colors with numbers. She had both the palette and the picture, but no way of knowing which colors went with which numbers. Concepts of colors of things were, before her color profiles were integrated into the network of her descriptive concepts, bled of phenomenal content.

8.2 INCOMPLETENESS?

This doesn't demonstrate the incompleteness of Mary's theory any more than the possibility of being lost through an inability to self-locate demonstrates the incompleteness of a map in your possession. There is a very deep confusion in holding representations to standards of completeness that undermines the very point of representation. If map-builders took to building red dots into maps, we could no longer carry them around. It's not an accident that self-locating building directories are fixed to walls or podiums. There are GPS locators (global positioning system), of course, but the self-locating arrow on a GPS bears exactly the same dynamic relationship to the first-order representational apparatus of the map that our reflexive expressions bear to their nonreflexive counterparts.

Did Mary learn a new fact when she saw the tomato? The terminology doesn't quite fit. But neither do I think we have to say, with Perry, whose account agrees with mine in other respects, that there is a species of nonfactual information that wasn't included in Mary's theory and that can only be acquired in this kind of episode. I think we should say that Mary's theory was both complete and fully coordinated with the world. The problem was all on Mary's side, just like the lost traveler staring blankly at his map. The map can be as complete and accurate as can be, but nothing in its first-order, invariant content will constitute, or supply, architectural connections to the landscape.[17] Compare a complete catalog of descriptive facts about a rare brand of ink, ink X (its chemical content, history, common uses, etc.), that happens to be written in that ink itself. Nothing in the first-order nonreflexive content of the description, be it ever so complete, will connect the properties it describes to the property it exemplifies. No set of nonreflexive truths will entail the sentence 'this-here, the ink I am printed in, is X'. That epistemic gap—the gap between properties described and properties exemplified—is not remediable by completeness or accuracy and can't be used to demonstrate the lack of

---

17. At this point, people often start thinking of ways of recognizing a point on the map by structural relations to the surroundings. One version of this is to think 'If the map is really complete, it should include a little representation of a lost traveler standing in front of a lake staring at his map, and even if there are many such travelers, I can do a little twirl or sachet to the left to identify the one that represents me so I am home free.' Of course, that's correct, but these ways of self-locating all at least tacitly invoke assumptions about architectural relations (e.g., that stick figures represent persons, that blue blotches represent bodies of water), and they all rely on contingent asymmetries in the domain. The point remains that maps are closed representational systems, and nothing in the in-house relationships between points on the map, so long as the map doesn't have a reflexive designator like a red dot, is going to establish an architectural relationship to anything outside.

either. Jackson's argument just brings out, in another way, the lesson of the Argument from Confinement. Only self-locating and self-describing acts will bridge the divide between a closed representational system and its subject matter, whether we are talking about minds or maps or physical theories.

8.3   REFINING IDEAS: THE DIRECTION OF DEVELOPMENT

I already mentioned that Mary followed a nonstandard program of development. Her conceptual training was completed before she could coordinate color profiles with any ideas so that she had the fully articulated network of concepts in place and coordinated with the world by links passing through brain-o-meters before she could associate any of them internally with color profiles. For her, the direct coordinating links between color profiles and ideas would not be, as they were for John, descriptions of the colors of external surfaces, but states of her own brain. She wouldn't say 'oh, that's what it's like to see red', she would say 'oh, that's what it's like for me when my brain is in state b'. That would be the place looks-talk doesn't have purchase for her; the place at which her ability to assign truth conditions to the claim that it seems as though her brain is in state b, but really it's not gives out. She doesn't know how to describe a possible world in which that is true. For John, before Jim forced him outside the shop, talk of colors of things had that character. John had to make room for the gap between looking green and being green before he knew what was being claimed by someone who said "I know that it looks green, but really it's not" and that requires articulation in his ideas of color that wasn't there originally. If his education in color perception stopped when he got to the part where light waves hit the eyeball, he might not have known how to give determinate sense to the claim "I know it seems like my retinal cones are activated in such and such a pattern, but really they are not." And let me emphasize again that this has to be understood very delicately. It's not that Mary can't recognize the abstract possibility that her whole theory is wrong or that it might develop in a way that makes room for the possibility of having a certain sort of experience and not being in the associated brain state. Nor is it that John could not recognize his own scientific ignorance and be prepared to defer to experts who claim that possibility of it seeming like one's retinal surfaces had a certain pattern without it actually being the case. It's that neither of them have, under the conditions described, the representational resources to explicitly describe conditions that would defeat the inference from the first to the second.

The fit between phenomenal profile and conceptual role is always provisional. A preliminary, tentative assignment is made and then refined in a way subject always to further refinement. The goal is to assign conceptual roles to phenomenal profiles that, in an increasingly accurate and robust way, expresses their informational content. It is a translation task and as hard as we know translation to be. The informational states in different media cut across one another in a way that makes translation an arduous, holistic, painful process. We can loosen the ties between concepts and phenomenal profiles by adding joints in the coordinating relation to get a better overall fit, but no matter how loose the fit, there will always be, somewhere in the network, fixed points: concepts tied so directly to their phenomenal profiles that looks-talk doesn't get ahold. The difference between 'this-here is what it's like for me when JI is looking at a red thing' and 'this is what it's like for me when JI is in brain state b'[18] is that the latter gives a more explicit, more invariant description of *this*, one that picks it out across a wider range of circumstances (e.g., those that include different ambient conditions or chemically induced hallucination). It is akin to the difference between 'this is JI's latest book' and 'this is JI's second book'.[19]

8.4 IN SUM

Here's how you achieve coordination between a pair of media. You identify points of extensional contact and put in place some physical procedure that transforms the output of the one into something that can act as input to the next. So, for example, recall the description in chapter 4

---

18. Assuming that the expressions on the right are indeed coreferential.

19. A few remarks about Perry's recent discussion of Jackson's argument. Perry assimilates learning what it's like to see red to recognizing that *that* man is Fred Dretske. On his account, it does two things: it forges an internal informational link between perceptions of red and ideas of red, and it adds a phenomenal profile of red (a 'Humean impression', in his words) to one's red ideas. The account has so much in common with the one I have given that I am tempted to say they are the same, but there are some differences in expression, and in the next section I draw conclusions I believe he would not endorse, so I don't make that assertion. For both Perry and me, what happens in Mary's mind is that an internal link is established between Mary's color ideas and color profiles. There were links in place before the episode, but they all passed outside the head. Perry, however, regards Mary as taking new information away from the episode with the tomato, information of a 'non-detachable', incommunicable kind. In *Knowledge, Possibility, and Consciousness*, Perry writes: "The problem, as I diagnose it, is that Mary's new knowledge cannot be identified with the subject matter content of the statement with which she expresses it, nor with the subject matter content of the thought with which she thinks it. Mary's new epistemic state, the one she expresses with 'this is what it is like to see red,' is of a certain type. States of this type are true only if the aspect of brain states to which their possessors attend is the aspect of brain states that normal people have when they see red. That is the reflexive content of her thought, and that is her new knowledge" (22).

of the transformations that occur on a ship when a landmark is sighted. Visual information is recorded by the alidade, then transferred to the gyrocompass card, before being converted to a digital representation and finally recorded as a written number in the column labeled with the name of the landmark in the bearing record log. Each of these is an information-preserving transformation that converts a representational vehicle belonging to one medium into a form in which it can interact computationally with the states of another. The transforming process can be automated like the transformation of a radio signal into sound, or it may be something as informal as a translation of a visual image into words. If it is information preserving, information will flow through the interface between the media without loss. If not, only some of the information will survive translation. I argued that thought coordinates itself with experience by self-descriptive acts that attach concepts to phenomenal profiles in 'this is what it is like to' thoughts.[20]

The error of mistaking cognitive relations for architectural ones replays itself here as the idea that if phenomenal states really are just physical states, we ought to be able to think our way from the physical *concept* to the phenomenal *property*. We ought to be able to get to phenomenal states by tracing out internal connections among physical concepts. The failure to do so is taken as evidence of a missing conceptual link. A gap between physical concepts and phenomenal states that can't be filled by physical knowledge shows that however tightly linked they may be dynamically, phenomenal states can't be *identical* with brain states. I have argued that this misidentifies the source of the gap.[21] Knowledge-about establishes an intentional relation between one idea and another; to know that Fred Dretske is a philosopher is to link the idea of Dretske to the idea of a philosopher. Recognition, by contrast, bridges semantic levels, establishing an architectural relation between an idea and something that is connected in the physical landscape. To think there is a chain of reasoning that takes you from purely physical knowledge to knowledge

---

20. The self-descriptive character of the contents associated with phenomenal states is obscured by the fact that, like the labels attached to pointers, they aren't obviously self-descriptive. We don't label the pointers on measuring devices with theoretical descriptions of the position of the pointer; we label them with theoretical descriptions of the quantities that the pointer indicates. This saves us from having to work out what quantity is being tracked by the pointer observable by going through the internal dynamics of the machine every time a measurement is made. The right way of thinking of what is going on is that the attached label is self-descriptive, but extrinsic. It has the form 'this is the dial position that (ordinarily) indicates such and such' where the such and such is what we're interested in. The same is true of the contents associated with phenomenal states, as I argue in chapter 11; they are implicit, extrinsic self-descriptions of the form "this is the taste/smell/look that ordinarily indicates such and such."

21. As has Perry, though without the intentional/arctitectural distinction.

of physical-phenomenal property identities is to make the same mistake as someone who thinks that staring at a map will by itself connect points on the page with the ground under his feet. Explanations, chains of reasoning, these link concept to concept. Hardware, wiring, that is what links concept to property. As indicated in the epigraph to this chapter, Jackson himself now rejects the conclusion of his argument and sees the philosophical task as that of identifying where it goes wrong. But the Jackson that put the argument forward, and those who still follow him where it leads, mistake a gap in the machinery for a gap in content, and try to fill it—futilely, as we will see again in the next chapter—by adding representational structure.[22]

8.5 THE SPACE OF REASONS AND THE SPACE OF CAUSES

There is one short addendum to all of this. I have said that transitions between media involve (more or less) information-preserving transformations of vehicles of content that convert the output of one medium into something that can interact computationally with the states of another. Just as the contents of observations have to be expressed symbolically before they can be fed into the computational apparatus of a physical theory, and English sentences have to be rendered in French before they can be combined in inferences with French expressions, phenomenal states have to be converted into an inferentially articulated form before they can interact with the machinery of thought.[23] So conceived, the transition from experience into thought involves little more than a simple transformation of vehicle.

Historically, this transition has been difficult for philosophers, sometimes for bad reasons. One worry is that experience is supposed to furnish the ground, or justification, for empirical belief, but it can't do so by supplying the premises on which empirical belief is based. It isn't inferentially articulated. It doesn't come packaged in a form that gives it any kind of rational connection with thought at all. This is sometimes stated by saying that experience isn't intrinsically 'conceptualized' and inference

22. You can get from an *idea* of a sensory state to an *idea* of a description of a sensory state and *vice versa*, but as Putnam emphasized, this is just a picture of a hook between the items you are trying to hook. And it is entirely internal to the space of reasons. There is both room and need for an explanation that connects these two ideas. Abner Shimony has called this, in a nice phrase, closing the circle.

23. And there are transformations that go the other way; one translates thought into finger motion, which is, in its turn, transformed into electrical signals and, ultimately, into a visual image on a computer screen.

doesn't get started until after conceptualization has been effected. Once we have a description of an experience, we are off and running, but the gap between the experience and the description is a yawning one that reason cannot cross. Experience can't engage the machinery of thought until it is translated into an inferentially articulated form, and this translation is not an inferential process. The reply to this is that the transformation is a physical one no less innocent than the one that translates English into French. It is part of the architectural background that supports thought, and that is all.

There is a different worry, not always carefully distinguished from the above. It has to do not with the transition from a noninferentially structured medium to an inferentially structured medium but with the transition from inference to Inference, where Inference is conceived not simply as computation, but as a practice subject to norms. There is an important divide here, and McDowell and Brandom, following the lead, respectively, of Kant and Sellars, have shed a good deal of light on it. Experiences are elements in the space of causes and ideas are elements in the space of reasons. These two spaces are held together dynamically by a physical process that transforms experiences into ideas of a kind no different from the kind that transforms an audio signal into sound or a light wave into a picture. But there is something special about the space of reasons that is not shared by these other media, and that may have its roots in social dynamics.

9

Inverted Spectra

We've been talking so far about the coordination of experience with thought in a single mind, and we've seen how self-descriptive acts can solve coordination problems. But there's a notorious problem about coordination of experience *across* minds that, although it's also been used to argue for dualism, raises quite different issues. The *locus classicus* of the statement of the problem, is given by Locke:

> Neither would it carry any Imputation of Falsehood to our simple Ideas, if by the different Structure of our Organs, it were so ordered, That the same Object should produce in several Men's Minds different Ideas at the same time; e.g. if the Idea, that a Violet produced in one Man's Mind by his Eyes, were the same that a Marigold produces in another Man's, and vice versa.[1]

The possibility to which Locke is adverting here has come to be known as the Problem of Inverted Spectra, and has been used as fuel against a number of different philosophical positions, for example, in attempts to analyze phenomenal properties in functional or behavioral terms, and recently by Chalmers as another argument for dualism. I'm interested in seeing whether it is indeed a possibility, how it arises, and what it shows. It

---

1. Locke, *Essay Concerning Human Understanding*, xxxii.

differs from the problem of coordinating experience with thought because there is no direct interface between the experience of different subjects, and it holds some important lessons about language.

9.1   IS SPECTRUM INVERSION POSSIBLE?

Is a prospect of the sort described by Locke really possible? If the question is whether there are structure-preserving automorphisms of color space, it turns out that the answer is no. There are subtle asymmetries in color space that would make such transformations detectable. A simple rotation of the hue circle that mapped blue onto yellow, for example, would carry an impoverishment of discriminatory capabilities (an invert would map distinct bluish reds to the same yellowish green). Similar things can be said for other transformations. But if the question is whether there are ways of permuting the properties that color one person's visual world, or transforming them in a manner that preserves their relations to one another, their roles in the production of behavior, and their causal relations to the environment, the answer is yes. Shoemaker, for example, considers an impoverished palette.

> I think we know well enough what it would be like to see the world nonchromatically, i.e., in black, white, and the various shades of grey— for we frequently do see it in this way in photographs, moving pictures, and television. And there is an obvious mapping of the nonchromatic shades onto each other which satisfies the conditions. . . . [2]

We could just as easily imagine changes induced by colored lenses, and we can conceive, if not imagine, substitution of qualities that are alien to our own phenomenology. So if we widen our gaze beyond the class of simple inversions, we have to agree with Locke that spectral inversion, if it occurred:

> could never be known: because one Man's Mind could not pass into another Man's Body, to perceive, what Appearances were produced by those Organs; neither the Ideas hereby, nor the Names, would be at all confounded, or any Falshood be in either. For all Things, that had the Texture of a Violet, producing constantly the Idea, which he called Blue, and those which had the Texture of a Marigold, producing constantly the Idea, which he as constantly called Yellow, whatever those Appearances were in his Mind; he would be able as regularly to distinguish Things for his Use by those

---

2. Shoemaker, The *First-Person Perspective and Other Essays*, 196, note omitted.

Appearances, and understand, and signify those distinctions, marked by the Names Blue and Yellow, as if the Appearances, or Ideas in his Mind, received from those two Flowers, were exactly the same, with the Ideas in other Men's Minds.[3]

The problem is not that properties exemplified in either your visual experience or in mine cannot be identified in terms of their role in the production of behavior or causal relations to features of the external landscape, it's that once we've identified the intrinsic properties of *my* experience by their causal relations to the environment and their role in the production of my behavior, and identified the intrinsic properties of *your* experience by their causal relations to the environment and role in the production of your behavior, this tells us nothing about the *internal* relations between properties that play parallel roles in our respective functional architectures. It tells us nothing, in short, about how the kind of experience you have when you see red relates qualitatively to the kind that I do when I see red. And this is a quite general problem. It goes not just for color, but for all of the qualities exemplified in experience: tactual, auditory, gustatory.... So, a worry that starts by exploiting superficial local symmetries brings into relief a large gap in our knowledge. If all I can know of the experience of others comes from how they behave, I can't establish whether their experience is intrinsically like mine. Why won't linguistic exchange settle the question? For just the reason that Locke says. The interpretation of one another's phenomenal vocabulary varies with the facts that we want to use it to convey in a way that renders it quite precisely uninformative. As I remarked in the last chapter when we wondered why Mary's teachers couldn't convey the information she needed to coordinate phenomenal profiles with concepts, the answer you get when you ask someone what yellow things look like to them is as informative as a French answer to the question whether 'oui' means yes in French. It's ultimately a lesson about language, and more generally about the kind of information that can be conveyed through a public medium, that we learn from reflecting on the epistemic possibility of spectral substitution.

9.2 EXEMPLARS

I'll assume that the story I've been telling so far is correct. Every subject has an internally exemplified palette of properties built up over a history of experience and coordinated with vocabulary drawn from a public medium

3. Locke, *Essay*, xxxii.

in Mary-style self-descriptive episodes. Judgments of phenomenal similarity, then, might work something like this. Experience—for example, the experience of having a migraine, looking at a tomato or tasting cardamom—leaves a blot on one's palette, equipping one with an internal exemplar that is used as a yardstick in judgments of future experience. When one makes a phenomenal judgment, for example, "This is the taste of cardamom", she looks to her palette, locates an internal exemplar derived from a previous cardamom-tasting episode, and applies the attached label to the new experience. We can think of blots on one's palette either as remembered experiences or ideas with remembered experiences as constituents. It's crucial to note the role of memory in the process of phenomenal recognition. It is past experience that prepares your palette; the labels you attach to new experiences in phenomenal judgments are connected to exemplars drawn from past experience. The labels can be passed through linguistic channels and compared with the labels that others employ, but the exemplars that act as yardsticks in judgments of phenomenal similarity can be passed only through the internal, intrinsic-property-preserving channels provided by memory. The thing about memory that distinguishes it from language, at least the kind of memory that is active in perceptual recognition, is that the memory of an experience resembles the experience. The upshot is that phenomenal similarity is well defined only over collections of experience that can be connected by memory.

There are some complex issues that I want to leave unresolved. I assume that an ability to judge phenomenal sameness in some cases precedes, and is a necessary condition for, the attachment of any labels.[4] So, for example, the Mary of the revised scenario who had had color experiences in visits to the Nida-Rumelin room, but had not yet attached any labels, could make judgments of sameness and difference in color, not just between simultaneously presented objects, but over time. She could compare past experiences with present ones and, in at least some cases, arrive at judgments of sameness and difference. We might say that she had rudimentary color concepts even at that stage, but a fully developed ability to judge phenomenal sameness coevolves with the practice of attaching labels and is heavily shaped by the labels one actually attaches.[5] Any account of phenomenal recognition in which memory plays a crucial

4. Quine's discussion in "Naturalizing Epistemology" of the need for preconceptual ability to judge phenomenal similarity is a *locus classicus* of what is now the received view among both philosophers and psychologists. On all of these points, psychological research should take the lead.

5. So, for example, it's been known for a long time that the more discriminating our concepts, the more discerning our judgments of phenomenal similarity, and some judgments of phenomenal similarity seem to require conceptual preparation of highly specific sorts, although the issue is complicated by the need to separate the role of conceptual preparation from its incidental effects in heightening attention, and so on.

role has the consequence that phenomenal similarity is well defined only within the closed circles of experiences connected by memory. So long as your experiences can't be measured against my exemplars or mine against yours, we are in the position of countries that have objects defining separate units of standard measure stored in government vaults, but who are unable to calibrate their spatial vocabulary against each other. If there is some one object to which they can mutually attach a spatial label, that object will provide the architectural rigging that coordinates their spatial vocabulary with each other.[6] But without these points of contact, their units of measure cannot be extended to cover each other's domain. Just so, calibrating my phenomenal vocabulary against yours requires the existence of experiences to which we can mutually attach phenomenal labels. If there is no overlap in the range of objects against which we can measure internal exemplars, that is, if there are no experiences that fall both in your psychological history and my own, we are out of luck. It doesn't matter that we can attach our experiences causally to common points in the external landscape; causal connections don't preserve intrinsic character. And it doesn't matter that we use the same words to describe our experience; it's the interpretation of those words in the mouths of others that is in question.

You and I can align our personal palettes structurally, but any transformation that preserves their structural relations to each other, causal relations to the environment, and role in the production of behavior will be undiscoverable. The problem is not one about knowing how to map our own experience into a shared description of a common world; it's a problem about knowing how to establish specifically internal relations between the properties exemplified in disjoint domains. So long as phenomenal similarity is defined only over presentational domains, and there is no overlap between these domains—no fixed points to which we could attach our respective phenomenal labels—there is just not enough fixed structure to allow us to align our personal palettes. The possibility that your experience is like mine only in structural respects will remain epistemologically ineliminable.[7]

9.3 LANGUAGE

Let's examine more carefully why linguistic exchange won't resolve the problem. If exemplars can be passed through memory, why *can't* they be

---

6. Length is a one-dimensional unit of measure, and so one measurement will suffice for complete coordination. In general, coordination of a pair of spaces along n dimensions requires n separate parameters.

7. I'll look below at the possibility that experience has no intrinsic properties.

passed through language? It's not as though I don't have a perfectly good vocabulary for talking about properties exemplified in your experience. The last seven words were an instance of such vocabulary, and this essay is full of such examples. If I want to refer to the property exemplified in Mary's experience when she sees a red thing, I say 'the property exemplified in Mary's experience when she sees a red thing'. What we don't have is a *nonrelational* descriptive vocabulary that spans the space between subjects. What I don't have is a way of referring to properties exemplified in Mary's experience without making explicit reference to her.

This brings out an important fact about the logic of 'what it's like to —' talk that's not always carefully attended to. The surface grammar is misleading in two respects: (1) There is a suppressed reference to a subject, and (2) The blank has to be filled not with a subjectless description of a property, but with an objective description of an event. There is just not something it is like *simpliciter* when something occurs. There is something it is like for you, something it is like for me, and something it is like for Bill Clinton and Tom Nagel. Much of what happens in the world—for example, things that happen on faraway times or places, or simply events that are hidden from view—has either a null effect, or effects so attenuated and diffuse that I can't attach any definite profile to them. This goes for happenings in Tom Nagel's brain as surely as it does for car crashes and cartwheels. There is something it is like *for Tom Nagel* when c-fibres fire in his brain, something it is like *for students* who feel the prick of his pain in a more attenuated, but still quite characteristic way, something it is like for his neuroscientist who is looking at the results of his brain scan. Tom Nagel's c-fibre firings have a different phenomenology for each of these subjects, and an effect too attenuated and indirect on the rest of us to attach any profile at all. 'What it's like to'-talk, properly construed, doesn't relate phenomenal properties to physical properties; it relates subjects to happenings. For every subject S and every worldly event, e, we can sensibly ask 'what is it like for S when e?' Most often the answer will be 'nothing *in particular*', but there will be an inner circle of events—a different one for each of us—to which we can rigidly attach profiles. And these, together with contextual support, will translate into profiles that can be attached a little less rigidly to a wider circle of events. When my c-fibres or x-fibres or y-fibres fire, they usually have pretty much the same effect, and as it turns out, the phenomenal profiles of all other events are determined by how they relate causally to these. Events in the proximal landscape have stable profiles if we control for standard conditions, but the farther out we get, and the more variation we allow in the ambient space, the less stable profiles get.

As a point of logic, to ask what is it like *simpliciter* when Tom Nagel's c-fibres fire—or worse, when c-fibres fire in general—is nonsense. We need to know *which* c-fibres we are talking about and we need to know *for whom* we are asking what it is like. Once the reference to a subject is made explicit it becomes clear that what-it's-like can't be an intrinsic property of an event, since what-it's-like for you when e is not in general the same as what-it's-like for me. And we know that to support the internal differences between what-it's-like for me when e and what-it's-like for me when f, when e ≠ f, they can't be relations simply to a single parameter. They have to be relations to something more complex, something with parts or dimensions, something structurally like personal palettes. Palettes serve as frames of phenomenal reference in the way the quantities associated with physical theory serve as frames of physical reference. They provide a descriptive basis that allows us to relate the properties of one object of perception to another. And a phenomenal profile is a set of coordinates on a personal palette. To know what an event *is like* is to know how to plot it on my personal palette. It is to know how it relates phenomenally to other things, not only whether it is exactly similar but also whether it is similar along particular dimensions, to a particular degree, or in particular respects. If the image of a palette suggests a disorganized collection of overlapping blotches, that is misleading. The color spectrum, rather than the painter's palette, is a better image to have in mind. Our personal palettes are highly organized spaces, rich with structure, that play an essential role in perceptual recognition. Perceptual psychologists make these spaces the focus of study, answering questions about their dimensionality and compositional structure (e.g., what are the simple qualities? how good are we imaginatively at decomposing and recombining them?).

So what-it's-like is not a property of properties, but a function from events to locations on a personal palette. This suppressed complexity is the source of some of the confusion about phenomenal properties. Every subject has *her own* palette, just as every subject has its own location in space and time. And these together comprise her personal experiential perspective on the domain of objective fact. What Mary should really say, when she is shown the tomato is not 'ah, so this what it's like to see red', but '*this-here*[8] is what it's like *for me* when a red thing is placed at p'. Now if we add Mary's brother, Mo, to the picture, placing him by her side when she has her revelation with the tomato, while Mary is framing the thought '*this-here* is what it's like *for me* when a red thing is placed at p', Mo is framing the thought '*this-here* is what it's like *for me* when a red thing is placed at p'. Each of them locates himself or herself with respect to p,

8. This, recall, is the descriptive analogue of an indexical.

takes stock of viewing conditions to be sure there's nothing out of the ordinary, and attaches the label 'seeing red' to a point on his or her palette.[9] Cognitively and semantically, these are self-locating thoughts but, unlike "here is <,>", thoughts that locate distinct places in the same space, they locate distinct properties on *separate* palettes. We suppress the personal parameter in ordinary English. We speak of sweet and sour tastes, high and low sounds, hot and cold sensations, leaving out the parameter that would raise the question whether we mean 'sweet taste' to attach rigidly to tastes of the kind that sweet things actually, ordinarily cause in ourselves or to change reference with changes in phenomenal profile. But it's an omission that's brought to the surface by reflection on inverted spectra. To wonder whether your reddish experiences are like mine is to wonder precisely whether what it is like for *me* to be looking at a tomato is the same as what it is like for *you*.

9.4   A LESSON ABOUT LANGUAGE

Let me cast all of this in the language of representational media and draw a general lesson. I've assumed that thought is the medium in which a subject expresses and combines information drawn from experience at different times and places. It is natural to think of it as the medium in which the events in a subjective history communicate with one another. Public languages are, of course, the medium in which distinct subjects communicate with one another. The information carried by a medium has to travel between interlocutors; it has to survive transport from one to another. Carrying a thermometer from A to B, for example, isn't a way of conveying the temperature at A to B. An invariant record of the information registered in a noninvariant way by the thermometer's state at A has to be made and sent in its place. Quite generally, a medium can only carry information that is invariant under transport between its interlocutors. A medium whose interlocutors are scattered through space can only carry information that is invariant under spatial translations. A medium whose interlocutors are spread out in time can only carry information invariant under temporal transformations. A medium whose interlocutors are members of different families, or are located in different countries can only carry information that is invariant under transformation of family and country. The invariance requirement acts as a sieve that filters out

---

9. There are two cases. In one we suppose Mary and Mo both had had red experience before, and it was just a matter of attaching labels. In the other, we suppose that one or the other of them had never had red experiences, and so they add a blotch to their personal palette at the same time that they attach a label.

information that depends on relations to features of context that are not shared by interlocutors.

As remarked in chapter 4, I speak mostly of media with relatively deep, natural boundaries, but I don't suppose that there are anything more than vague, pragmatic general criteria for identifying and individuating media. Whenever we've got a collection of situated systems exchanging information and a more or less implicit delimitation of the class of possible interlocutors, we have a representational medium and the invariance requirement can be applied. Any group of speakers sharing a local bit of landscape can set up a provisional medium that exploits the momentary confluence of context. There are as many actual media of this sort as there are conversational interactions, and as many possible media of this sort as there are contexts. Apparent counterexamples to the invariance requirement can be understood as involving temporary employment of context-bound media. This doesn't render the requirement empty, as we will see. It still yields quite powerful consequences when applied to particular media.

There is a very particular type of information that may be lost when one moves from a medium to one with stricter invariance requirements. I will provide examples of cases of external media in which this happens— one in detail, two in passing—and suggest that this is precisely what happens to the intrinsic properties of experience when we move from thought to language. There is a broadening of the class of interlocutors and a concomitant strengthening of the invariance requirement that results in a loss of information. The information lost is, as one would expect, information tied reflexively to the context of the original medium. In this case, that is information about the intrinsic nature of the properties that color our personal palettes.

9.5   INTERPLANETARY ANALOGY OF 'LEFT' AND 'RIGHT'

The first example concerns leftness and rightness (or properties interdefinable with leftness and rightness) in an interplanetary language on the supposition that there are no asymmetric objects that can be ostended from both planets. The technical term for these properties is 'chiral properties'; I will sometimes use 'handedness'. Consider my hands, ignoring the incidental differences, and suppose that each is a perfect mirror image of the other. They have the same color and the same parts. Their parts have the same lengths and are separated by angles of the same magnitude. For all marks on one there is a corresponding mark on the other. In short, aside from the different orientations, they are duplicates. Any sentence we can construct that does not contain chiral terms is either true of both of my hands or true of neither. I'm going to make one controversial metaphysical assumption and one actually false physical assumption about chiral properties. Since it matters for our purposes only that the case presents a coherent possibility, this shouldn't affect things. The metaphysical assumption is that leftness and rightness are distinct intrinsic properties of hands. The empirical assumption is that the physical laws are invariant under spatial reflection.[10] If two objects can share all other intrinsic[11] properties and yet be mirror images of each other, handedness can't supervene on those other properties. And what goes for objects *in* the world, goes for the world as a whole; it will be invariant global transformations that everywhere invert left and right.

Now, consider the following problem, borrowed from Martin Gardner's *The Ambidextrous Universe.*

> [How can we] communicate the meaning of 'left' [to the inhabitants of some Planet X in a distant galaxy]? . . . We may say anything we please to our listeners, ask them to perform any experiment whatever, with one *proviso:* There is to be no asymmetric object or structure that we and they can observe in common.[12]

It should be clear from the terms of the problem that it can't be done. There is no way of telling how to map Planet X chiral vocabulary onto our own by exchange of nonchiral information, and hence no way of coordinating our use of the terms 'left' and 'right' with theirs if we respect the proviso. If we had a single point of common reference to which we could both attach chiral labels, that would provide the architectural rigging that would coordinate the labels with one another. But without a common point of reference there is no way to do it. There will be different ways of mapping their terms onto left and right on Earth that preserve all relations to coordinating links between their vocabulary and ours and no way of breaking the symmetry. The upshot is that although 'left' has a perfectly definite *intra*planetary reference (it is coordinated unambiguously with its extension both on Earth and X), and although 'left-on-Earth' and 'left-on-X' have a perfectly definite *inter*planetary reference, 'left,' by itself, does not. The same goes mutatis mutandis for 'right'. There simply *is* no way of coordinating a term in an interplanetary language with a chiral property in

---

10. It was assumed for a long time that this was so, but it turns out that there are some asymmetric probabilistic laws associated with the weak nuclear interaction.

11. I'll suppress this, and specify only when I mean to include relational properties.

12. Gardner, *The Ambidextrous Universe,* 70.

an invariant way. The residents of a planet coordinate chiral terms individually with properties on their planet, but there is no way of translating across a planetary divide without making reference, implicit or explicit, to planets, and there is no way of establishing whether left-on-Earth is the same as left-on-X.

To put it in a way that recalls the vocabulary introduced in section 1, planets are unarticulated constituents of handedness talk that have to be made explicit for purposes of coordinating across a planetary divide. They provide the frames relative to which 'left' and 'right' are coordinated with extensions and, because of the contingent limitations on objects of common ostension, no direct coordinating links can be established between frames. This doesn't mean there is anything metaphysically extraordinary about left-ness and right-ness. There are simply contingent epistemic limitations that keep planetary residents from coordinating frames with one another. The indeterminacy in how to map 'left' and 'right' doesn't carry over to the rest of their spatial vocabulary, and 'left' and 'right' are perfectly well defined on each planet nondescriptively by relations to orientable objects. The problem is simply that there's no way of coordinating across a planetary divide, because there is simply no way of comparing an object to which 'left-on-A' applies with one to which 'left-on-B' applies, and no way of breaking the symmetry in relations between these expressions and the rest of the vocabulary. It's a coordinating problem, and we are dispossessed of our ordinary ways of solving coordinating problems by the proviso against ostension.

We can say that 'left' and 'right' have an implicitly indexical, or frame-dependent content that is revealed by the problem of coordinating, but we should recognize that this kind of indexicality is a perfectly general phenomenon. *All* of our (non-mathematical) concepts are, in this sense, frame-dependent. The frame-dependence can always be eliminated by explicit relativization, and in most cases we can replace the explicitly relational description that makes reference to a frame with an intrinsic one that spans frames. This is what happened for instance with John in chapter 6, whose scientific education allowed him to replace frame-dependent color concepts tied directly to profiles and relativized to lighting conditions (*green-in-electric-light vs. green-in-sunlight*) with an unequivocal concept that spanned both contexts and provided the conceptual and epistemic means of coordinating the frame-dependent concepts with one another. The implicit relationality of his immature concept was revealed by failure to coordinate across lighting conditions. It doesn't matter that John uses the same word for the new concept; he distinguishes it from the frame-dependent concepts by retrospectively reconstruing his previous uses as relativized versions of it. The Planet Xers cannot complete this progression, but for reasons that are quite contingent and metaphysically unmysterious.

Let me describe another case—even more apropos—where we have the same inability to coordinate directly across frames, because I think it's useful to see the relationships reproduced in a range of cases to make it clear that it's a perfectly mundane phenomenon. Imagine a pair of texts that coin their own descriptive vocabulary. Each introduces a term 'grishy' with the sentence 'grishy is the color of this ink'. If you could only get a look at *one* of the texts, you wouldn't be able to tell whether 'grishy' refers to the same color in both. You wouldn't be able to establish any kind of internal similarity between the properties referred to as 'grishy' in the separate texts. Each could refer in an unambiguous way to the color the other calls 'grishy', if they have names for each other and quotation. A could use 'the color that B calls "grishy"' to refer to the extension of B's term, and B could use 'the color that A calls "grishy"' to refer to the extension of A's term, but the textual parameter would be ineliminable and internal relations (is grishy-in-A *like* grishy-in-B?) would be impossible for either to determine.[13]

9.6 LANGUAGE AND PHENOMENAL CONTENT

What these examples teach us is that if there is no overlap between phenomenal histories, if I can't, for example, compare your exemplars against mine, and if there is no single experience to which we can both attach phenomenal label (e.g. a pain or a tickle that falls in both of our histories) it is quite open to hold that the properties exemplified in experience are perfectly real properties fully integrated into the natural order and represented in an objective way in our shared conception of the world, but that they are represented in an extrinsic form that, because of contingent limitations on access, can't be translated into an intrinsic representation. Just as each planet in the imagined universe with Planet X has to supply its own standards of leftness and length, each of us has to paint the world in colors drawn from our own palettes. There's no option of *thinking* in a medium that lacks phenomenal content; all links between concept and property pass through phenomenal profiles. Phenomenal profiles occupy the interface between the space of concepts and the space of causes; and

---

13. We have to suppose also that they contain no indirect links that would permit coordination, so they can't contain sentences like, e.g., 'She threw away the grishy part of the egg, and ate the yolk', or 'It was an even lighter grishy than the color of freshly fallen snow'. We could suppose they are short texts, that contain just that sentence and, say, stock prices for noon, January 2, 2002.

the conceptual labels attached to phenomenal properties provide the architectural rigging that coordinates elements in the space of concepts with elements in the space of causes. If we purge thought of phenomenal content, we sever the connections with experience that give it external significance. As I put it at the end of chapter 7, we sever the channels by which information flows from property to concept. But the lesson of this section is that we do have to *speak* in a medium purged of phenomenal content. The links between concept and phenomenal properties have to be made, they can only be made in individual self-descriptive acts à la Mary and Mo, and no amount of linguistic interaction will enforce conformity. None of this has any effect on the use of language to exchange information either about the public landscape or about aspects of another's internal lives that has any effect on behavior, which is to say, none of it has any practical effect at all. And it doesn't supply any support for the kind of dualistic ontology that bifurcates the universe into two fundamentally different, ontologically incommensurable realms.

The example of the Planet Xers also illustrates two themes from other sections: (1) that frame dependence (which is just a kind of implicit relationality) is relative to the class of interlocutors, and (2) that it is discovered not by introspection but communication. It's not by looking inward that our planetary friends discover the frame dependence of left and right. If they discover it at all, it's by talking to their neighbors. Nor does a child discover the parochiality of the concept 'yucky' until she meets people who apply it differently. The articulation in concepts, that comes with the revelation of hidden contextual parameters, is in no way intrinsic to the internal states we use to get information about them. As an epistemic matter, it is discovered by comparison across contexts.

The stricter invariance requirement imposed on language than on thought that comes with the widening of the class of interlocutors to include multiple subjects has the consequence that there are thoughts that can only be linguistically expressed in a manner that relates them explicitly to the frames of subjects. There's what-it's-like for you for when such and such and what-it's-like for me when such and such, but there's no way of removing the reference to a subject and speaking of what-it's-like *simpliciter*, and no way of establishing internal relations between what-it's-like for you when such and such and what-it's-like for me when such and such. These concepts are irreducibly, ineliminably relations to collections of exemplars that define the frame of thought for particular subjects, and they don't travel across frames any more than the 'here' of one observer travels across spatial frames. Intercontextual representational media always leave behind the noninvariant features of their situated counterparts. The what-it's-like properties of the world are precisely those that are reconstructed as relations to subjects by explicit representation of a personal parameter when the noninvariant description is traded in for one that is invariant under transformations between subjects. There is no nonrelational vocabulary for describing experience that spans the space between subjects. We use the properties exemplified in our own experience as points of reference in identifying events in the public landscape. When we take what is invariant under transformations between arbitrary choices for points of reference, what remains is bled of phenomenal content, and has to be coordinated individually with the properties that define our personal palettes. The procedure is exactly the same as that we go through in representing space, substituting 'spatial' for 'causal' relations. It loses information about all but structural relations between the starting points.

Descriptions in vocabulary drawn from a public language are like maps without a red dot. We have to coordinate descriptions individually with colors borrowed from (or properties exemplified in) our own experience, in the same way we each have to coordinate a shared map with the common landscape from our particular location in it, and in the same way that self-interpreting texts have to coordinate their descriptive vocabulary with the world individually, using the properties they exemplify as their own points of reference. The problem is not that the experiences of others can't be *represented* in an invariant way; it's that invariant representations are always relational and irremediably extrinsic. Extrinsic descriptions are perfectly objective, however, and they allow all the coordination that is needed for practical purposes.

One final analogy, with the focus on the lesson about language. Imagine that the United Nations automates simultaneous translation by developing a kind of Esperanto box that translates speech into a universal language that is then translated into the respective languages of delegates. Imagine two people who don't know each other, who are from a part of the world in which more than one language is in common use—say, Switzerland—communicating through the device. If we suppose that the box is impoverished in two very specific ways—it doesn't understand names for languages and has no means of quoting speech—and we fictionalize the facts about languages to remove identifying structural differences (e.g., we imagine that words for the same property have the same number of letters, that they are spoken by the same number of people, not associated geographically with any region, and so on), there will be no question that the interlocutors could put to one another that would allow them to establish whether they speak the *same* language. They could establish structural isomorphism and sameness of content, but nothing will allow them to decide whether the words and sounds that act as vehicles of content are *intrinsically* similar, the sort of thing they could determine if they could just hear each other, or get a look at the movements of each other's lips.

What the Esperanto box does for different languages, language does for the thought of different subjects, and, for that matter, so does physical experiment. Translation through any medium that transforms the vehicles of content will filter out content that is tied reflexively to properties of the vehicle. This is for the same reason that the invariant content of a mobile map filters out information tied reflexively to its location. Information about the properties of a medium doesn't survive the passage through intermediaries. Every language user has to coordinate the descriptive vocabulary of a language with her own palette in the same way that every user of a map has to coordinate it with his own location. The upshot of all of this is that questions about the intrinsic similarity of the experiences of different subjects are linguistically and epistemologically undecidable. You and I can make structural comparisons, but if there are no fixed points, no particular experiences to which we can both attach phenomenal labels, or nothing to provide the architectural rigging that will let us align our phenomenal vocabularies, no more is possible.

9.7 QUINING QUALIA

I have left the very hardest issue until last. I have been speaking as though the problem of establishing internal relations between properties exemplified in the experience of different subjects is a purely epistemic one, that is, that there are facts about whether your green experiences are like mine, but it just happens that we have no way of ascertaining them. God could tell, as we might say, were he to look. That suggestion was supported by the examples. There were facts about chiral properties left out of the invariant descriptive interplanetary vocabulary,[14] and there were facts about languages that didn't survive the pass through Esperanto. But there are other cases in which the ontological ruling goes the other way. Consider the question of whether a pair of events, a and b, are simultaneous. Specify a frame of spatial reference and the question has an answer. One gets different answers relative to different frames, so no invariant description says anything about simultaneity. The standard of simultaneity that one will use in judging temporal relations between events will be supplied by the frame

14. The existence of frame-independent chiral properties was a point of metaphysical dispute for centuries. By 'descriptive vocabulary', I mean nonrelational descriptive vocabulary, i.e., vocabulary that doesn't contain any explicit or veiled reference to particulars.

one happens to occupy. But we don't say that there are facts left out of the invariant description; we say that simultaneity is a frame-dependent way of describing relations between pairs of events that is completely captured in the invariant description. We say, that is, that there *are* no non-frame-dependent, or nonperspectival, facts about temporal relations between events. From a God's-eye point of view, there are only spatiotemporal intervals and the frames occupied by situated perceivers. There are more mundane examples of cases in which we eliminate the structures that would make it possible to raise questions about facts not captured in the invariant description. We don't think that there are nonperspectival facts about whether someone is a foreigner, whether spinach is delicious, or what time of day it is. These are reconstructed without remainder as relations to places, conative palettes, and time zones, respectively.

Structurally, the cases are analogous. Each subject has a frame defined by her personal palette and the function *what-it's-like*(e) gives the phenomenal profile of different types of event relative to her palette. If we take these cases as models, we say that *what-it's-like*(e) describes a subject's experiential perspective on the world, but there are no nonperspectival facts to support internal comparisons between what the world is like for you and what it's like for me. To wonder whether what it's like for me when I'm looking at a tomato is the *same* as what it's like for you when you're looking at a tomato is as nonsensical as wondering if an event that occurs at t in my frame is simultaneous with an event that occurs at t in yours. Wittgenstein seems at times to have held such a view. In connection with the claim that one can entertain thoughts about the quality of pains that are not one's own, for instance, he writes:

> It is as if I were to say: 'you surely know what "It is 5 o'clock here" means; so you also know what "It's 5 o'clock on the sun" means. It means simply that it is just the same time there as it is here when it is 5 o'clock'.[15]

Wittgenstein doesn't spell out his own position, but the more interesting versions of this kind of position wouldn't deny there are phenomenal properties, but merely that they are intrinsic to vehicles of content. The idea would be to reconstruct them at the impersonal level as relations to subjects.[16]

---

15. See Wittgenstein, *Philosophical Investigations*, 350. See also, Nagel, *The View from Nowhere*, 23.

16. This is a coherent position so long as one doesn't go on to say that subjects themselves are nothing but strings of psychological events. For if one says that, then one has to say that psychological events are distinguished from one another intrinsically and this is supposedly what was being denied.

So we are faced with the question:

Q) Are there or are there not, facts left out of the invariant description? Have we said all that there is to say once we have answered all
the questions about whether e and e* have the same profile in the
experience of one or another subject, or are there additional facts
about the similarity or difference of experiences of *distinct* subjects
that can't be gleaned from descriptions in the invariant vocabulary?

In considering Q, we are faced with symmetrically related, frame-
dependent representations and we have to decide whether to retain or
eliminate the structure that would allow for objective, intrinsic differences
between the situations they represent. This form of question is very familiar in physics; many of the most historically important theoretical disputes and interpretive controversies hinge on questions of precisely this
sort. Some of these examples go one way, some go the other. Many are
still hotly contested. The search for general principles for distinguishing
significant from insignificant theoretical structure is one of the most important ongoing research programs in philosophy of physics. We can
distinguish two possible answers to Q:

Realism: each of us has an internally exemplified palette of properties
that are real, intrinsic properties of experience that appear as ineliminable constituents in any complete, frame-independent account
of the world's contents. Structure-preserving permutations of phenomenal properties produce distinct possibilities.

Elimativism:[17] phenomenal properties are different kinds of relations to
subjects. They don't appear as constituents in the frame-independent
representation of the world. Structure-preserving permutations of
phenomenal properties don't produce distinct possibilities.

Everything that has been said so far is compatible with both realism
and eliminativism about phenomenal properties. The choice between
these positions it is not only linguistically irresoluble, but phenomenologically irresoluble.[18] If there is a way to decide the case, it has to come
either from an argument that one or another of the positions is incoherent, or from general principles governing the separation of significant
from insignificant theoretical structure.

17. 'Relationism' is a better name because it is more apt and less prejudicial, but familiarity favors
'eliminativism'.

18. In this respect, it replicates the situation with spatial reflection. There is also a formally and
phenomenologically undecidable dispute between realism and eliminativism in that case (does spatial
reflection, or does it not, leave an object unchanged?). See note 14.

9.8 WORRIES ABOUT REALISM

My instinct is to defend a realistic view, best captured by the analogy with self-interpreting texts, extended so that the printed shapes have a variety of colors, textures, and smells, and so that all (primitive) descriptive vocabulary is interpreted by association with internal exemplars. Each text has a palette of internally exemplified properties and each uses the same self-describing expressions ('this is the color/smell/texture/taste called so and so') to interpret its predicates, but the meaning of the predicates potentially varies with texts in a way that robs them of invariant content. The result is that the descriptive vocabulary in the shared part of the textual language is not descriptive of the *intrinsic* properties of the texts. It carries only structural information. The position is a kind of naturalistic phenomenal realism. It holds, against the eliminativist that experience *has* intrinsic properties, and against the dualist that those properties are fully integrated into the natural order (i.e., causally efficacious, entering into laws, interacting with other physical properties in all of the ways that they interact with each other).

There are two general worries that threaten the view. The first concerns arguments that Wittgenstein gave against the possibility of a private language. The second concerns the trouble one has of imagining inter-subjective comparisons of experience without falling back on deceptive perceptual metaphors. The nature and validity of Wittgenstein's arguments are heavily contested both philosophically and exegetically and I'm only going to indicate briefly how I understand their bearing here. The heart of Wittgenstein's arguments, on one way of understanding them, is that the possession of a concept requires normative constraints on its reapplication. On the story I have told, there are no intersubjective norms that govern which phenomenal profile I attach to a term like 'salty taste' or 'red sensation', and so, as Wittgenstein says, "... whatever is going to seem right to me is right. And that only means that here we can't talk about 'right'."[19] I have agreed with Wittgenstein that it does mean that the phenomenal profile can't be part of the linguistic meaning. I denied that descriptive vocabulary in a public medium has phenomenal content, but I added that the internal links between phenomenal properties and descriptive terms play a crucially important causal role in recognition.

---

19. This doesn't conflict with the recognition of norms governing application of concepts like 'tastes like/looks like/smells like, etc.' derivative of their role in classification of objects in the public environment. Nor does it conflict with the recognition of norms governing application of concepts like 'is in pain/ is thinking, etc.', derivative of their role in production of publicly observable behavior. It is only the quality of the profile that is essentially private in the objectionable sense.

Reddish experiences ('sensations', in Wittgenstein's terminology) aren't part of the meaning of the term 'red', but they are an ineliminable part of the process that supports its application. If I couldn't recognize a reddish *experience* when I had one, I couldn't recognize a red *thing* when I saw one. Reddish experiences are part of the architectural background that supports linguistic practice. I cannot find in Wittgenstein an argument that this amounts to recognition of a private language in an objectionable sense.

Now, to the second worry. Intersubjective comparison of phenomenal properties requires the existence of an encompassing frame with a standard of similarity that covers the whole domain, in which the experience of distinct subjects can be simultaneously located. There's a puzzle here about the encompassing frame. The examples I used encouraged the suggestion that it was all a matter of getting a look from the outside. In interplanetary handedness comparisons, if we just see an exemplar of left-ness-on-X next to an exemplar of leftness-on-Y, the question is resolved. Likewise in intertextual comparisons of grishiness; we just need to get a simultaneous look at a pair of exemplars. In the case of the Esperanto box, we just need to hear speakers in their native tongue. But ask yourself if this really makes sense in the case of phenomenal experience. If we take the perceptual metaphor seriously, we have to think of the encompassing frame as provided by an external perceiver that takes my experience and yours as intentional objects and compares them by the standard of similarity imposed by its own perspective. What kind of a perceiver are we to imagine? One like ourselves, presumably, but if I ask myself what it would be like for one person to *get a look at* the experiences of a pair of others—that is, to take them as intentional objects and compare them by the standard of similarity imposed by his own perspective— the most I can do is imagine a neurosurgeon peeking in the brains of, say, Mary and Mo as they look at the tomato. Clearly that's not what we mean when we ask whether Mary's experience is like Mo's. None of us looks *at* our own experiences when we judge them similar or different to one another and we shouldn't think of intersubjective judgments of phenomenal similarity in this way either. Phenomenal states are *vehicles* rather than the objects of experience.[20] What we really want when we attempt intersubjective comparisons of color experience is to extend the standard of similarity we each apply to our own phenomenal states to cover those of others. The same is true of the Planet Xers. They don't want to know whether the Planet Y exemplars of leftness are the same as theirs by some

---

20. Thought is quite singular in being able to take its vehicles as intentional objects. In chapter 6, I proposed it as the mark of an intrinsically intentional medium.

external standard; they want to extend their own standards of handedness to cover Planet Y. As they would put it, they want to know whether what the Yers call 'left' is *left*. We quite illegitimately import our own experiential perspective into the situation when we imagine looking at things from the outside.

But once this is made clear, a difference between the cases I proposed as models and the case of phenomenal properties may be significant. Extending their own standard of handedness to cover Planet X made sense for the Yers because they could make sense of the operation of carrying their exemplars across the planetary divide, bringing a left-on-Y mitten over to Planet X, and seeing whether they could lay it overtop a left-on-X mitten, in just the way they do to carry out handedness measurements on Y. There may be epistemological questions about whether the mitten changed in transit, but those are questions they face even on their own planet when they carry their mitten from one place to another or perform measurement at different moments in time. And they have the same techniques at their disposal for satisfying themselves that no change has taken place. We have become accustomed to the fact that there is no proof, in such matters, just common sense. The significant point is that a left-on-Y mitten located on Planet X is a perfectly coherent scenario. This process of comparison against exemplars is how we measure not only length or orientation, but also, duration, taste, color, smell, and so on. And we can extend our judgments about length, duration, taste, color, smell, and so on to any domain to which we can, in principle, transport our exemplars. But here's where a problem arises about the phenomenal case. If we add to the account of perceptual recognition sketched above, a Lockean theory of personal identity of the sort defended in the next section, it turns out that the barriers against comparing phenomenal properties across a subjective divide are not merely contingent. It turns out, that is to say, that we cannot transport exemplars across a subjective divide without literally merging minds. The account of perceptual recognition held that exemplars have to be passed through internal channels that don't transform the properties of the medium, exemplars are passed through the perceptually unmediated channels provided by memory (and their synchronic analogues[21]). The Lockean theory of personal identity defended in the next chapter holds that memory links are criterial in determining personal identity. This means that any two events that are related in the way they need to be to permit internal comparison belong, by definition, to the same mind. If what it is for two experiences to be intrinsically comparable is just what it

21. I'll suppress this unless needed.

is for them to belong to the same mind, it's a flat-out contradiction to talk about comparing someone *else's* experiences against your own.

This is a bit of an in-house worry; these pieces of the puzzle are separable. But if it makes the very thought of intersubjective comparisons of phenomenal properties incoherent, it looks like the combination of phenomenal realism and a Lockean theory of personal identity won't work. I think the right response is that while it's true that we cannot carry internal exemplars across the divide between minds without merging, we can give sense to the question of whether your experience and mine are similar by asking: If you and I merge, would we find that we had been speaking the same phenomenal language or would we find ourselves with descriptive terms associated with exemplars that differ intrinsically? So I think that this worry can be deflected, after all.

To sum up, then, I've defended the view that phenomenal properties are real, intrinsic properties of experience that fall through the net of description in any public vocabulary, leaving us with substantive, but irresoluble epistemic questions about whether the phenomenal states of others are intrinsically like our own. But I've recognized the eliminativist alternative as a defensible position.

9.9 CHALMERS

I did not include, with realism and eliminativism, David Chalmers's property dualism, the most currently influential view about the metaphysics of phenomenal properties, as an option. I'm not certain that, for all of its apparent clarity, I understand what the view is. In its early, seemingly subjectless form, I don't see how to make sense of it. Recent discussions make reference to subjects, but raise more questions than they answer. Before examining the question of subjects, there are some other things to say about Chalmers's view that this is probably the right place to say. I emphasized that Jackson's argument, if successful, reveals not just the incompleteness of a physical description but also its incompletability. If it is successful, it doesn't show merely that the physical story as we understand it is incomplete, or even that there are merely nonnatural or nonphysical facts. It shows that there are facts that can't be included in any story that can be conveyed in a lecture or textbook. If successful, it shows that there are facts that literally defy description. This means that we can't just expand the list of facts and complete the description in a way that is not itself susceptible to the argument. Chalmers's 'fundamental theory of consciousness', however, sounds like an attempt to complete the description. Here is his proposal:

[T]o bring consciousness within the scope of a fundamental theory, we need to introduce new fundamental properties and laws....

There are two ways this might go. Perhaps we might take experience itself as a fundamental feature of the world, alongside space-time, spin, charge, and the like. That is, certain phenomenal properties will have to be taken as basic properties. Alternatively, perhaps there is some other class of novel fundamental properties from which phenomenal properties are derived. Previous arguments have shown that these cannot be physical properties, but perhaps they are nonphysical properties of a new variety....

And later,

In a way, what is going on here with consciousness is analogous to what happened with electromagnetism in the nineteenth century.... To explain electromagnetic phenomena, features such as elecromagnetic charge and electromagnetic forces had to be taken as fundamental, and Maxwell introduced new fundamental electro-magnetic laws. For a theory of consciousness, new fundamental features and laws are needed.[22]

So let's try this: we add a new quantity $Q = \{q_1, q_2, q_3, \ldots\}$, a kind of juice that comes in a variety of flavors (one for each distinguishable phenomenal property) which, after he had fixed all the physical facts, God squeezed onto some events in the world. We call the juice 'consciousness' and each of its flavors, a 'phenomenal character'. The flavors have an internal structure that sensory psychology investigates (there is the space of visual experiences, auditory experiences, tactual experiences ... each with its own internal geometry), and they bear nomological relations both to one another and to brain states, which are to be the subject of Chalmers's new science. But once we catalog them, ascertain the laws that relate them to physical quantities, and assign them to events, our description of the world will be, Chalmers suggests, complete.

Once we have a fundamental theory of consciousness to accompany a fundamental theory in physics, we may truly have a theory of everything. Given the basic physical and psychophysical laws, and given the distribution of the fundamental properties, we can expect that all the facts about the world will follow.[23]

But it's not. Go through Jackson's argument, adding all the facts about Q, and the psychophysical laws that relate it to physics, to the stock

22. Chalmers, *The Conscious Mind*, 127.
23. Ibid., 126–27.

of knowledge Mary had before she is shown the tomato. Chalmers's extended theory (physics + science of consciousness) will be as provably incomplete, by his own arguments, as physics itself. I call it a diagonal argument to evoke Cantor's famous proof of the existence of non-denumberable sets. It has the form; give me a list, and I'll demonstrate that it is incomplete. The only way to block the argument is to allow (as Jackson did in his original reply to Churchland) that the completed science defies expression in language, and that is because the only way to complete the description is by reinstating immediate connections to experience. This renders the theory incommunicable, in the same way, and for the same reason, that building the red dot into a map renders it (on pain of inaccuracy) immobile.

There is something more than just superficially misconceived about trying to complete physics in a way that would make it immune to Jackson's argument. What the arguments of this section and the preceding really show is that completeness of the sort to which Chalmers's special science aspires can be bought only at the expense of communicability, and communicability isn't an *incidental* feature of physical theory. Physics is defined by the project of giving an objective description of the world in the sense of 'objectivity' expressed by invariance across transformations between interlocutors, where 'interlocutors' are understood, in the widest sense, as including not just perceiving subjects, but any kind of situated physical system. To talk of a 'science of consciousness', once 'science' is properly understood, and giving 'consciousness' Chalmers's reading, is to come pretty close to contradicting oneself. And this contradiction comes not just in physics. The point of representation quite generally, from a dynamical point of view, is to *break* the contextual constraints on the propagation of information—that is, to fashion information-bearing states whose informational properties are fully intrinsic to them, so that they can be moved around, sent forward in time, and exchanged without loss or change of content. Reinstating immediate connections to experience is a retrograde step. If description is linguistic representation, and language is a public medium, descriptions are, by their *nature* communicable. Wittgenstein's remark seems an apt response to Chalmers's complaint to the physicist: "Isn't what you reproach me of as though you said: 'in you language, you are only speaking'!"[24]

Putting aside the general difficulty with attempts to complete the description, let's look at the form of this special science whose subject matter is the relations between physical events and Q. Property dualism,

24. Wittgenstein, "Notes for Lectures on 'Private Experience' and 'Sense Data'."

defined as the view that Q is distinct from but nomologically related to the physical properties is susceptible to a straightforward objection that arises from the points made earlier about the logic of what-it's-like talk. There is just not something it is like *simpliciter* when, for example, c-fibres fire. There is something it is like *for particular subjects* when *particular* c-fibres fire, and the relations between particular subjects and the firing of particular c-fibres make any invariant description of relations between physical and phenomenal properties that do not make reference to subjects impossible. In a recent paper on phenomenal belief, Chalmers acknowledges the subject-relativity of what-it's-like-to facts. Subjects are explicitly mentioned in the new picture, and phenomenal properties are apparently no longer conceived as intrinsic properties of physical events, as they were on the earlier picture. On the earlier picture, phenomenal properties were conceived as irreducible properties of events occurring in certain brains. On the new picture, they are intrinsic properties either of subjects or special mental 'entities'. In his words:

> It is natural to speak as if phenomenal properties are instantiated by mental states, and as if there are entities, experiences, that bear their phenomenal properties essentially. But one can also speak as if phenomenal properties are directly instantiated by conscious subjects, typing subjects by aspects of what it is like to be them at the time of instantiation.[25]

But I confess to being still confused about the form of that the science of consciousness is supposed to take. We have the objective facts (which are just what we always thought they were, and which include the common intentional objects of experience, and which include also the causal base for the experience of different subjects, that is, the brain states that nomologically determine the experience of different subjects) and we also have subjects, each with their own experiential histories. And we are to conceive of phenomenal properties as intrinsic properties of subjects or their experiences. But now we have to decide what experiences are and what subjects are, and how they relate to one another and to the material contents of the universe. Are subjects substances, or are they *constituted* by their experiences? *Where* are they? Do either they, or their experiences, have spatiotemporal locations? If experiences are located in space and time, is it supposed to make sense for one subject to take the experience of another as an *object* of experience? If property dualism gets the structure of our concepts right, it seems that *ought* to make sense, and a different sort of sense than that in which I can have experience of the

---

25. "The Content and Epistemology of Phenomenal Belief," 2.

brain state of another, for the view is defined by the distinction between phenomenal properties and brain states. But I don't know what it could mean.[26]

The passage continues, but not in way that helps:

> These ways of speaking do not commit one to corresponding ontologies, but they at least suggest such ontologies. In a *quality-based* ontology, the subject-property relation is fundamental. . . . In a more complex *experience-based* ontology, a subject-experience-property structure is fundamental (where experiences are phenomenal individuals, or at least something more than property instantiations), and the subject-property relation is derivative. In what follows, I will sometimes use both sorts of language, and will be neutral between the ontological frameworks.[27]

Chalmers doesn't say more, and I won't speculate. The only way I can see to make sense of the view that physical and phenomenal properties are distinct existences, related as cause to effect, is by assimilating it to the option I called 'subject dualism'. We give up the idea of building phenomenal properties into the world, think of them instead as properties of subjects or experiences of subjects, where subjects are not conceived as located in space or time, not included implicitly or explicitly in the material universe. We allow, then, that the world is completely characterized by physics, and let the science of consciousness chart the relations between the intrinsic properties of subjects and those of the world. There will be a separate set of psychophysical laws for each subject, which map physical events onto their own intrinsic properties, or properties of their experiences and systematic relations between the laws, but no direct internal relations between subjects. The resulting picture will be Leibnizian with some extra stuff (it contains the full Leibnizian universe of monads, but adds a physical world, and laws relating properties of monads to worldly events). I think this is a stable position, it gets the structure right, and as I mentioned earlier, I think it comes closest to the unreflective view we have of ourselves. My picture is a way of trying to find that structure in the natural world, instead of reifying it in separate mental substances. It is a straightforward generalization of the way of finding the changing

---

26. "Can the property of being in a certain brain state be the very same property as that of having a certain sensation? . . . Can we really make sense of the thought that this feeling, this aspect of what goes on inside me that makes it a toothache or a headache or the smell of a gardenia or the taste of turnips, is an aspect of my brain that someone else . . . could, in principle, see?" Perry, *Knowledge, Possibility, and Consciousness*, 9. Perry, of course, goes on to argue that we can, but only in the sense that I have allowed, that one can have experience of the brain state of another.

27. "The Content and Epistemology of Phenomenal Belief," 2.

sequence of A-series in the B-series that I will propose next in response to McTaggart's argument for the unreality of time.

In sum, I think property dualism in its early form is missing an argument place. Once subjects are included, a menu of options becomes available, depending on how subjects are conceived. The only way that I can see of maintaining a genuine dualism of properties is by holding subject dualism. If that is Chalmers's position, I think it is a stable one, but it involves a quite different extension of physical ontology than the one involved in bringing electromagnetic phenomena into the fold.

A couple of addenda about my own position: first, there are some well-known arguments that there couldn't be facts about the *contents* of our thoughts (our own as well as those of others) that aren't in principle decidable by linguistic means. Even if these arguments are correct, they don't apply to facts about the properties *exemplified* in experience. We can model the relations that media would have to bear one another to make this kind of incommunicability possible, and if we accept the assumptions I started with (descriptive vocabulary is interpreted by exemplification, and there is no nonlinguistic access to the experience of others), thought and language bear each other just such relations.

Second, I have argued that thought has content—phenomenal content—that language, and other interpersonal representational media, lack, but it is worth emphasizing that there is no prospect of retreating to a more neutral level of representation in thought, one that would permit complete communication, without severing the links that coordinate it with the world. Links between ideas and the external landscape *have* to pass through experience, and they are as essential to the role of thought in navigating the world as the red dot on a map, to its role in guiding motion.

9.10 CONCLUSION

I have suggested that by recognizing the ineliminable relationality of thought about the experience of others, we can acknowledge the epistemic and cognitive gaps brought out by the Knowledge Argument and the possibility of inverted spectra, while restricting them to purely epistemic ones. We capture, in this way, the kind of privacy that experience actually has without bifurcating ontology. The position is still naturalistic and compatible with the strongest forms of phenomenal realism; it simply recognizes epistemic boundaries, of a not particularly mysterious sort, that can't be bridged by language. As I mentioned, in part III I will argue later that the very boundaries that keep us from unmediated access to the thoughts and experiences of others are what make *selves* out of us. They are as necessary to our existence as the doughnut is to the hole's. From a naturalistic point of view, experience *has* intrinsic properties for the same reason that any information-bearing medium has intrinsic properties. We need enough internally distinguishable vehicles to provide an alphabet for thought, but it doesn't matter what the vehicles are like, and it doesn't matter how yours relate to mine. Mother Nature needn't have used the same palette to paint our inner lives, and if she did (for, she tends toward frugality in production of types), there's still no reason not to get creative in distributing them. Differences will get conveniently filtered out in the pass through language, and we will be none the wiser.[28] Nothing in the epistemological situation supports a dualistic ontology or impugns the completeness of physics. That is the lesson to highlight. Physics is as complete as it can be, as complete as it can coherently aspire to be without relinquishing communicability. Physical concepts aim for publicity, they aim to eliminate the reflexive elements that tie concepts to a particular medium.

It's not that physics removes all mystery, but that there's something wrong with standards of completeness that demand that it should. A representation doesn't have to look, smell, or feel like the object or property it represents, nor stand in any particular spatial and temporal relation to it. If all reflexive traces are removed, a representation is transportable across time and space, translatable into any medium. The quality of our mental lives is precisely what's left behind when they're described, but the attempt to recapture that quality by extending descriptive resources reveals a very deep misconception about the nature of description.

---

28. Notice, indeed, that our peculiar capacity for internal self-design may have the consequence of preserving individual discrepencies by automatically correcting for them by internal adjustments. Individual mutations of certain kinds wouldn't have the kinds of practical ill effects that would select against them in organisms that were, unlike us, hardwired on the inside, meaning that perhaps we should actually *expect* inversions and structure preserving mutations of all kinds.

IO

Grammatical Illusions

"The (deeply rooted) grammatical illusion of a subject is what generates all the errors...."

—Anscombe, "The First Person, 81."

So far we've been looking at cognitive and epistemic gaps that arise in the spaces between media. I want to shift focus to expose a grammatical illusion generated by the formal interaction between reflexive devices and the nonreflexive apparatus of a medium that lies behind another influential batch of arguments for dualism. The illusion receives its purest expression in a famous argument presented in 1908 by John McTaggart that was actually targeted at the reality of time. I'll use that argument to introduce this illusion and then show it at work in the arguments for dualism.

10.1 McTAGGART'S ARGUMENT

McTaggart's argument is as simple as it is baffling. There are exegetical disputes and a long history of fascinating philosophical commentaries on the argument that I'll bracket, since they are tangential for my purposes. McTaggart begins by distinguishing positions in time, which he calls *moments,* from their contents, which he refers to as *events.* He uses *quality* to refer to intrinsic properties and *characteristic* to refer indifferently to intrinsic and relational properties.[1]

The argument concerns the relations between two different series in which events are located:

1. He doesn't distinguish between internal and external relations—relations that, respectively, do and don't supervene on the intrinsic properties of their *relata.* I'll follow suit.

A-series: the series of moments running from the past through the present and into the future.[2]

B-series: the series of moments ordered by the relation is-earlier-than.'[3]

It proceeds in three stages, with an interlude between the second and third to fend off an objection, and I'll take them up in turn.

Stage 1

Time involves change.

If there is to be change it must be change of what occurs in time.

What occurs in time are events, so if there is change, events must possess characteristics at one time that they do not possess at another.

But events themselves neither come into or go out of existence, nor change either intrinsically or in their relations to other events.[4]

The only respect in which they change is in whether they are past, present, or future, which is to say, in their position in the A-series.[5]

Stage 2

If pastness, presentness, and futurity are characteristic of events, they must be either intrinsic properties, or relations that events bear to something else.

Suppose they are relations.

It is part of logic of 'past', 'present', and 'future' that they are incompatible with one another; no *single* thing possesses all three.

2. See McTaggart, "The Reality of Time."

3. Actually McTaggart defines three series. The third is effectively the B-series without a direction. It doesn't play a role in the argument and I'll follow most commentators in ignoring it.

4. "Take any event—the death of Queen Anne, for example—and consider what change can take place in its characteristics. That it is a death, that it is the death of Anne Stuart, that it has such causes, that it has such effects—every characteristic of this sort never changes" See McTaggart, "The Reality of Time," 459.

5. "In every respect but one [Queen Anne's death] is equally devoid of change. . . . It began by being a future event. . . . At last it was present. Then it became past" see McTaggart, "The Reality of Time," p. 460.

All of them, however, are predicable of each element in the B-series.

This, however, is a contradiction, so past, present, and future cannot be relations.[6]

Interlude

McTaggart pauses at this stage to consider the objection that the contradiction is defused by saying that pastness, presentness, and futurity are characteristics that events possess at different times. This is the crux of the argument. McTaggart asks what it can mean to say that an event possesses pastness, presentness, and futurity at different times. What are these things—these *times*—in relation to which it is being supposed that events are past, present, or future? Presumably they are elements in the B-series. If that is right, the objection is that pastness, presentness, and futurity are relations that an event—itself an element in the B-series—possesses relative to different elements in the B-series. But we know already that there is no change in relations among elements in the B-series. So if this is the suggestion, it doesn't involve real change, and McTaggart has the conclusion that he wants.

So the times in relation to which events are said to be past, present, or future must lie *outside* the B-series. To make this work, we have to think of the B-series as embedded in some external timelike dimension, and pastness, presentness, and futurity as relations they bear to different elements in this new dimension. But now consider this expanded universe. Since being past, present, and future in relation to the *same* time, are incompatible relations, they must be relations between elements in the B-series and *different* times. But if they are relations to different times, they're not really incompatible characteristics. For each event is always and unchangingly present in relation to this time, past in relation to those, and future in relation to others. And if they are not incompatible characteristics, there is no change and, consequently (for McTaggart), no time.

So, if there is to be real change, the relations between elements in the B-series and elements in the new timelike dimension must change. But then we're right back where we started, because it is no easier to make out what it means to say that the relations between events and times change than it is to say that events do. For, to say the relations between an event e and a time t changes must mean that e is present with respect to t at one time, and past with respect to t at another. But *presentness-with-respect-to-t*

---

6. It conflicts both with (iv) and, as McTaggart remarks, with the presumption that there is change. See McTaggart "The Reality of Time," 468.

and *past-ness-with-respect-to-t* are incompatible relations, so either there is a contradiction, or they are not both *schtimultaneously* predicable of A, that is, there are objects outside of time—'schtimes'—that are such that e is *present-with-respect-to-t* at one *schtime* and *past-with-respect-to-t* at another. This way, it should be clear, lies regress. To try to escape the contradiction that arises from the incompatibility of pastness, presentness, and futurity, on the one hand, and the fact that all are predicable of each event, on the other, by insisting that elements in the B-series don't bear them *simultaneously* is either to contradict the assumption that there is change or to push the question back a step by embedding both the B-series and times in yet another dimension, with respect to which the very same problem will arise. Either way, McTaggart has his conclusion.

The fundamental difficulty here is that time is *constituted* by the relations among the elements of the B-series. The B-series *is* time, and there is nothing whose relations to these changes in a way that would allow us to regard transitions from present-ness to past-ness, for instance, as changes in relations to *it*. Nothing that is itself an element of the B-series can play that role, and nothing outside the series will evidently do the trick either. The idea that pastness, presentness, and futurity are characteristics that events possess *at different times*, is an attempt to resolve the contradiction involved in their attribution to a single object by relativizing. The heart of the problem is that we are not supposed to be able to consistently suppose the existence of anything to relativize *to*. There are no objects, in the B-series or outside it, that *could* bear its elements the sort of relations that would order them in an evolving sequence of A-series's.

Stage 3

The third stage of the argument parallels the second; in McTaggart's words:

> If the characteristics of the A series were qualities, the same difficulty would arise as if they were relations. For, as before, every event has all of them. This can only be explained, as before, by saying that each event has them successively. And thus the same fallacy would have been committed as in the previous case.[7]

The conclusion is that presentness, pastness, and futurity are not real characteristics of events; they are neither intrinsic properties of them nor relations that they bear something else. And if they are not real characteristics, if there is nothing in which the presentness of the present

---

7. Ibid., 470.

moment consists, something which we can say *changes* as it becomes past, if all there is in the world is the set of events with the fixed temporal relations between them, then the idea that time passes or that there is change, that is, that the universe as a whole is not the same from one moment to the next, is a myth. Mellor summarizes the point nicely:

> [Positions in the B series], unlike [positions in the A series], are outright, unqualified properties of events. . . . The A series is neither: it has to be defined in terms of the B series plus a present instant. And the present instant has to *move*: There has to be McTaggart change, or the A series would be identical with the B series. Past, present and future, therefore, as aspects of reality, stand or fall with McTaggart change.[8]

And what McTaggart argues, of course, is that there is no McTaggart change. He does show—quite conclusively, to my mind—that being past, present, or future is neither an intrinsic property of an event nor a relation it bears to something outside the set of events.

The problem, in a nutshell, is that pastness, presentness, and futurity cannot be intrinsic properties of events because the intrinsic properties of events don't change, so they must be relations to something else. But since the same events are past, present, and future at different times, they have to be relations to something—the *Now*—that changes its position in the B-series. But *nothing* changes its position in the B series. Whatever the Now is, we have a rock solid argument that it is not identical with anything that has a fixed position in the B-series. Its connection to any B-series element is *temporary*. The argument is so simple and so general, it seems utterly intractable. I would bet the farm on its validity. There is nothing in the B-series—or consistently addable to it—that bears the right relations to its elements to order them in a continuously changing sequence of A-series.

10.2   THE RESOLUTION

McTaggart is right that we have to find something that relates to elements in the B-series in the way that now does to speak of past, present, and future, and he is right that there's nothing in or consistently addable to a B-series that will do the job. He is right, moreover, that embedding the B-series in a higher timelike dimension doesn't ultimately help. The image of the Moving Now is a mental picture that most of us employ

---

8. Mellor, "McTaggart, Fixity and Coming True," p. 85–86, my emphasis.

intuitively in flipping back and forth between speaking in temporal and atemporal terms, locating moments both on an ever-changing now-centered calendar and an eternal, uncentered map of time, but it can't be the right metaphysics. The solution to the problem is this. 'Now' doesn't refer to a *thing*. It's not a singular term, but a *function* with a suppressed temporal parameter supplied by context whose value is the local value of the temporal parameter. If $f(t) = t$ and Now$_t$ is a token of 'now' produced at t, Now $f(t) = t$. So, for example, Now$_{June\ 9,\ 2005}$ is a token of 'now' produced on June 9, 2005. It refers to June 9, 2005. This gives Now$_{June\ 9,\ 2005}$ the double life I emphasized earlier. Because it is tied semantically to the expression 'June 9, 2005' and architecturally to the day itself, it acts as a bridge between the semantic network and elements in the temporal landscape binding dates (elements in a representational medium) to days (elements in a temporal ordering). The same goes for utterances that occur at different times. Now$_{June\ 10,\ 2005}$ is a token of 'now' produced on June 10, it is tied architecturally to June 10 and semantically to 'June 10'. It binds June 10 to 'June 10'. Now $_{June\ 12,\ 2005}$ is a token of 'now' produced on June 12. It binds June 12 to 'June 12', and so on.

Since tokens of 'now' that occur in the same context have the same semantic values, the expression can function as a singular term in a fixed temporal context. No harm will be done so long as we confine our rea-soning to one context, but as soon as we intersubstitute occurrences drawn from different contexts or existentially generalize across contexts we are reasoning invalidly. All the trouble arises because we forget that the expression is a function. We begin to think of 'now' as a name and when we string together a sequence of 'now' occurrences, we are left with the illusion whose incoherence is correctly diagnosed by McTaggart, of an object tracing a path through the temporal landscape. McTaggart's Mov-ing Now isn't a mobile particular but the range of a function from tem-poral contexts to times.

To accept this is to accept McTaggart's conclusion: events change from one moment to the next in respects defined by relations to now—that is, respects like pastness, presentness, and futurity—only in the way that emeralds change from grue to bleen at the millennium.[9] It's not change of a kind that McTaggart would recognize as real, that is, not

9. O is grue just in case O is (examined before the millennium and green) *or* (examined after and blue). O is bleen just in case O is (examined before the millennium and blue) *or* (examined after and green). Grue and bleen were introduced by Goodman in *Fact, Fiction, and Forecast*. These are adaptations of his definitions that did not involve change. The original definitions were: O is grue just in case O is (first examined before the millennium and green), *or* (first examined after and blue). O is bleen just in case (first examined before the millennium and blue) *or* (first examined after and green).

change in the characteristics of events but in a universe in which the basic particulars are events, it's the only kind of change there is.[10] This doesn't mean that there aren't ways of reconstructing our ordinary ways of speaking of change in this kind of universe, nor that there aren't alternative ontologies that incorporate real change in the characteristics. Much of the debate spawned by McTaggart's argument is devoted to discussion of these alternatives. Another good chunk of it centers on questions about whether, and in what sense, time can be said to pass. Neither of these issues is central to our concerns.[11] I have focused on bringing out the mistake to which McTaggart succumbs in thinking that talk of past, present, and future requires the ontological support of a Moving Now in anything but the trivial and perfectly coherent sense described above because I see it as the archetype of a mistake that we make when we think of selves or phenomenal properties as somehow outside the natural order. The conundrum presented by the difficulty of integrating the B-series and the A-series ontologically—finding a way of making sense of *the relative motion* of those series, given that they are composed of the very same elements—is a fundamentally formal one. And the resolution, likewise, is purely formal. McTaggart rightly saw that there is a puzzle, and his argument brought into stark and elegant relief the incoherence of the imaginative picture of the supposition that there is any *thing* in a B-series relation to which could generate the changing sequence A-series. His mistake was entirely about the grammatical category of 'now'. It's not the kind of expression that requires the ontological support of an object. This is something we all know on reflection, but that it is convenient to forget for everyday purposes, for a reason I'll say below.

10.3   OTHER EXAMPLES: SPACE AND FAMILY TREES

We can reproduce the formal relationships between the A- and B-series in contexts in which there is little inclination to succumb to the illusion. Consider the function that assigns to each point in space a representation of space centered on it. You get a representation of a structure S centered on an element e by replacing every relation $R(x_1 \ldots x_n)$ in S of a type that takes e as an argument with the relation $R(x_1 \ldots x_{n-1}, e)$ and then suppressing e. A representation centered on e is just a representation from

10. Haslanger, "Persistence through Time" contains a nice survey of options. See also Sider, *Four-Dimensionalism.*

11. In the case of passage, in particular, I think there are very hard questions, but they should be separated from the issue of integrating the A-series and B-series. The real difficulties lie elsewhere.

e's perspective. In the spatial case, relations like 'is to the east of y' 'is far away from z' are replaced with 'is to the east' and 'is far away'. A place that is far away and to the east from one perspective may be close and to the west from another.[12] For another example, consider the network of familial relations depicted on a family tree and the function that assigns to each node in the tree a representation of the family centered on it. A representation of Bob's family tree centered on Bob will relate everyone in his family to him. A representation centered on his father will relate everyone to his father. A person who is an uncle from Bob's perspective may be a brother from his father's. In both the spatial and familial case, we have the same formal relationships that we have with the A- and B-series. We have an objective ordering, on the one hand, and a set of perspectival orderings, on the other, one attached to each element in the objective ordering. The association with elements in the objective ordering imposes an ordering on the perspectival orderings. Just as there was a temporal ordering to the A-series, there is a spatial ordering to the spatial perspectives and an ancestral ordering to the egocentric familial perspectives. And we also have analogues of the Moving Now. Where the Moving Now seemed to give us a moment that appeared to travel through time, turning future into present and present into past, the spatial case gives us a Wandering Here that moves through space, turning near into far, is-to-the-east-of into is-to-the-west-of. And the familial case gives us a Roaming Relative that travels to different nodes turning mothers into daughters, brothers into husbands. Of course, there are not really any times that move through time, places that move through space, or relatives that travel through family trees. There are only the grammatical illusions created by forgetting that 'now', 'here', and 'me' are functions rather than singular terms.

An indexical, S, provides us with a symbol, any *occurrence* of which acts like a singular term (picks out an object, is intersubstitutable with coreferential terms, falls within the scope of quantifiers, flanks '=', and so on), and which is ascribable a changing repertoire of properties (different sets of 'S is —'-sentences are true in different contexts). We succumb to illusion when we suppose that there is a thing in the world, denoted by S, with the evolving repertoire of properties ascribed in 'S is —'-sentences: a continuant across contextual shifts that now has this set of properties, now a different set, and is now at one place, now at another. The illusion evaporates as soon as the relativization of reference to context is made explicit and it is observed that the context is changing. What we really have is a

---

12. In the terminology of chapter 5, a representation of S centered on e has e as an unarticulated constituent. In this case, e can be an element in the structure or outside of it.

set of things, each with its own evolving repertoire of properties, and an expression that changes its reference as it is moved from context to context. But there is not an object denoted by the expression whose biography is given by the set of 'S is —'-sentences. I move through space, saying, successively, "here is green," "here is red," "here is blue,"[13] but it doesn't follow, obviously, that there is a place that is green, red, and blue. I stand at a fixed location and, letting days pass between utterances, say "today is sunny," "today is cloudy," "today is raining," but it doesn't follow that there is a day that is sunny, cloudy, and raining. There is not in general continuant identified and then reidentified on separate occasions of use.

10.4   McTAGGART MODALIZED

I'm going to suggest now that we can discern the same mistake in modal reasoning that is used in arguments for dualism. Dualism, of course, comes in many flavors. I'll focus on dualism about phenomenal properties and the *locus classicus* of dualist views: Cartesian dualism about the self. That way we cover the most currently popular form of dualism as well as a perennial favorite. Consider a set of elements bearing one another a network of external relations: objects arranged in space, for example, moments in time, relatives in family trees, or properties in a causal network. Introduce names for each of the elements, predicates for their properties, and relation terms for the relations they bear one another. Compose a complete catalog of truths about the elements arranged in these spaces using this vocabulary. Now add reflexive expressions, expressions whose semantic value varies with position in the space.[14] The reflexive expressions associated with space and time refer, respectively, to positions in a spatial and temporal ordering. Those associated with family trees and causal networks refer, respectively, to family members and nodes in the networks. We can generate epistemic and modal arguments for the falsity of identity statements linking reflexive expressions to nonreflexive ones by reasoning as follows. Consider any proposed identity $I = A$, where I is an indexical and A is a nonreflexive name for one of the elements in your set.

---

13. Letting colors stand in for arbitrary properties, the simplest cases involve incompatible intrinsic properties.

14. For simplicity, we can suppose that it refers reflexively to *this thing here*, but really, it's only the variability of its semantic content with location in the space that matters. It could just as easily refer to my neighbor to the left.

1. Epistemic argument: Any identity statement that links a reflexive expression with a nonreflexive one will exhibit cognitive and epistemic gaps that can't be resolved by first-order knowledge. I can know everything there is to know about the intrinsic properties of items on the list and how they relate to one another, without knowing that $I = A$.

2. Modal argument: Facts described reflexively vary independent of the facts that can be described in nonreflexive terms. I can hold fixed all of the facts about the intrinsic properties of and relations between elements in the space and imagine distinct possible worlds corresponding to $I = A$ and $I \neq A$.

See how this plays out with time. Suppose that now is January 1, 2006:

1. Epistemic argument: I can know everything there is to know about the intrinsic properties of moments in time and how they relate to one another without knowing that now is Jan. 1, 2006.

2. Modal argument: I can hold fixed all of the facts about the intrinsic properties of and relations between moments in time and imagine distinct possible worlds in which now is Jan. 1, 2006, Jan. 2, 2006, Jan. 3, 2006, . . . and so on.

Here's how it plays out with phenomenal properties. Suppose that *this-here* exemplified property is the one produced in ordinary perceivers in standard conditions when they are visually presented with a ripe tomato:[15]

1. Epistemic argument: I can know everything there is to know about physical properties and how they relate to one another, without knowing that *this-here* is the one produced in ordinary perceivers in standard conditions when they are visually presented with a ripe tomato.

2. Modal argument: I can hold fixed all of the physical facts and imagine distinct possible worlds in which *this-here* is the property produced in ordinary perceivers under standard conditions when they are visually presented with a ripe lemon rather than a tomato.

Here's how it plays out with the self.

1. Epistemic argument: I can possess a complete and correct impersonal description of the world without knowing who I am (if, for example, I awake in an amnesiac fog like Rudolph Lingens in the Stanford Library with all of the impersonal knowledge about

---

15. Recall that *this-here* was introduced as a reflexive property designator. It refers demonstratively to an exemplified property.

myself contained in a biography at my fingertips but no egocentric memories to link me to it).[16]

2. Modal argument: I can hold fixed all of impersonal facts about the world and imagine distinct possible worlds in which I am Napoleon at the Battle at Waterloo, Mother Teresa administering to the poor, or Sergio Leone directing *Once Upon a Time in the West*.

The modal arguments are nothing but McTaggart with 'temporary' replaced by 'contingent'. Or perhaps we should say that McTaggart's argument is just a particularly strong version of the modal argument. Instead of appealing to imaginative cases to support the claim that there is counterfactual variation in the association between now and any moment in time, McTaggart points to the indisputable existence of actual variation in time. The contingency of the connection is what really matters. The modal argument for property dualism contends that phenomenal properties can't be identified with physical properties because the connection between physical and phenomenal properties is broken in other possible worlds. The modal argument for the nonidentity of the self with any objective particular contends that the self's connection to anything that has a place in the objective order is broken in other possible worlds.

The diagnosis of the fallacy is the same as in McTaggart's argument. The imaginative scenarios used to break the link involve contextual shifts that alter the semantic value of one of the expressions that flank the identity sign. In the cases of 'now' uttered at different times, 'here' uttered at different places, first-person imaginings that adopt the perspective of another person, it's the reflexive expression whose reference is altered by the shift in context. In the case of *this-here*, our reflexive property designator, it's the semantic value of the nonreflexive one.[17]

The root mistake behind the epistemic and modal arguments is to fail to attend to the fact that reflexive expressions don't have a fixed semantic value. They bind to elements in the semantic network only fleetingly, temporarily, insecurely. They bind only as tightly as the agent that uses them is bound to the features of context they articulate. The reason we get misled is that reflexive expressions add degrees of epistemological and imaginative freedom to a language. They introduce terms, that is to say, that behave in their logical, cognitive, and epistemic relations to nonreflexive terms, in ways characteristic of noncoreferring terms. By criteria that we have developed for judging the truth of identity statements

16. Perry, *The Problem of the Essential Indexical and Other Essays.*
17. See 10.8.

involving coreferential names or descriptions, identity statements linking them to nonreflexive expressions will always come out false. The important thing about these arguments is how general they are. Nothing needs to be supposed about the nonreflexive vocabulary on your list except that its semantic content is invariant under transformations that alter the semantic value of the reflexive device. Nothing needs to be supposed about the nature of temporal vocabulary except that it binds to moments in a way that is invariant under translation in time. Nothing needs to be supposed about the nature of physical vocabulary except that it binds to properties in a way that is invariant under transformation of the properties of the medium in which it is expressed.[18] Nothing needs to be supposed about impersonal vocabulary except that it binds to people in a way that is invariant under transformations of speaker. These aren't just arguments for the incompleteness of some list. If they are valid, they are perfectly general arguments for the *incompletability* of any list. Extend your list how you like, they will furnish arguments that something is left out, that there has been an omission that no addition can redress.[19]

The general phenomenon is easy to state in abstract terms: reflexive expressions are linguistic examples of what are called coupled representations. They're bound architecturally—that is, causally or spatiotemporally—to what they represent. Decoupled representations, by contrast, can be moved around without altering their content. Their semantic role doesn't depend on context. Decoupling is a relative matter. A term is decoupled from space if it can travel without alteration of content, decoupled from time if it can be stored without effect, decoupled from temperature if its content is indifferent to changes in temperature, and decoupled from medium if content is unaffected by translation into other media. The semantic relations between coupled and decoupled representations will vary necessarily with transformations of context and this means that they can't be incorporated into a medium that is used to communicate across those contexts. Modal and epistemic arguments of the form above work only for in-house relationships among terms that are connected in a single semantic web, terms whose semantic relations to one another are fixed. Reflexive devices *cannot* acquire fixed semantic relations to the other terms of a medium. Their job is precisely to vary

18. Spectral inversion, thought of in these terms, involves a transformation of medium that permutes intrinsic properties. Transformations to alien phenomenology involve substitution rather than mere permutation. It may be that only the former are imaginable; we lack the internal exemplars needed to imagine the latter.

19. I call them diagonal arguments because they bring to mind Cantor's proof of the existence of nondenumerable sets. Give me a list, says Cantor, and I'll show you it's incomplete.

their location in the semantic network to counteract variation in relations between the network and its subject matter.

10.5   WHY THE ILLUSION IS COMPELLING

The illusion of the extra property or particular is generated by—to steal a term from the mathematicians—an abuse of notation.[20] You abuse notation when you fudge a distinction that doesn't make a difference in some restricted context. So, for example, you let 'A' stand in for 'B' in contexts in which they are coextensive, even if they come apart in other contexts. There's nothing wrong with abuses of notation if they're used carefully. We make them quite deliberately all the time. 'A' can be a function and 'B', one of its values, or 'A' can be a name for 'B', or 'B' a name for 'A'.[21] Wherever there's a one-one correspondence across the contexts relative to which the abuse is perpetrated, no harm will be done. Indeed, there may be some good. If one is designing a computer language, or carrying out a mathematical computation, one will quickly discover that they can be cheap, efficient devices for avoiding unnecessary structure. If the distinction between 'A' and 'B' isn't relevant and we already have 'A', who needs 'B'?

When we use an indexical as a singular term, we make a linguistically licensed abuse of notation. When I am in c, I can use the reflexive function-name, F, that takes every context of type c onto itself as a substitute for 'c'. If I don't have a name or identifying description that applies to c, it may be my only way of referring to it and it has the indispensable virtue of providing a way of doing so that bypasses the ordinary route through senses, allowing me to refer to things for which I don't possess an individuating concept. So long as I don't extend patterns of reasoning appropriate to singular terms across contexts, everything will work out fine. While in c, intersubstitution of one 'f'-occurrence for another, and existential generalization from $P_1(f), P_2(f), \ldots P_n(f)$ to there is an s—namely, *the f*—such that $P_1(s), P_2(s), \ldots Pn(s)$ will be truth preserving. Across contexts, they will not. The grammatical illusions of the Moving *Now*, the internally exemplified properties that fall outside the scope of physical description, and the self that can't be captured in the net of objective representation are products of invalid existential generalizations, artifacts of an abuse of notation carried across contexts.

20. I'm adapting the term.
21. Of course, use/mention confusions are other examples of the kinds of mistakes to which forgetting about an abuse of notation can give rise.

If we widen the notion of an abuse of notation so that it applies to natural, nonsymbolically structured media, we can see that Mother Nature, a consummately efficient designer, exploited them everywhere. She is, to recall Dennett's words from the passage of earlier, "a stingy, opportunistic engineer who takes advantage of rough correspondences whenever they are good enough for the organism's purposes."[22] All over the place, she has put states with context-dependent informational content in control of behavior where the context wasn't one that the organism didn't need to wander out of. And what is a state with a context-dependent content but a state with the context-independent content of a relation to contexts? We do the same when we let phenomenal profiles stand in for what they indicate in a fixed context. The invariant content of a phenomenal profile is a function of an unspecified, and unspecifiable, number of features of context. We learn to articulate those features as we move across contexts in the kind of process John went through in chapter 6. Our overall functional organization recognizes the relational character of the content of phenomenal profiles, even if we don't typically incorporate it into the contents of our states, that is, even if the complexity isn't represented explicitly in the 'labels' we attach to them. Even after revelation of the hidden contextual parameter, John doesn't think of color profiles as relations between surface properties and ambient conditions. He continues to think of them as representations of surface properties and adjusts which properties he thinks of them as representing when he changes contexts. Adjusting labels behind the scenes gives him the internal fluidity he needs to move across contexts, without imposing more structure on content. It allows him to exploit the efficiency of coupled representation without limiting mobility.

This may cast light on the peculiarly ambiguous psychological status of phenomenal profiles. We are reminded of the distinction between reddish experiences and surface red when we enter blue light, have colored drops placed in our eyes, or move outside of our standard contexts. But for everyday purposes, we ignore it. The less frequent these reminders, the more entrenched the abuse of notation.

10.6 THE SELF

When we replace maps of space or time with representations of all of space-time and string a bunch together in a sequence that reflects their spatio-

---

22. Dennett, "Ways of Establishing Harmony," in *Dretske and His Critics*, ed. McLaughlin, 122.

temporal ordering, the illusion takes the form of a picture of an unchanging manifold of events with a singular object—*me*, or *my consciousness*—tracing a path through it.[23] The vision is beautifully articulated by Weyl in this passage from his elegant 1949 book *Philosophy of Mathematics and Natural Science:* "The world *is*, it does not *happen*. Only in the gaze of my consciousness, crawling up the life-line of my body, does the world fleetingly come to life."[24] The Weylian gaze of consciousness is the purely reflexive 'I' of the individual thought mapping itself into the spatiotemporal landscape; it's the 'here-now' of a mind engaged in a continuous cycle of self-location and relocation. As soon as we begin to treat it as a referring term, we are led by the modal argument from its imaginative separability from anything that has a fixed location in the landscape to conceive of it as a primitive locus of mental life, a basic, ineliminable degree of metaphysical freedom.

It's the same mistake that we have seen. We use the 'I' that represents the function from experience into thought as though it were a singular term referring to an object whose changing repertoire of properties is given by the range of the function. Then we notice that we have the imaginative capacity to string together arbitrary sequences of thoughts and experiences, and we represent some of these imaginative feats by holding fixed the facts depicted in an invariant form on our maps of space-time, and tracing different trajectories through them with the red dot that identifies our personal perspective. We imagine the world being just as it actually is in all objective respects, that is to say, except our*selves* tracing different subjective paths. And then we give the modal argument; if I can hold fixed all of the facts about the world, including the facts about material bodies and imagine my*self* traveling different paths—for example, inhabiting the body of Napoleon, or Oprah, even a cockroach—then I cannot *be* my body, my brain, or anything that supervenes these. And we get to thinking of the body as a sort of camera that registers information about the world on its sensory surfaces and the self as a separate object that receives its signals and controls its movements.

And the problem doesn't depend in any way on a restriction to physical vocabulary. We can hold fixed all of the facts, including the facts about souls or individual essences, if these can be characterized in impersonal terms. Nor am I confined within the boundaries of a single skull. I can imagine jumping around quite arbitrarily and discontinuously through history. One moment, I'm Napoleon at the Battle of Austerlitz, the next I'm Nelson Mandela addressing the United Nations, and then Hume on

---

23. This image recurs often in Strawson's *Individuals.* See also Nagel, *The View from Nowhere.*
24. See Weyl, *A Philosophy of Mathematics and Natural Science,* 116.

the eve of the publication of the *Treatise*. Or I can begin by imagining as Nagel does,

> my house burning down and the individual T. N. standing before it, feeling hot and miserable, and looking hot and miserable to bystanders.... If I add to all this the premises that I am T. N., I will imagine feeling hot and miserable, seeing the sympathetic bystanders, etc.[25]

I can then change the premise and imagine that I am one of the bystanders, out in my pajamas, warmed by the flames, enjoying the spectacle, and flip back and forth between the two. If you are any good at this, you will find that there are no imaginative restrictions on the trajectory you can imagine following. If you can describe it, you can self-ascribe it. And each of these trajectories will have its own imaginative content. No matter how you expand your catalog of the world's contents, the self will behave inveterately, incurably, as an extra degree of freedom.

It's important to understand, as I emphasized in chapter 10, that there is no middle road, no comfortable Chalmers-style halfway house. If one accepts these arguments, one accepts them at full strength. If the self is a thing, it's not just nonphysical; it cannot be captured in the net of objective representation. It is a simple, irreducible substance logically and metaphysically separable from all of its properties, forging an experiential path through an otherwise dormant world. It is, as Vendler puts it "a frame in which any picture fits."[26] If we are going to stop this line of thought, we have to stop it before it starts.[27] And we should; it got off on the wrong foot. 'I' is not a singular term. It can act as a convenient proxy for one in a fixed context by an abuse of notation, but intersubstitution across contexts of precisely the sort needed to establish the general claim of modal separability from objective particulars is invalid.[28] There is no continuant reidentified across these imaginative transformations of first-person perspective. They involve contextual shifts that block the existential generalization to a thing with the full complement of ascribable modal properties.

25. See Nagel, *The Possibility of Altruism*, 103.

26. See Vendler, *The Matter of Minds*. Perhaps it isn't an entirely unattractive picture; it comes close to the unschooled view of the reflective layperson and, if one were choosing metaphysical building blocks, subjects, space-time, and matter aren't especially extravagant choices.

27. And it doesn't help to say that the self isn't a singular term, but a predicate, and that when I say "I am JI," I attribute *me-ness* to JI. The same form of argument will establish nonsupervenience of *me*-ness on any basis of objective fact.

28. What kinds of transformations of context invalidate inferences will depend on the type of function. They will be those that transform the value of the argument, or, equivalently, that take you from one intersubstitution context to another.

10.7 THE LESSON

Everybody knows that indexical expressions are functions from contexts to objects. But string a bunch of occurrences drawn from different contexts together, forget about the abuse of notation that allows you to use them provisionally as singular terms, and you have a recipe for confusion. There is a general lesson here; whenever you are given an argument that purports to show that there are things in the world that can't as a matter of metaphysical necessity be incorporated in an objective description, things that by their very nature defy invariant representation, look for an abuse of notation. It is a sign that we are letting a function from contexts to objects stand in for one of its values by letting the context itself effectively play the role of the suppressed parameter in disambiguating noncoreferential uses. Add functions from contexts to semantic values to your vocabulary, choose symbols of the same graphical or grammatical type that you use to represent objects, allow the abuse of notation that permits you to use them as singular terms in a fixed context, and you are inviting a mistake. If you forget about the abuse, and reason in ways that apply to singular terms, you will conclude that there is an object distinct from anything named or described by your other singular vocabulary, a degree of semantic and metaphysical freedom that it has failed to capture and that it peculiarly cannot be extended to include. The lesson here is that whenever you have an object or property, something you assign as a semantic value to a term in a representational medium, that exhibits one or all of the following syndrome of properties, you should look for an abuse of notation. If it seems to slip irremediably through the net of objective representation, if there are contextual constraints on reference to it, or if reference to it is immune to failure, there is likely to be a hidden parameter that relates it reflexively to the context of use. Weyl's four-dimensional generalization of McTaggart's Moving Now, the 'gaze of consciousness' crawling, against the background of a static space-time, up the world line of his body, brings together the various components of perspective—spatial, temporal, phenomenal—that I have treated separately until now. The unseen seer tracing the path it carves out is pure illusion, an artifact of unfolding psychological history characterized by a continuous cycle of self-location.

There are some metaphysical pictures that are the result of philosophical miseducation and some that arise organically. I have argued that the grammatical illusion plays a role in philosophical argument, but the roots of the Weylian vision are deeper. The man on the Clapham omnibus shares something quite like that vision and he doesn't reason himself to it by philosophical argument.[29] I conjecture that it may have its roots in something as simple as the grammatical illusion.

10.8 PHENOMENAL PROPERTIES

Before moving on, I want to turn to an issue that I postponed earlier concerning phenomenal properties. I have claimed that the imaginative scenarios that are supposed to establish the contingency of the connection between reflexive and nonreflexive expressions involve contextual shifts that alter the semantic content of one of the expressions that flank the identity sign. There are two ways in which this can happen. I can render 'here is <,>' false, for example, by either holding fixed the interpretation of coordinates and altering my location or by holding my location fixed and altering the interpretation of my coordinates. The former is what physicists refer to as an active transformation; the latter is a passive transformation. In the first, there is actual movement; in the second, only a shift in the frame of reference. The truth value of 'here is <,>' is not invariant under either kind of transformation. The cases of 'here', 'now,' and 'I' involved active transformations that altered the semantic value of the indexical. The imaginative scenarios that are used to establish the contingency of '*this-here* = c-fibre firing', by contrast, involves passive transformations that alter the interpretation of the physical vocabulary.[30] In cross-world comparisons involving phenomenal properties, the reference of *this-here* is held fixed, although there is a tacit shift in the frame of descriptive reference that alters the interpretation of 'c-fibre-firing'.

This claim leads into contentious waters. There is no settled agreement among philosophers of science on what determines the interpretation of physical vocabulary. But we can bypass the difficult issues by showing that it follows from a principle that is not in dispute. First, we need to look at the imaginative scenarios that are used to establish contingency. Try to imagine worlds that are phenomenally indistinguishable from our own but which differ with respect to the distribution of physical properties. You do it by holding fixed all of the physical properties of persons and their functional relations to the environment and imagining that the phenomenal properties are entered into this causal network in a different way. Because the physical properties fix phenomenal structure only up to isomorphism, this seems perfectly possible. You can either fix

29. I take this character from David Lewis, but I thank Huw Price for informing me that it is an old English representative of the common man.

30. I follow the practice of talking in terms of states rather than properties here.

the physical properties and play around with different ways of entering the phenomenal properties into the causal order or fix the phenomenal properties and imaginatively reshuffle the physical ones. Either way, there don't seem to be any a priori constraints on how the physical and phenomenal properties are distributed with respect to one another. Notice, however, that filling out the cases in imaginative detail requires a break in the causal connection that holds in our world between phenomenal states and the visible colors, audible sounds, discriminable textures, tastes, smells, and so on, that we use them to track.

I'll refer to these properties as observable properties, and the predicates that refer to them as observational, without taking on the objectionable assumptions of the traditional notion of observability. All that I mean by calling a property observable is that it can be tracked under ordinary conditions without sensory implementation. Although the causal relations between phenomenal states and observable properties are attenuated and the dynamical relations are vague and context-dependent in all of the ways that were brought out in chapter 6, observable properties are the most direct epistemological interface between phenomenal states and the public environment. Now, any account of the interpretation of physical vocabulary that makes it dependent on the interpretation of observational vocabulary will entail that the interpretation of physical vocabulary is not invariant under alterations of the causal relations between phenomenal states and their distal causes, and this will mean that imaginative scenarios that alter these relations will induce a change in the interpretation of physical vocabulary.

Is there reason to think that the interpretation of physical vocabulary depends on the interpretation of observational predicates? Yes. Observational properties are the touchstones in the public landscape by which the quantities that figure in scientific description are identified.[31] It is tempting to be overly simplistic about the relationship here. No explicit definition of theoretical terms in observational vocabularly is possible. We might, as a first pass, suppose something like the following. Consider Mary from chapter 8. She is a scientifically informed student of the brain. She has studied c-fibres, she has memorized the textbook that contains the full compendium of scientific truth about c-fibres. She is the personal embodiment of scientific knowledge about c-fibres. To Mary, c-fibres are the things that make true all or some central core of the statements made about c-fibres in the text. In metalinguistic terms, the reference of

---

31. The question of whether the concept is defined by all or just some central core of these truths need not have a determinate answer, and it doesn't matter for our purposes.

'c-fibres' is whatever satisfies the open sentence we get by taking the c-fibre textbook and adding a variable wherever the word *c-fibre* occurs. We haven't yet identified the extensions of Mary's 'c-fibre' thoughts because the text is full of other scientific terms and we haven't said what their extensions are. But we do the same for that vocabulary. For every scientific term T that appears in the text on c-fibres, there is another text that contains the full compendium of T-involving truths. We conjoin them into a single volume, replacing scientific terms with variables so that we are left with an open sentence that contains only logical vocabulary and terms referring to observable properties. All talk of c-fibres, d-fibres, neurons, and neurotransmitters has been removed so that the only remaining descriptive vocabulary refers to properties we can relate directly to phenomenal states. The physical quantities are implicitly defined by this expression as that set of quantities that jointly satisfies the open sentence.

This view of how theoretical vocabulary is interpreted was proposed by Ramsey, and later developed by Lewis and Horwich. The problem with it is that we need a lot more flexibility, both in the internal relations between theoretical terms and the relations between theoretical terms and their extensions than is allowed by the standard ways of elaborating it. Whether it can be developed in a manner that allows a realistic fluidity on both sides remains to be seen, but all we need for our purpose is the somewhat weak tenet, central to any empiricist philosophy of science that our referential grip on the extensions of theoretical terms is mediated by their relation to observable properties.[32] I know of no empiricist account of the interpretation of scientific vocabulary that doesn't make it dependent in some way on the interpretation of observational vocabulary. If physical vocabulary depends for its interpretation on the interpretation of observational vocabulary, and observational vocabulary is, in its turn, anchored to phenomenal states, then the physical correlates of conscious states are known only by attenuated, extrinsic descriptions that ultimately relate them to phenomenal states. It follows that the interpretation of physical vocabulary transforms with shifts in causal relations between phenomenal states and the observable properties we use them to track.

Let's break this into smaller chunks. The claim is that

1. The interpretation of theoretical terms depends on the interpretation of observational vocabulary. (This is the empiricist tenet).
2. The interpretation of observational vocabulary depends on causal relations to phenomenal states. What my red concepts refer to

---

32. I would like to thank Paul Teller for warning me away from too simplistic a conception of this dependence.

depends on their causal connections to red profiles. (This follows from the view that observational vocabulary is interpreted in self-descriptive thoughts of the form 'red is the property that ordinarily causes *this-here*'.) Hence,

3. The interpretation of theoretical terms is not invariant under transformations that alter the causal relations between phenomenal states and their distal causes.

Consider a world in which we are all spectral inverts, for example, and suppose we use colored lights as pointer observables on our measuring instruments for electric charge: green lights indicate positive charge and red ones indicate negative. Clearly, the terms 'positive electric charge' and 'negative electric charge' refer to different properties in that world than they do in ours. The interpretation of all terms whose reference depends in whole or in part on the interpretation of color vocabulary will be shifted. Just so, in ways that are more complex and harder to gauge, it follows from the empiricist tenet, together with the view that the interpretation of observational vocabulary depends on relations to phenomenal states, that the interpretation of the terms that science uses to describe the brain will be shifted in a world in which the causal relations between phenomenal states and observable properties is broken. All descriptive vocabulary— whether it's the descriptive vocabulary of everyday English or vocabulary drawn from a formal scientific theory—has a hidden reflexive component that relates it ultimately to phenomenal states. And this means that we don't, after all, have the kind of independent grip on physical and phenomenal that is needed to support the modal argument.

A spatial analogy that reproduces some of these features might help. Suppose that I live three blocks east of a visual landmark that I can identify from my window—a clock tower, say—to which public officials assign the coordinates <0,0>. And suppose I discover my own coordinates by working backward from my spatial relation to the tower. I measure my distance and direction from the tower, consult a local map that tells me that the house that lies at the relevant distance and direction from the tower is at <n,m>, and I conclude that my coordinates are <n,m>. 'Here' in my mouth refers to the place represented in an invariant way by '<n,m>'. That is a true identity. There are ways imaginatively to break the connection between 'here' and '<n,m>'. There are worlds, that is to say, in which "here ≠ <n,m>," worlds, for example, in which the tower is stipulatively assigned a different address, worlds in which it is located in the next block, and worlds in which I live in a different part of town. But none of these are worlds in which here ≠ <,>. If we hold fixed my location, the metalinguistic link between the tower and its address, and the spatial relation between the tower and me, there is no more room for variation. The same goes for phenomenal properties. The descriptive coordinates employed by physics get their meaning from stipulative assignments to public landmarks. The public landmarks, in this case, are observable properties that we identify from our respective phenomenal windows. We work back to a physical characterization of our phenomenal states in a manner no different from that in which city-dwellers work back to a coordinate representation of their spatial location. If we hold fixed the phenomenal property as we compare worlds, rigidify the links between the distal causes and their physical descriptions, and rigidify the causal links between distal causes and brain states, there is no room for variation.

The relationships are obscured by the very dim conception that most of us have of the physical. The layman's concept of a neuron is largely deferential; I mean by 'neuron' whatever the neuroscientists do. To the neuroscientist, neurons are those things that they observe and manipulate in the laboratory through microscopes, MRI images, and so on. Neuroscientists' concept is deferential to the extent that they rely on physicists for understanding of the instruments they use to observe and interact with neurons. Neuroscientists need have no more explicit understanding of these than we have of the sensory machinery through which we view the world. And there is nothing in this to undermine a robust realism about the objects and structures neuroscientists view through these instruments. But whether we are talking about the ordinary objects of everyday sense or the neurons and synapses that appear in scientific descriptions, the interpretation of our descriptive vocabulary is dependent on the causal relations between phenomenal states and the environment. And any account of the interpretation of theoretical terms that makes their semantic values dependent on causal relations to phenomenal states will have the consequence that the referent of the physical predicate in physical-phenomenal property identities is not invariant under transformations that alter causal connections between phenomenal states and their distal causes. Observable properties are touchstones in the public landscape that are used to identify the properties employed in physical description. If they are, in their turn, identified by relations to phenomenal states, the interpretation of theoretical vocabulary cannot be invariant under transformations that alter causal relations between phenomenal states and physical vocabulary. The concept of a c-fibre has a computational role within a theoretical framework interpreted by connections to other phenomenal states that can seem to give it a life independent of any connection to pain, although the whole body of physical concepts is dependent on relations to phenomenal states in a way that ultimately belies any claim to have clear and distinct conceptions of the two.

This doesn't rule out property dualism. Even if the central tenet is correct, our phenomenal states might be merely epiphenomenal effects of brain states. But it does shift the burden of proof. A defender of the modal argument has to either defend an account of the interpretation of theoretical terms according to which it is unaffected by reinterpretation of observational predicates, or he has to provide a convincing description of worlds that differ from ours in the distribution of physical properties without breaking the causal links between phenomenal states and observable properties (or assuming what he set out to prove). I don't myself see how to do this. It's not enough to show that there's no contradiction in assuming that the relationship between brain states and phenomenal states is not identity. The modal argument was supposed to that it *couldn't* be.

Defenders of the modal argument have rested much in the fact that we have a substantive and determinate mental grip (to use Levine's phrase) on phenomenal properties which assures us of their identity in cross-world imaginings. This fact has played an important role in defeating attempts to account for the apparent modal separability along the lines of Morning Star/Evening Star cases as being due to a difference in modes of presentation. I think defenders of the modal argument are right to do so. Where they go wrong, in my view, is in imagining that our less determinate grip on the physical properties is not mediated by their relations to phenomenal properties.

PART 3

Selves

This section shifts gears from negative arguments back to elaborating the more positive story begun in part I. In this section, the focus is not on the general question of how selves are situated in nature, but on issues concerning the identity and individuations of selves.

11

Identity over Time

I ended part II by saying that the Weylian gaze of consciousness is the *here-now* of a mind engaged in an ongoing cycle of self-location. But I haven't said anything yet about what makes two self-locating episodes, episodes in the history of a single mind. I haven't, that is to say, said anything about the identity of the self over time. We all think of ourselves as more or less temporally extended beings. The self who rolled out of bed with a thought about the morning's lecture is the same one who delivered the lecture and the same one who will recall it before the next. The self who hated school in second grade is the same one who lectures now twice a week and the same one who will retire in old age. To bring out the gap between the momentary subject of the reflexive thought and the temporally extended subject to which we attribute thought and experience, I'll start with an objection that Anscombe lodged against Descartes. I will defend a familiar view about identity over time, underscoring again how some of the most puzzling features of thought about ourselves can be resolved by focusing on the architectural underbelly of thought.

11.1 REFLEXIVE ACCOUNTS

There are two ways to define self-representation. One characterizes it by its subject matter; self-representation is representation of *selves*. The other is subject neutral. Self-representation is simply reflexive representation.[1] The 'self' in 'self-representation', on the reflexive account, is not different from the 'self' in 'self-supporting' or 'self-contained'. It modifies the verb and indicates only the reflexive nature of the relation in question. A self-representation is one that takes itself, or the system that produces it, reflexively as intentional object. One way to bring the difference between reflexive and nonreflexive accounts is to think about self-portraiture in art. We usually think of a self-portrait as a painting of a self, the artist, the portrayer. A reflexive self-portrait eliminates the middleman. It is its own proper subject. The simplest kind of self-portrait represents itself under the identity mapping. Everything is a self-portrait in this sense. This is a degenerate form of representation because there is no risk of misrepresentation. More interesting self-portraits depict their situation in the wide environment, relating themselves to their surroundings. A self-centered representation like a map with a red dot or a sentence that describes itself is a self-portrait of this kind. How do we identify the subject of a self-portrait? That depends on the portrait. A map with a red dot is a representation of a part of space: a city, a building, a room, or the part of a room occupied by the map, depending on the map's resolution. I'm inclined to think that the subject of a self-portrait is only as well defined as the content of the portrait permits. As that content gets refined, the subject becomes correspondingly more well defined. A coarse-grained portrait has a coarse-grained subject.[2]

I have been implicitly defending a reflexive account of self-representation. I have nowhere made use of an unreduced notion of self, but spoken instead of the activity of self-representation and this means that I avoid the difficulties inherent in a subject/object model of knowledge or representation. The subject/object model requires a cognitive interaction between distinct existences, beginning a regress that seems to place the subject always outside of its own cognitive grasp, making it the ultimate unknowable. The subject of thought is what *does* the thinking. In an evocative image, it is like the reaching arm, always itself

---

1. It is important that the reflexive nature of the representation is part of its content. In a truly reflexive representation, there is a level bridging semantic route from the object to representation and back again. This is what distinguishes self-representation from mere representation *of* self.

2. This is one sense in which one defines oneself by representing oneself.

outside of reach.[3] Two premises are needed to generate this regress: (i) there is a subject for every object and (ii) that no subject is its own object. The reflexive account collapses the regress by simply denying the second premise. Thoughts, unlike arms, can reach back and grasp themselves.[4]

If you hold a reflexive account of thought about the self, you have an explanation of peculiarities of occurrent thoughts about oneself (immunity to failure of reference, guarantees of existence), and you explain why Hume, for example, couldn't find a self lurking among the various thoughts and impressions he found when he turned his thought upon himself.

> For my part, when I enter most intimately into what I call myself,
> I always stumble on some particular perception or other. I never can
> catch myself at any time without a perception, and never can observe
> anything but the perception.

But it encounters a special problem with identity over time that can be brought out with an objection that Anscombe raised against Descartes' discussion of the self. When Descartes raises the question of what he is, he writes

> I know that I exist and I am seeking to discover what I am, this
> "I" that I know to be.... But I, who am certain that I am, do
> not yet know clearly enough what I am; so that henceforth I

3. The image comes from Ryle.

4. In the contemporary literature, John Perry and David Velleman are the primary proponents of reflexive accounts. From Perry, see most recently, *Reference and Reflexivity*, and *Knowledge, Possibility, and Consciousness*. From Velleman, see "Self to Self," "The Objective Self," "A Sense of Self," "Identification and Identity," and "Identity and Identification" all in *Self to Self*. I am not sure that Perry's account is purely reflexive in the sense intended. Perry holds that the idea of self is the idea of a person under the agent-relative role 'being identical with'. This seems to make the notion of a person a constituent of that of a self. The notion of a person is too closely related to that of a self to make this a purely reflexive account. Velleman is more explicit in rejecting the idea that 'self' denotes an ontological category. As he says: "Some activities and mental states have an intentional object ... of these, some can take their own subject as intentional object; ... of these, some can be mentally directed at their own subject conceived as such— conceived, that is, as occupying this very state or performing this very activity. A reflexive mode of presentation is a way of thinking that directs an activity or mental state at its own subject conceived as such." See *Self to Self*, 2.

Velleman emphasizes that if self-representation is just a reflexive mode of presentation, then 'self' isn't a univocal notion. It is possible that we have many partially overlapping selves, as many selves as there are proper subjects of self-representation, and our I-thoughts range over different ones in different contexts. I have focused on the momentary subjects of Cartesian I-thoughts and the temporally thick selves that span the psychological history of an individual consciousness. Velleman explores other-kinds of selves as well, more deeply involved with ideas of responsibility and agency. The reference in his presentation of the view above, to the subject as that which performs the activity or occupies the representational state suggesting that this is conceived as distinct from the state or activity itself is unnecessary. I would have chosen a locution that emphasizes one of the primary virtues of the reflexive account, viz., that it obviates the need for subjects in that sense.

must...retrench from my former opinions everything that can be invalidated by the reasons I have already put forward, so that absolutely nothing remains except that which is entirely indubitable.[5]

He goes on, notoriously, to argue for an ontologically inflated conception of the self, but Anscombe's objection takes effect before the argument gets off the ground. She charges that Descartes' argument fails because he pulls a bait and switch, overtly declaring the object of his inquiry to be nothing other than that whose existence is made known in the act of trying to deny that it exists, but then tacitly appealing to a richer notion in allowing that it can be reidentified in different thoughts. She writes:

> People have sometimes queried how Descartes could conclude to his RES cogitans. But this is to forget that Descartes declares its essence to be nothing but thinking.... His position has, however, the intolerable difficulty of requiring an identification of the same referent in different I-thoughts.[6]

The thought here is that Descartes has to begin with a purely reflexive conception of self if he sticks to the letter of his definition. For, the existence of the self is guaranteed only if it is the purely reflexive 'I' that picks out the thought itself. If the thinker outlives the thought—that is, if the 'I' in one thought is even *potentially* intersubstitutable with the 'I' in others—it would seem that there is some nonreflexive notion licensing the substitution, something whose existence can't be revealed in the mere production of an 'I'-thought. On the one hand, the concept needs to be kept bare to guarantee existence, but on the other, the bare concept doesn't support reidentification. If I cannot be something whose existence is not made known in the production of an I-thought, something whose existence can be coherently doubted while I am thinking of it, then I cannot be something that even potentially recurs.

Anscombe is not the first to make this objection. It can be traced at least to Lichtenberg's famous remark that Descartes should have concluded 'it thinks' rather than 'I am thinking'. Russell made this objection. Wittgenstein appears to have endorsed it. Strawson does as well.[7] They reacted in different ways—some of them accepting richer notions of self and denying guaranteed existence, others denying that 'I' is a referring term at all—but each of them regarded the objection as devastating to Descartes. The objection is effectively that Descartes implicitly professes a purely reflexive

5. See Descartes, *Meditations*, 103
6. See Anscombe, "The First Person," 67.
7. See Strawson, *Individuals*, 97.

understanding of 'I' in identifying his subject matter, but makes use of something richer in allowing intersubstitution. Once the difference between the purely reflexive 'I' of the single thought and the temporally extended subject of repeated I-thoughts is made explicit, it becomes a real question how a self-directed thought captures past and future 'I'-occurences in its referential scope. At this stage in his argument Descartes and the defender of a reflexive account of self-representation have the same task: to find a way of turning the purely reflexive 'I' of the individual thought into something that ranges over things with temporal extension without assuming anything but a purely reflexive understanding of 'I'. The reason it presents a difficulty is that all that the reflexive account supplies us with is one 'I' thought and then another, with nothing to bind the 'I's in these thoughts into coreferring bundles. Unless this piece of the puzzle can be supplied, there's not enough structure in the reflexive account to support reidentification.

11.2   PROBLEMS WITH IDENTITY OVER TIME

How do we get from the purely reflexive 'I' of the individual thought to the 'I' of the temporal continuant? Let's look at how it works with other indexicals. An indexical or demonstrative expression ordinarily comes with an associated sortal. In some cases, the sortal is a part of the semantic content of the expression, as in the case of 'today' or 'this country' or 'this car'. In others, it is made clear by the conversational context, for example, you say 'now' and the conversational context makes it clear that you mean in the next few minutes rather than in the next few years.[8] In formal terms, indexicals and demonstrative expressions are functions. They have a descriptive component and a reflexive one. It is the descriptive component that proscribes the range of the function and supplies criteria of identity that govern substitution.[9] The

---

8. The 'here' of 'do you live here?' is not well defined until you know whether you are being asked about your home or your country. The conversational context can settle these questions without verbal exchange, and boundaries can remain vague, but the extension of a 'here'-use is only as determinate as the sortal that we can contextually associate with it, however vague its boundaries and tacit the association. There are two potential sources of indeterminacy; indeterminacy in which sortal is being tacitly invoked (is he asking whether I live in this house or this neighborhood?) and indeterminacy in the extension of the sortals being invoked (where, exactly, do the boundaries of my house lie? Do they include the guesthouse out back?).

9. This has to be qualified to recognize a preconceptual ability to track objects. When 'this' is used in application to an object through an unbroken sequence of experiences, there are subpersonal perceptual mechanisms attending to visual cues that appear to kick in, allowing us to track the object without application of concepts. These mechanisms have to be subpersonal if neonates are to be able to track objects before acquisition of concepts. It's plausible that this ability is a condition of the possibility of concept acquisition and is perhaps not properly described in terms of identification and reidentification.

reflexive component delivers value. The sortal associated with the referential act is what draws the boundaries around the extension. It is what determines, to the extent that it is determinate, which parts of space or time, or which bits of matter, fall under the scope of a particular occurrence. It is what determines which other occurrences of the indexical can be intersubstituted *salva veritate*. The reflexive component is only centering reference on a part of space or time, or on a bit of matter.

The famous immunity of indexicals to certain sorts of errors of identification is connected to this division of labor. So long as there is a thing of the sort to which the sortal applies present (in cases like 'today' and 'now', there is guaranteed to be, but this is not generally so), then reference can't be misdirected by a mistaken conception of the thing. Rip van Winkle might mistakenly think it's the year 1200, but his 'today' utterances in 1968 refer to days in 1968. I might mistakenly think that the train I'm pointing at is the newest member of the German fleet on its way to Brussels when it is in fact the oldest member of the French fleet on its way to Frankfurt, but my 'this train' utterance will still refer to the Brussels-bound coach. Immunity to errors of this sort, however, does not guarantee immunity to errors *re*identification and substitution. I can easily be wrong that two 'today' thoughts refer to the same day or that a pair of 'this-train' pointings refer to the same train because reidentification and intersubstitution require judgment, and where there is judgment, there is the possibility of error. Indeed, we can think of indexicals as buying ease of reference at the price of difficulty in reidentification and intersubstitution. All I have to do to identify a particular instance of an X is produce a tokening of 'this X' in its presence, but I (ordinarily) need to apprehend and apply individuation conditions for X's in order to apply the substitution rule for 'this X'. The syntactic criteria that govern reidentification and intersubstitution in the ordinary case (*modulo* ambiguity) provide no guide here.

To understand 'I' on this model we have to recognize the same division of labor. We have to think of 'I' as meaning 'this self' and suppose that criteria of identity for selves are employed in reidentification and intersubstitution of tokens of 'I' occurring at different times. And we have to recognize the possibility of errors of reidentification and substitution. But here 'I' parts company with other indexicals. One doesn't need criteria of identity to reidentify oneself over time, or to intersubstitute the 'I' of one thought or impression with the 'I' of another. And not only are one's occurrent references to oneself immune to error, one cannot make an error in *re*identification. You cannot mistakenly intersubstitute two noncoreferring 'I'-occurrences. No criteria of identity are employed, and no errors are possible at any stage in identification, reidentification, or substitution.

These facts are wholly unique to 'I' and capture much of the very special mystery in thought about the self. It's not just that we can refer to ourselves without an individuating conception; that much, as I said, is true of any object that can be referred to indexically. It's that we can refer to ourselves without any conceptualization at all. We can refer to ourselves without so much as an idea of the *kinds* of things we are; we can identify and *re*identify ourselves without being able to say what unites our parts or being able to pull ourselves under a single concept. Kant and Strawson both identified this as the central mystery of the self and recognized it as deeply implicated in supporting the intuitive view of the self as a simple, enduring substance. As Strawson says:

> And now we come to the fact that lies at the root of the Cartesian illusion . . . when a man (a subject of experience) ascribes a current or directly remembered state of consciousness to himself, no use whatever of any criteria of personal identity is required to justify his use of the pronoun "I" to refer to the subject of that experience . . . there is nothing that one can thus encounter or recall in the field of inner experience such that there can be any question of one's applying criteria of subject-identity to determine whether the encountered or recalled experience belongs to oneself—or to someone else.[10]

Few philosophers any longer dispute these facts about reference to the self.[11] The difficulty can be compounded by noting that not only *do* we not judge that the proper subject of one thought or impression—the 'I' of any self-ascribed thought or impression—is the same as the 'I' of another, we *couldn't*. There's a well-known circularity in any attempt to establish that a past or future thought is *mine*. It's easy to think 'every thought or impression that presents itself to me in a certain way—as Strawson put it above, any thought or impression that I encounter within the field of experience—is *mine*'. The problem is that the numerical identity of 'I' that is doing the encountering is presupposed in such thoughts. It *has* to be presupposed if it is used to proscribe the class of same-self-related states.[12] There is a thought that is being encountered at t and a thought that is being encountered at t*, but if the identity of the 'I' doing the encountering at t and t* is an open question, no judgment of this form will

---

10. Strawson, *Bounds of Sense*, 165.

11. Evans and Shoemaker discussed them extensively. Ascombe and Wittgenstein appreciated their importance. The emphasis on the difference between 'I' and other indexicals is clearest in Kant.

12. Ask yourself wherein lies the unity of the *one* who is doing the encountering? What is that in virtue of which there is a *one* who encounters all of my experience, for example, and a one who encounters all of your experience, but no one that encounters mine and yours together?

settle it. The same goes for perception. One can't *observe* that *this* impression and ... (letting time pass) ... *this* one belong to the same subject, because the numerical identity of the perceiving subject is presupposed by any perception that spans the two. The difficulty is nicely captured in a remark of Bennett's[13] "to think of *myself* as a plurality of things is to think of my being conscious of this plurality, and that pre-requires an undivided me."

Kant argued on these grounds that it simply cannot be part of the cognitive burden of the mind to sort its own thoughts and experiences from those of others. In his words,

> the mind could never think its identity in the manifoldness of its representations ... if it did not have before its eyes the identity of its act, whereby it subordinates all [the manifold] ... to a transcendental unity.[14] ...

> I am conscious of myself as the single common subject of a certain group of experiences by being conscious of the identity of the consciousness in ... conjoined ... representations[15]

If establishing its own identity over time is a burden that the subject can't meet, it's easy to fall into the idea that the unity of the thinking, perceiving self is an absolute and unassailable presupposition of all empirical cognition. Kant's response, on one interpretation, was to provide a positive account of the synthesis that organizes experience into a conception of oneself as a subject of experience, but insist that the transcendental unity of the subject, at and over, time is a condition of the possibility of the whole process of synthesis. What this means, however, is notoriously difficult to understand. He writes:

> The I that I think is distinct from the I that it, itself, intuits [perceives] ... I am given to myself beyond that which is given in intuition [perception], and yet know myself, like other phenomena, only as I appear to myself, not as I am.[16]

Another response is to simply deny that the self can be decomposed into temporal parts. Thoughts and impressions that occur at different times must be conceived as modifications of a simple substance and

---

13. See Bennett, *Kant's Dialectic*, 83.
14. Kant, *Critique of Pure Reason*, 1781/1787. Translations taken from Brook, "Kant's View of the Mind and Consciousness of Self," 2004.
15. Ibid., B133.
16. Ibid., B155.

their identity is partly dependent on the identity of the substance they modify.

11.3 POST HOC CONCEPTUALIZATION

Let's descend from these airy heights and see if we can get a clearer view from the ground. How can there be reidentification without application of criteria of identity? From our perspective, immunity to error is an important clue. It suggests strongly that architectural links are somehow regulating intersubstitution. The fact that the answer to the question 'is this thought mine?' is, on the one hand, contingent (there are thoughts that are not mine), but on the other hand, always positive, suggests that there is something that is keeping us architecturally confined to a context in which the positive answer is correct. Let's see if we can capitalize on this suggestion by returning to the example of the Z-landers that we took from Perry in chapter 1. Recall that the Z-landers are unadventurous folk who never travel and who never meet, or have occasion to talk to, people from other places.[17] They talk about the weather, and their weather beliefs play an important role in their practical lives. What they plan and how they act depends on their beliefs about the weather. What is striking about their weather talk is that it never includes an explicit reference to a place. They never mention or make any reference to Z-land in their reports. The nightly news, for example, says simply 'rain today, sun tomorrow, storms on Wednesday' without any mention of place, and that tells them everything they need to know in order to decide whether to cancel the picnic or carry an umbrella.

We agreed with Perry that Z-land appears in the specification of the truth conditions of their Z-land utterances and beliefs even though they make no mention of place. The Z-landers can make the spatial content of their weather talk explicit by adding 'here' to their reports. This is a practically trivial addition; so long as they remain at home 'here' can function grammatically in that context as a name for Z-land, and unconstrained intersubstitution of tokens of 'here' will preserve reference. Inferences will go through unproblematically, information will flow smoothly from Z-land to Z-lander weather beliefs, and from one Z-lander to another in talk about the weather. The sheer mechanics of the situation will ensure coordination without any need for a mediating concept of the

---

17. We suppose, also, that the weather is uniform across Z-land.

place. If Z-landers begin to move, however, or communicate with non-Z-landers, unconstrained intersubstitution will lead to faulty inferences, and they will need something in the head that can serve as a constituent of beliefs about the weather there and distinguish those beliefs from beliefs about weather elsewhere. They will need, in short, an idea of Z-land that occurs as an articulated constituent in beliefs that are sensitive to the state of, and guide behavior in, Z-land. The links between perception, belief, and action will be less direct than they were before, mediated now by a representation of place and self-ascription of location. Z-landers will not respond immediately to reports of rain by grabbing an umbrella. They will ask *where* it is raining, and they will stop to check it against the place they are *at*.

For another example of the process by which unarticulated constituents are articulated, think of the child who learns to use 'Mom' and 'Dad' to refer to his own mother and father, without understanding that motherhood and fatherhood are relations.[18] So long as the child remains in the family circle, this isn't something he needs to worry about.[19] If he hears that Mom is in the garden, he will know whom to find there. And if someone tells him that Mom is wearing a straw hat, he will conclude correctly that there is someone in the garden who is wearing a straw hat. 'Mom'-occurrences in his restricted world will all lead to the same place, and there is no need to interpose a parameter to coordinate them either with one another, or with their common referent. For him, 'Mom' functions as a singular term. As soon as he leaves the family circle, however, he will discover that 'mother' refers to other people in the mouths of his friends, he will need to keep explicit track of *whom* is speaking, and he will need to know something more about motherhood. What he needs to know, precisely, is a complex matter, and depends highly on particularities of his situation. The general rule is that he needs a way of getting from an utterance of 'mother' to its referent and a way of determining whether a pair of 'mother'-occurrences corefer. What this requires will depend on how many mother-son pairs he knows, and whether there are general ways of identifying speakers' mothers. If sons never leave their mothers' sides or if sons were always the spitting images of their mothers, the task would be easier than in a world like ours in which there are no

18. In formal terms, the process of articulating unarticulated constituents is that of representing one's frame of reference. One makes concepts drawn from different frames of reference communicable by plotting them jointly in a frame that includes a dimension in which their relations can be made explicit. The new constituents are values of parameters in added dimensions.

19. Supposing that he doesn't get information from other sources (books, radio, television), or at least that those sources don't use the terms 'mom' and 'dad'.

foolproof visual ways of recognizing mothers. How much structure he needs in his own head to keep the information flowing smoothly, so that information about a particular mother is collected, combined, kept safely separate from information about others, and brought to bear in the right way in his interaction with her will depend on which other mothers he gets information about, and how he gets that information. Mom-talk in the child's environment, and mom-thought in the child's head, while he is confined to the family circle, like Z-lander weather reports, have a hidden contextual parameter that can remain hidden so long as he remains in a context in which it has a fixed value (not hidden in the sense that it corresponds to anything in his head, but in the sense just described, in the sense that it plays an unacknowledged role in coordinating his thought with its extension), but that needs to be articulated when he is exposed to contexts across which its value varies.

Focus on the process of replacing unarticulated constituents with representations. Recall how things went with the Z-landers. They began by talking freely of the weather, without overt acknowledgment of the spatial relativization of weather talk. Making the spatial relativization explicit proceeds in two stages; they learn first to attach 'here' to their weather reports as a caution against unconstrained intersubstitution. The 'here' signals to them that they shouldn't infer disagreement from differences in reports, for the reporters may live in different places. But before they can begin to use weather talk again in inferences, before their weather thoughts can be properly integrated into the web of belief, and before they can coordinate their own weather reports with weather reports of their neighbors, they will need to replace 'here' with a parameter that explicitly represents, by varying in value with, their own location. Before they can be used effectively in reasoning, that is to say, weather reports and weather beliefs that concern different places will have to be made *internally* distinguishable. Indexicals are a perfectly legitimate way of securing reference; and they have the critical advantage of securing it in a way that bypasses the ordinary route through ideas, placing less conceptual burden on their users. But they have the disadvantage of concealing relations of intersubstitutivity. One cannot tell from an internal perspective—by inspection, so to speak, of the beliefs themselves— whether a pair of 'here', 'this', or 'today' occurrences are intersubstitutable. From the inside, one 'here' or 'today' thought looks like any other. Something more is needed before one can reidentify an indexically identified particular, that is, recognize it as the same as that encountered under different conditions or on another occasion.

This second stage, at which the indexical is replaced with explicit representation, is highly nontrivial. It is here that Z-landers will have to come to appreciate and employ criteria of identity for places.[20] They can no longer rely on the fixed architectural link to keep their here-occurrences divided into intersubstitutability classes. They will have to learn to identify and individuate places. They will need a concept of places that are not their own, and an understanding—both practical and theoretical—of criteria of identity for places. The same story could be told about sheltered children. Once they have left the family circle and can no longer rely on the context to coordinate reference, if they are to use 'mother' effectively in reasoning, they will need to develop an understanding of familial relations, and learn to apply criteria of identity in deciding whether distinct 'mother'-occurrences are intersubstitutable. As soon as they begin to move around, Z-landers no longer have the kind of built-in, invariant informational link to a place that allows it to act as an unarticulated constituent in their thought, and they need something a little higher up in the representational hierarchy, something with a looser connection to experience, to hang their Z-land thoughts on.

Returning, now, to bridging the gap between the purely reflexive subject of the individual thought and the 'I' that ranges over whole extended streams of them. How can present I-occurrences capture a collection of parts under its scope if there are no criteria associated with the term to proscribe its extension? I want to suggest that we learn to use 'I' by a mechanical procedure: producing tokens, and allowing unconstrained intersubstitution, relying on the external relations among the tokens to preserve reference. Reference is thus secured without explicit representation of the intersubstitution context. This reverses the ordinary direction of determination. We do not introduce the concept of a self to proscribe the intersubstitutivity context for 'I'-tokens; it is the de facto relations among tokens that get intersubstituted by application of the mechanical procedure that determines the criteria of identity for selves. You have to possess criteria of identity for days and mothers to sort 'today' and 'mom' occurrences into intersubstitutability classes, but it is the singular oddity of 'I' that no conceptualization of this sort is provided by the rule of use. In practical terms, the rule of use is trivial; it says "attach 'I' as proper subject to all thoughts and impressions, intersubstitute indiscriminately."

---

20. A criterion of identity for a type of object is that in virtue of which one object of that type is identical to, or distinct from, another of the same type. If the object is complex, a criterion of identity is the principle of unity for its parts. It tells you that in virtue of which two X-parts are parts of the same X. There is a large and well-developed literature on the notion of a criterion of identity. Particularly apropos here are Strawson and Evans. See, in particular, Evans's discussion of 'fundamental grounds of difference'. I'm remaining neutral on the question of whether any real identification has taken place at the stage before the conceptualization that allows reidentification. There is, at that stage, the internal *form* of reference and coordination with an extension partly secured by contextual restrictions.

Conceptualization is, however, needed to integrate 'I' inferentially with other terms, and many authors in the contemporary literature have emphasized that it is essential to being properly ascribable a genuine idea of self. Evans, for example, holds that in order for 'I' to be recognized as a semantically significant component of thought,

> one's Idea of oneself must also comprise, over and above [un-mediated links to perception and action], a knowledge of what it would be for an identity of the form 'I $= \gamma$' to be true, where γ is a fundamental identification of a person: an identification of a person which—unlike one's 'I'-identification—is of a kind which could be available to someone else.[21]

Kant made the same point in distinguishing 'I think' as an empty accompaniment of every thought from meaningful self-ascription. For Evans, the requirement is an instance of a general condition on identifying thought that gets its justification from an understanding of the role of thought in mediating perception and action. He writes:

> Sensory input is not only connected to behavioral disposition in the way I have been describing . . . but also serves as the input to a thinking, concept-applying, and reasoning system . . . it is only those links which enable us to ascribe content (conceptual content now) to the thoughts.[22]

The requirement follows also from the criterion I gave for recognizing the semantically significant components of a representational medium. A representational medium, recall, is identified by a set of information-bearing states and content-preserving transformations. It follows that the semantically significant components are those transformation of which is not content preserving. Using a medium demands an understanding of which transformations of state are content preserving. This requires two things. It requires knowing whether, and when, one term, or occurrence of a term, can be substituted for another in inference, and it requires knowing how this term interacts inferentially with other terms. When it comes to indexicals, transformations of context that leave the intrinsic

---

21. See Evans, *Varieties of Reference*, 209. Conceptualizing oneself for Evans means conceiving of oneself as one among a range of entities, any of whom can bear the properties that one ascribes oneself on the basis of experience. Evans thinks that this means conceiving of oneself as an occupant of space.

22. The condition, which he calls the Generality Constraint, formulates the conditions under which an internal symbol makes a contribution to content, and can be said to stand for, or *represent*, a thing. In its general form, the condition requires us to see "the thought that a is F as lying at the intersection of two series of thoughts: the thoughts that a is F, that a is G, that a is H, . . . , on the one hand, and the thoughts that a is F, that b is F, that c is F, . . . , on the other." See Evans, *Varieties of Reference*, 209.

properties of an expression untouched are not, in general, content-preserving and this makes intersubstitution a little more difficult because the recognitional ability required to use indexicals is shifted down a semantic level. Instead of requiring an ability to reidentify the same word in different sentences, it requires an ability to reidentify an object on different occasions or in different contexts. Knowing how a token of an indexical interacts inferentially with other terms is also more difficult. For nonreflexive expressions, inferential connections with other terms are built into the inferential structure of the language, are learned when one learns the language, and are as stable as the inferential structure of the language.[23] Indexical expressions can't be integrated inferentially into the language in this way. The inferential properties that attach to the reflexive component vary as quickly as its reference changes. Aside from those that derive from its descriptive component, an indexical has no intrinsic inferential connections to other terms. A token of 'here' or 'today' or 'I' inherits inferential connections to other terms from the objective truth conditions that attach to the nonreflexive expressions it is associated with in indexical identity sentences. The process by which the purely mechanical procedure of attaching indexicals to thoughts is transformed into real, identifying thought—for example, the process by which one goes from merely producing mental 'I'-tokens to actually *thinking about oneself*—then, involves grasping the truth of an indexical identity sentence. To represent oneself in the sense of being able to take oneself as an *object* of thought requires more than the ability to produce mental tokens of 'I'. It involves grasping the objective truth conditions that integrate those tokens into an articulated network of concepts. To be able to entertain thoughts not only about our own selves, but those of others, we have to understand, moreover, what would make true an identity of the form $I = \gamma$, where γ is an arbitrary name or identifying description.

The repeated pattern is the one that we saw with the Z-landers. There is a suppressed parameter with a fixed value that is first expressed indexically and later replaced with a singular term. We get a closer analogy if we allow ourselves to embellish. Instead of Z-landers, imagine a population of conscious, weather-sensing trees: Tree-landers. Tree-landers can tell sunny weather from rain and each has a repertory of actions suited to weather in its own locale. Perhaps, for example, they open their leaves in rainy weather and close them in sun. They get information about rain

---

23. The inferential structure of natural languages evolve, of course, but evolution of inferential structure is different from context-dependence. The inferential properties of a context-dependent expression change spontaneously with context and without any kind of reorganization of the inferential structure of the medium.

in other locales only indirectly through reports from birds that bring news from distant lands. Their weather thoughts and reports start out, like those of the Z-landers, without explicit spatial content. They learn to attach 'here' mechanically, allowing unconstrained internal intersubstitution but refraining from substitution in connection with reports from outside. The conceptualization needed to integrate their 'here'-thoughts properly into the web of belief occurs at a later stage, if it occurs, and involves apprehension of objective criteria of identity for places.

In apprehending criteria of identity for selves, we face something like the task that Tree-landers face in apprehending criteria of identity for places. Ideas of other locations are for them, in the beginning, slots where they funnel information about weather that is not weather *here*, that is to say, weather that doesn't make itself felt in *this* way and have a direct, regulative bearing on the opening and closing of leaves. And just so, ideas of other *selves* are for each of *us* places where we house thoughts and experiences that are not our own, that is to say, thoughts and experiences other than *these*, thoughts and experiences that don't make themselves felt in this way and have a direct regulative bearing on activity. They are whatever lies at the other end of the linguistic chains that bring us news of such thoughts.

There is nothing inherently mysterious, if we focus in this way on the sheer mechanics of securing reference, in the fact that each of us can refer to one object in thought in a way that is immune to failure of reference (i.e., whose existence is ensured and reference to which is secured in the very production of the thought), which is nevertheless distinct from (because it possibly outlives) the thought, and yet with no conception of what kind of thing we are referring to.

This account gives us

1. identification without application of criteria of identity;
2. reference to a continuant, and;
3. immunity to mistakes in reidentification.

Moreover, since no criteria of identity are employed in reidentification, apprehension of criteria of identity, if and when it is made, will present itself as a *discovery* and show all of the psychological signs of contingency. Suppose R is the relation that turns out to unite the thoughts and experiences of a self, which is to say, the relation that 'I'-occurrences that get intersubstituted by application of the mechanical procedure bear one another. It doesn't matter what R is, so long as it doesn't make explicit and ineliminable reference to a self, the proposition 'S and S* belong to the same self *if* S R's S*' will not look like a conceptual truth.

1. It will be dubitable.
2. Being told that S R's your present thoughts will seem to leave it as an open question whether S is nevertheless *yours*.
3. It will seem as though you can imagine scenarios in which all of the objective R-relations remain fixed, although the gaze of your consciousness crosscuts them, alighting now here now there, at will.

These facts, stated in general form, will seem to rule out any reductive candidate for a constitutive relation between temporal parts of a self to anyone in the grip of the Fregean Model of Thought. As Nagel has said:

> The very bareness and apparent completeness of the concept [of the self] leaves no room for the discovery that it refers to something that has other essential features which would figure in a richer account of what I really am. Identification of myself with an objectively persisting thing of whatever kind seems to be excluded in advance.[24]

And earlier:

> My nature . . . appears to be at least conceptually independent not only of bodily continuity but also of all other subjective mental conditions, such as memory and psychological similarity . . . at the same time it seems to be something determinate and nonconventional. That is, the question with regard to any future experience, "will it be mine or not?" seems to require a definite yes or no answer. . . .
>
> This seems to leave us with the conclusion that being mine is an irreducible, unanalyzable characteristic of all my mental states, and that it has no essential connection with anything in the objective order or any connection among those states over time.[25]

We have seen repeatedly when and why these kinds of arguments fail. A proper understanding of the mechanics of securing reference provides a mundane explanation that avoids this metaphysically inflationary conclusion.

Two brief qualifications. First, there is a disanalogy between 'I' and the Tree-lander 'here'. It's a contingent fact that Tree-landers are rooted to their location. They could conceivably pick up and move. We can hold fixed the identity of the Tree-lander and vary the value of the hidden spatial parameter. We can't, however, hold fixed the identity of the subject and alter the value of the personal parameter. That is a context to which each subject is *constitutively* confined. Second, I suppressed the question

---

24. See Nagel, *The View from Nowhere*, 35. He is expressing but not endorsing the view in this passage.

25. Ibid., 34.

of why we should think that the Tree-lander 'here' means 'this place', rather than, for example, 'this tree' or any one of the other candidates that are undiscriminated by the rule of use applied in a fixed spatial setting. The answer to this question is that we shouldn't. To get their 'here' uses tied determinately to a place, we would need to add something to support the counterfactual: 'If the Tree-landers began to move, their 'here'-uses would remain spatial locations'. My inclination is to think that rules of use, and the semantic properties that they ground, are in general only so determinate as they have to be in order to discriminate cases that arise within the contextual niche that users occupy. And that means that until the practice becomes more articulated, there simply is no fact about which of the indefinitely many objects undiscriminated by the rule of use *as applied* the Tree-lander 'here' refers to. None of this damages the example. It was intended only to illustrate how reidentification without criteria of identity works provided where architectural constraints keep one confined to an intersubstitutability context.

11.4   FROM INFORMATIONAL
TO CONCEPTUAL CONTENT

The progression from opening and closing leaves in response to external stimuli, on the part of the Tree-landers, to having thoughts with the contents given in 2–4[26] mirrors our progression from moaning in pain to having thoughts with the contents given in 6–8.

1. opening leaves
2. 'Rain!'
3. 'Rain, here!'
4. 'Rain at $<,>$!'

5. moaning in pain
6. 'Pain!'
7. 'Pain here!' or 'Pain at me!'
8. 'JI is in pain'.

1, is a reaction, not a representation; it carries information, under the right conditions, by indicating the presence of rain, but it has no conceptual content, no role in inference or communication. 2, has-conceptual content, but it is, we might say, 'placeless'; it doesn't contain an articulated spatial constituent. 3, has an explicitly spatial content, but it has no intrinsic

---

26. I have suppressed temporal parameters, and the accompanying, insignificant 'it'.

connection to a place. Only 4, has, as I will put it, a *fully expressed* content; only 4, contains an explicit representation of the place that it is about. A content is fully expressed just in case it has a semantically significant constituent that represents, in a context-free manner, each property and particular that enters into its truth conditions, just in case, we might say, its information-bearing properties are entirely intrinsic to it.

Likewise, 5–8. 5, is a reaction, not a representation; it carries information, under the right conditions, by indicating something about a subject, but it has no conceptualized content, no role in reasoning or inference. It is not connected in the inferential web.[27] 6, has conceptual content, but it is 'subjectless'; the relativization to a subject is not reflected internally. In 7, the content is explicitly ascribed to a subject, but only in 8, once the blank is filled, will the content fully and finally be expressed.

Each step in the progression is epistemically innocent, but conceptually loaded. Each involves expressing, in an increasingly conceptually articulated, increasingly invariant form, the informational content of the kinds of experience that are the direct cause of leaf-opening in the Treelander's prereflective states, and moaning in our own.

The task is for us if we want to understand what kinds of thing we are to furnish objective criteria of identity for 'me', as it occurs in 7,[28] that delimits the intersubstitution class of 'I'-occurrences, that is, that determines the conditions in general under which inferences of the following forms are valid:[29]

"Pain at me at t"
"Pain at me at t*"[30]

There is someone who was in pain at both t and t*.

"Pain at me at t"
"Itch at me at t"

There is someone who was both in pain and itchy at t.

27. It has a role in communication, but only in the way that smiles have roles, i.e., by indicating pleasure. It is a primitive precursor of talk.

28. I don't distinguish between 'me' and 'I'.

29. There are two sorts of criteria of identity; there are just objective truth conditions for 'I'-involving statements, and then there are what Evans calls 'fundamental ideas'. To have fundamental ideas of a and b is to know in a perfectly general way, under all possible conditions, whether a = b. Only fundamental ideas will tell us the nature of the objects in question. For purposes of simply keeping track of, and coordinating information about, selves only objective criteria of identity are required. The distinction between objective criteria and fundamental ideas dissolves in the case of the self because we are, as pointed out below, constitutively tied to an intersubstitution context.

30. The quotes are intended to indicate that these are particular, situated thoughts.

Representing ourselves in this sense is as inessential for internal purposes (i.e., for purposes of coordinating experience with action and our own thoughts with one another) as representation of their own location was to the Tree-landers, for the purposes of coordinating the opening of their leaves with rain in their locale. When we begin to communicate, making the personal content of our own thoughts explicit is necessary in order to coordinate it with other sources of information about our own thoughts and with the information we get about thoughts and experiences that are not our own. We begin to *self*-ascribe thoughts, pains, and itches if and when we find a use for ascribing them to others.

11.5   DRAWING THE BOUNDARIES

So let's return to the question of what makes one I-thought fall within the scope of another. What makes a pair of 'I'-occurrences intersubstitutable for each other? What makes two—in particular, two thoughts or experiences that occur at different times—thoughts or experiences of the *same* self. Anscombe thought that Descartes' argument foundered on what she called the "intolerable difficulty" that if the thinker outlives the thought—that is, if the 'I' in one thought is even *potentially* intersubstitutable with the 'I' in others—its existence can't be revealed in the mere production of an 'I'-thought. Her worry was that the notion of an I, in a sense that allows *different* occurrences of 'I' to refer to the *same* self must be prior to and cannot be *constituted* by the mere production of those thoughts. We have seen why Anscombe's difficulty is not, after all, so intolerable. There are two ways to define an intersubstitutability context: implicitly and explicitly. Explicit definition does indeed require prior conceptualization of the referent, but if we can learn how to use 'I' by a purely mechanical procedure, one that can be described without any explicit reference to or conceptualization of selves, we can let the de facto relations among tokens that in fact get intersubstituted when 'I' is used in accordance with the procedure implicitly define the principle of unity for selves. Reference—even reference to a continuant—can in this way *precede* apprehension of criteria of identity. Apprehension of such criteria will be unnecessary for purposes of coordination and if it is ever made, it will present itself as a discovery. We don't need semantic links between the terms where there are architectural links in place. It is only when we break architectural links by moving to different contexts that mediating concepts become necessary. That was the insight in Perry's original example, but it has been extended here to apply the links between the parts of the self in a way that explains some of its most intractable peculiarities. The extension shows how it can turn out to be news to us that the thing we've been identifying and reidentifying all along is really one whose parts are held together by such and such connections.

If we specify the rule of use ("attach 'I' indiscriminately to all thought and experience, allow unconstrained intersubstitution") and let the intersubstitutability contexts be implicitly defined by the rule of use, then finding out what selves are, and in particular, what *I* am will be a matter of determining what the intersubstitution context in fact *is*, a matter of figuring out what turns out to unite occurrences that get intersubstituted by the procedure specified in the rule of use. The crucial insight here is that we don't need to represent those relations in order to reidentify the self. What do we get if we apply this strategy? We get—I propose—external informational relations, the direct causal links inside the head that permit information to flow without passing through perceptual or linguistic channels. These are what tie the events that lie along a single stream of consciousness to one another; they are what tie the temporal parts of a self together; they provide the principle of identity for selves over time. A self is nothing more than a sealed pocket of world-representing structure, communicating with its environment[31] through controlled channels. Each of us applies 'I' mechanically by attaching it as grammatical subject to internal states and, only later, once we have worked up a rudimentary picture of the world, raise questions about our nature. It is really the existence of these sealed pockets that provide the contexts of intelligibility for 'I'-use: Humean bundles, connected by architectural connections that let information flow between them in a manner that is unmediated by anything in the intentional foreground. Information is conveyed from one part of these bundles to another along channels that are not explicitly represented in the signal. The intelligibility of 'I'-use doesn't depend on the existence of simple enduring substances for thoughts to inhere in. It requires nothing more than the various 'I'-thoughts, the psychologically unmediated informational relations they bear one another, and enough informational segregation from the environment to make 'I'-use unproblematic. It requires nothing more than the closed internal environment inside a mind that forces all communication with the environment, including all communication with other selves, through the broadband connection provided by experience. There is a lot of causal substructure,

---

31. The environment is understood here as including everything external to the subject, so the body is a fixed part of the environment of thought. For a very probing comparison of this view of the role of the body with the strong embedded/embodied view associated with, e.g., Noe or Regan, see Clark, "Pressing the Flesh."

invisible to thought, that supports this cozy informational arrangement, but the channels through which information flows internally from past to future and from one part of the mind to another are all a part of the architectural background. The flow of information is unmediated by anything in the intentional foreground of thought.

It is crucial to this way of understanding things that connectedness is an architectural relation, one that is independent of the contents and qualitative character of mental states. It is true that 'I' can meaningfully occur only in the context of articulated world-representing structure, that this requires a certain amount of continuity of content, and that given certain assumptions about how world-representing structure is formed, this in its turn may demand continuity in qualitative character. And it is also true that causal connectedness of the sort that permits experientially unmediated flow of information ordinarily has the *effect* of imposing continuity in content. But no continuity of content or qualitative character plays a role in individuating selves. Psychological continuity of either of these kinds is in no way constitutive of the relation belongs-to-the-same-self-as.[32] This brings out a critical divide among forms of psychological reductionism often overlooked in the literature on personal identity. If we call views that share this feature 'Pure Lockean' and views that include internal criteria among the conditions for identity over time 'Parfittean', after their most famous examplar, Locke holds a Lockean view. As does James, who writes:

> My present Thought stands...in the plenitude of ownership of
> the train of my past selves, is owner not only *de facto*, but *de jure*,
> the most real owner there can be. Successive thinkers, numerically
> distinct, but all aware of the past in the same way, form an adequate
> vehicle for all the experience of personal unity and sameness which
> we actually have.[33]

According to James, the self or subject

> is a Thought [mental state], at each moment different from that
> of the last moment, but appropriative of the latter, together
> with all that the latter called its own. All the experiential facts
> find their place in this description, unencumbered with any

---

32. We might want to say that internal criteria are important and relevant to *personhood*, for that is a rich notion entangled with concepts of agency and responsibility. The existence of persons, in this richer sense, is not guaranteed by the production of I-thoughts.

33. See James, *The Principles of Psychology*, 1.360.

hypothesis save that of the existence of passing thoughts or states of mind.[34]

Velleman has made this distinction and provided the most psychologically convincing defense of a Pure Lockean view of which I know in the contemporary literature in a manner almost tailored to fill the gap pointed out by Anscombe in reflexive accounts of self-representation. He writes:

> Past persons are reflexively accessible via experiential memory, which represents the past as seen through the eyes of someone who earlier stored this representation of it; and future persons are accessible via a mode of anticipation that represents the future as encountered by someone who will later retrieve this representation of it.[35]

As a theory of the self, only a Pure Lockean view—that is, one that allows no admixture of internal criteria into the constitutive relations between the parts of a self—shows how intersubstitution can be internally unregulated in the right architectural setting, how we can identify and reidentify ourselves over time without application of any criteria whatsoever. It is the only view that explains the fact, wholly unique to self-identification and critical to Descartes' argument, that we can make repeated identifying reference to ourselves in thought without having (or needing to have) any conception of what unites our temporal parts. It's the only view that reproduces the peculiar patterns of cognitive gaps and epistemic guarantees that characterizes past and future-directed thought about oneself. Epistemic guarantees come with cognitive gaps, and they're signs that architectural rather than conceptual links are holding together some of the pieces of the cognitive machine.

So I agree with Kant that the numerical identity of the thinking, perceiving subject is presupposed by every judgment that spans a pair of thoughts or impressions, whether they occur together or at different times. And instead of looking above to some intrinsically unified unifier to provide the unifying principle, I look below, at the hidden underbelly of thought, at the wiring and connections in the background that keep the information flowing smoothly across the intentional foreground.[36] What unites the states of a subject on a Pure Lockean view are the causal relations that preserve all or most or some of the information in the intentional foreground of thought. A good bunch of what is contained in explicit memory and belief gets transmitted to my future selves, and what

---

34. Ibid.
35. Ibid., 1.6.
36. Remaining neutral on how this relates to Kant's position.

makes them my future selves is precisely that they are connected to my present self by those lines of transmission. Communication with others is mediated by the production of publicly observable symbols or behavior. Others have to talk, write, or behave in ways that I can see, ways that can be designed either to mislead or clue me in. There are immediate connections among the mental states of a single subject, but the brand of immediacy in question doesn't come with the traditional encumbrances of transparency and certainty. It is compatible long chains of mediating action behind the scenes, and it can accommodate the kinds of inaccuracies, pathologies, and internal divisions of self that we know to arise when psychological boundaries inhibit the flow of information.[37] There is no contradiction in supposing the immediate informational connections that unite the temporal parts of a self cutting across the boundaries of bodies, but as a matter of contingent fact, the body provides the physical context in which they are realized. It protects the architectural links that convey information between parts of the self and keeps them not directly permeable to other minds.

There is room in what I have said for both indeterminacy and legislation. We're all familiar with thought experiments that raise questions about the application of 'I' in circumstances in which the architectural scaffolding that supports the informational arrangement in which 'I'-use has its normal application is broken, for example, thought experiments in which information is coming from or flowing to multiple sources (fission and fusion), through artificial channels (memory insertion), or from subjects that aren't psychologically connected to us in the ordinary way (you wake up with memories of the experiences of a sixth-century Russian monk). How indirect and artificial can the causal relations in question be if there is a difference between recovering memories of one's own and acquiring someone else's? Do there have to be constraints on the causal route by which they come to me? There need not be anything in our present use that decides these cases. If enough of the architectural background that supports 'I'-use is broken (and it is characteristic of architectural connections that they *can* be broken; they're just "wiring and connections" to recall Peter Godfrey-Smith's phrase), the notion of a temporally extended self, as we know it, will no longer have application. If, for example, fission, fusion, and amnesia become common, or memories can be uploaded with no internal signs of inauthenticity and a black market develops in which this kind of exchange becomes commonplace, we will need a more

37. For an account of immediacy also shorn of those traditional encumbrances, see Moran, *Authority and Estrangement.*

articulated set of concepts to accommodate the full range of relations one can bear to the ancestors and downstream descendants of one's thoughts.

What is special about 'I', wholly unique to it as a term in thought, is that the facts that govern intersubstitutability of 'I'-occurrences are external to and need not be represented in thought. The mind doesn't represent its boundaries so much as bump up against them. I don't have to know what I am in order to know which thoughts, memories, experiences, and hopes are mine. I don't have to know anything *about* my future self in order to have thoughts about, make decisions on behalf of, have hopes and fears and such centered on *her*. The ideas I have about how my history will unfold play no role in determining which of the world's future inhabitants is me. If I think that I will be the first woman president of the United States, but Marla Maples beats me to it, that doesn't make my present thoughts about my future self thoughts about Miss Maples. Whoever gathered these memories and sent them to me along the discriminating internal channels that Mother Nature has provided inside the head, with whatever internal embellishments and emotional resonances that were added by that past self, that was me. And whoever receives these thoughts and experiences along the same channels will be me as well. When I talk or think about myself, I talk or think about the connected, and more or less continuous, stream of mental life that includes this thought, expressing the tacit confidence that that is a uniquely identifying description (in the same way I might speak confidently of this river or this highway pointing at a part of it, expressing the tacit assumption that it doesn't branch or merge), but it need not be. There is no enduring subject, present on every occasion of 'I'-use, encountered in toto in different temporal contexts. The impression of a single thing reencountered across cycles of self-re-presentation is a grammatical illusion of the sort exposed in chapter 10.

11.6 CONNECTING WITH EARLIER THEMES

To recap, part II ended with of grammatical illusion; the Weylian gaze of consciousness crawling up the lifeline of a body understood as the here-now of a mind engaged in a continuous cycle of self-location. This section raises the question of what ties a sequence of 'here-now's into a single, temporally extended consciousness. What makes thoughts that occur at different times thoughts of a single self, or what makes the 'I' in one thought inter-substitutable with that in a later thought? 'I' was distinguished from other indexicals by the fact that no criteria of identity are applied at any stage in identification and reidentification. These facts revealed another of the holes that we saw in earlier chapters emerge when the mind reflects on itself, and they were resolved like other such blindspots by focusing on the hidden underbelly of thought. We've learned by now to recognize immunity to error and cognitive separability from identifying concepts as signs of architectural links playing a role in securing reference. What 'I' added to our understanding of how indexical thought works generally is an understanding of how architecture could also play a role in governing reidentification and intersubstitution.[38] It showed us how architectural facts could not only pick the value of a function whose range has been proscribed but also how they could help proscribe the range of the function. A substitution rule that doesn't require any application of concepts is combined with constraints on movement to divide 'here'-occurrences into equivalence classes as surely as a generally applicable substitution rule that contains criteria of identity. Tree-lander 'here'-use is described by the rule 'attach as proper subject to all happenings and intersubstitute freely'; 'there is rain' becomes 'there is rain *here*', 'there is sun' becomes 'there is sun *here*', and so forth. And every 'here' in these occurrences is intersubstitutable with every other. The physical ties that bind Tree-landers to their locations do all of the work in governing intersubstitution that criteria of identity do for mobile beings. Our 'I'-use is, likewise, described by a rule that doesn't require any application of concepts 'attach as proper subject to all happenings and intersubstitute freely'; 'there is pain' becomes 'I feel pain', 'there is thinking' becomes 'I am thinking', and so on. And every 'I' in these occurrences is intersubstitutable with every other. The physical boundaries that close minds off from one another do all the work in governing intersubstitution. Reflexive constructions showed us how we bypass the need for something in the foreground of a representational state by relying on discriminating architectural links to secure reference. We now see how, in special cases, we can even bypass even the need for criteria of reidentification by relying on architectural constraints that keep us confined to intersubstitutability contexts.

11.7 WHY THE TEMPORALLY EXTENDED SELF?

I spoke only briefly, at the end of part I, about the importance of the historical dimension of self-representation. I want to say a little more here. Why do we represent our pasts, not simply why do we represent *the* past, but why do we each represent our *own* pasts? Why do our *self*-representations have

---

38. Indeed, that phenomenon is quite general. Even where criteria of identity are employed, there needn't be apprehension of fundamental grounds of difference, to use Evans's term. As in the case of the Tree-landers, we can rely on contingent conditions—architecture—for discriminating informational links to them.

a historical dimension. The reflexive, or first-personal, content of a GPS device or a self-guided missile is 'here I am now'. We, by contrast, keep a dynamic record of personal past, written and rewritten with each passing moment. To say that we look at the past through the lenses of the present doesn't begin to capture the complexity. We look at the past through the layered lenses of all of the presents that separate us from it, and each of these lenses has its own transforming effect. If we have learned anything from studying situated cognition it is that Mother Nature doesn't reify structure without purpose. The reification of structure along the temporal dimension of our psychological histories engendered by autobiographical memory is extravagant and demands explanation. It is important to understand just how extravagant that reification is; every momentary cross section of our internal lives contains a partial, selective, backward-looking image of the whole, one that is not only updated, but subjected to ongoing, retrospective revision.

In psychological terms, the importance of the addition of the historical dimension cannot be overestimated. There is a lot to say here, and what preceded is really a kind of prelude to understanding the role of auto-biographical *memory* in the cognitive life of a self-representing agent.[39] The answer is simple: autobiographical memory brings information about personal past into the deliberative loop. A system that retains an explicit record of its past can make promises, accept and acquire commitments. It can form developing relationships and personal projects. It has interests of its own and can systematically carry out parts of an extended plan. All of this depends on retaining information about personal past in an explicit form. Each temporal part of a life is guided by the developing narrative it receives from its forebears, a transformed version of which it passes to its descendants. That narrative functions as a vehicle by way of which variables pertaining to the whole can acquire a role in determining the behavior of parts. The temporal parts of an agent that represents its past can act as a team, guided by their contribution to a collective goal against the background of an accomplished past.[40]

11.8   OTHER VIEWS ABOUT IDENTITY OVER TIME

A comparison of the Pure Lockean view with other views of identity over time will help to bring out important points of contrast. The distinguishing

---

39. Dennett, again, has an answer: we keep an explicit record of personal past so that we can retrace steps and check mistakes. I think that's partly right; it's certainly why it is useful to equip computers with a personal memory. But it's not the whole story.

40. I'm emphasizing the similarities, but there are important differences.

feature of the Pure Lockean view is that it's the chains of transmission that determine the proper subject of past and future directed I-thoughts. The 'I' in an I-thought refers to the connected sequence of psychological states into which it is entered where connectedness is a causal link that supports psychological continuity. The Pure Lockean view doesn't have to explain the 'special access' one has to one's past and future thoughts; what makes a thought *mine* is that it lies within the unmediated psychological reach of *this* one.[41] It's important to understand, in order to avoid shallow objections to the view, that psychological immediacy of the relevant sort doesn't entail either that our pasts are transparent to us or that the information we have about them is perfectly reliable. The distinction between the foreground and background of thought allows us to see that connections that are immediate from a psychological perspective can be underpinned by attenuated causal chains, making room for error and unreliability.

The defining thesis has two corollaries: (1) that the sense associated with "I" or the self-conception embodied in one's explicit beliefs about oneself plays no role in determining its reference, and (2) that there are no constraints on internal relations (i.e., relations in content or qualitative character) between states of the same self. The first corollary leads to a contrast with views I'll call 'Fregean', which allows that self-conceptions play a role in identification; the second corollary leads to a contrast with Parfittean views, which holds that some kind of internal unity is a necessary condition for identity either at, or over time. The labels are mnemonic only. I call Parfittean views *Parfittean* because Parfit held that some persistence of belief, desire, memory, and so on is necessary for identity over time. His account may be a better fit with a richer notion of personhood. I call Fregean views *Fregean* because Frege held that the reference of any term in thought was determined by an associated sense. But he invented some very special kinds of senses to play that role in the case of 'I', and I use the label for views that give any kind of sense even a small role in reference determination. The Pure Lockean regards all internal accord as the contingent product of the external causal and informational links that are the real, constitutive ground of identity. She regards internal criteria, definable in terms of content and qualitative character, that is to say, as neither necessary nor sufficient for identity. And she holds that our beliefs *about* ourselves—'self-conceptions'—play no role in determining the target of our 'I'-thoughts.

---

41. A connection is psychologically immediate just in case unmediated by anything in the intentional foreground, i.e., by anything that is explicitly represented in thought.

11.9 PARFITTEAN AND FREGEAN VIEWS

Against Parfittean views, there is what I take to be the nonnegotiable intuitive datum that I could suppose that my thoughts and experiences have any motley content or qualitative character you please over time without contradicting myself. As a conceptual matter, their being *mine* is independent of any internal characteristics. As for the Fregean view, in its most extreme form, the Fregean holds that we have a defining idea, or set of ideas, that determines who we are. Less extreme versions hold that our self-conceptions play some role in identification. We can avoid questions of which of a subject's beliefs about herself plays an identifying role by conjoining all of a subject's explicit beliefs about herself. No Fregean will identify self-conceptions with the full set of a subject's first-personal beliefs, but if these thick self-conceptions don't play a role in determining reference, then no thinner conception obtained from a subset of these beliefs will do so either, and no way of weighting them to give some ideas larger roles will make any difference. If we can show that the thick conceptions don't play a role in reference-determination, we will have a general argument against the Fregean. But we've already seen an argument of this sort in chapter 1. We saw examples—staples of the literature on self-identification—of people either without an individuating conception of themselves (Rudolph Lingens waking up in the Stanford Library in an amnesiac fog) or with a rich self-conception that is in fact satisfied by someone else (the misguided Heimson who thinks he's Hume). We can make sense of successful reference in the absence of identifying beliefs about oneself—indeed, in the absence of any beliefs except that one is having certain thoughts and impressions—and complete delusion only because the reference of 'I'-occurrences is independent of self-conception. Barring Frege's extreme measure of recognizing an infallibly present, unassailably accurate, trumping sense that each of us possesses of ourselves, and that is, as a matter of *logic*, inaccessible to anyone else,[42] only the view that the facts that are constitutive of identity are *external* to psychological states gets this right. It doesn't matter *what* you believe about yourself, the facts that determine *who* your beliefs are about are independent of content. In the case of indexicals quite generally, it's the external architectural links that are determinative of reference. These are independent of descriptive contents. There's no way of misdirecting the connection between 'I'-uses

---

42. I won't say anything about this view. It has received some defense as an account of 'I', but doesn't have much support, and it's hard to see how it could be extended to accommodate the semantic facts about temporal indexicals without near absurdity. Once temporal indexicals are given a non-Fregean account, there's no longer any reason to resort to these extreme measures. See Burge, "Sinning against Frege."

and their referents by having a mistaken self-conception, because the connection doesn't pass through conceptions. It's not that we don't *have* self-conceptions, it's that they play no role in identifying the target of our 'I'-thoughts, no role in determining what those thoughts are thoughts about. This is why ideas about ourselves are externally constrained; the direction of fit is not from self-conception to self, but from self to self-conception. We've got to fit the conception to the referent of our 'I'-thoughts if we want to get things right. Fregean views get it wrong.

That much is true of other indexicals as well, but in other cases we have, if not an identifying conception, at least some conception, of the kind of thing we are referring to when we use an indexical, in the form of criteria of identity needed to govern intersubstitution. We might not have an identifying description of tomorrow in mind when we use 'tomorrow', but we know it's a *day* we're referring to. With 'I', we don't even need that much. We can be perfectly competent users of the expression without any conceptual demarcation of intersubstitutability context. The rules of use give us a mechanical procedure that requires no restraint on the part of the subject (it says, simply, 'intersubstitute freely'), but still divides 'I'-occurrences into classes of intersubstitutable tokens. If it's hard to see how that's possible when one is in the grip of a Fregean Model, that is, how one can identify and reidentify something in thought without employing an individuating concept, the Lockean gives us a perfectly straightforward account. Reference is secured by the external relations that divide 'I'-occurrences into mutually accessible clusters, informational links that make some 'I'-containing thoughts accessible to *this* one and put others outside its reach—that is, *immediately* accessible, accessible without any intervening experience, they communicate with one another through internal pathways that obviate the need for publicly accessible, linguistically mediated interaction. The boundaries of the self are drawn in this way from the outside. We don't need to represent them in thought to keep from making accidental, invalid 'I'-intersubstitutions any more than the dog needs to represent the length of its chain to keep from overrunning it. There is resonance here with some of Wittgenstein's later remarks. On the idea that we don't confront ourselves in thought as an object, but rather bump up against our boundaries, for example, he writes:

> I objectively confront every object, but not the I[43] . . .

> The philosophical I is not the human being, not the human body or the human soul with psychological properties, but

43. Wittgenstein, *Notebooks*, 79.

the metaphysical subject, the boundary (not a part) of the world.[44]

11.10   NO-SUBJECT VIEWS

Turning, now, to a very different class of views the so-called 'no-subject views' whose popularity in Britain at one time can be traced to some other remarks of Wittgenstein's. Those remarks are worth quoting in full. Wittgenstein begins by drawing a distinction between two types of 'I'-use:

> Now the idea that the real I lives in my body is connected with the peculiar grammar of the word "I," and the misunderstandings this grammar is liable to give rise to. There are two different cases in the use of the word "I" (or "my") which I might call 'the use as object' and 'the use as subject'. Examples of the first kind of use are these: 'my arm is broken', 'I have grown six inches', 'I have a bump on my forehead', and 'the wind blows my hair about'. Examples of the second kind are: 'I see so and so', 'I hear so and so', 'I try to lift my arm', 'I think it will rain', 'I have a tooth-ache'.[45]

He then points out that uses in the first class are susceptible to errors of use to which the second are immune:

> One can point to the difference between these two categories by saying: The cases of the first category involve the recognition of a particular person, and there is in these cases the possibility of an error, or as I should rather put it: The possibility of an error has been provided for.... It is possible that, say in an accident, I should feel a pain in my arm, see a broken arm at my side, and think it is mine, when really it is my neighbor's. And I could, looking into a mirror, mistake a bump on his forehead for one on mine. On the other hand there is no question of recognizing a person when I say I have a toothache. To ask 'are you sure that it's you who have pains?' would be nonsensical ... and now this way of stating our idea suggests itself: that it is as impossible that in making the statement 'I have a toothache' I should have mistaken another person for myself, as it is to moan with pain by mistake, having mistaken someone else for me.

44. Ibid., 80.
45. Wittgenstein, *The Blue and Brown Books*, 66–67.

Wittgenstein draws from this the conclusion that the 'I' in the second kind of use does not really involve reference; the statements into which it enters aren't really about anyone.

> To say, 'I have pain' is no more a statement about a particular person than moaning is.[46]

No-subject views are characterized by the denial that 'I' is a semantically significant constituent of mental self-ascriptions, that is, that mental states, as distinct from corporeal properties, are genuinely ascribed to anything, and the denial is based on the immunity of the 'I' in such ascriptions to the ordinary kinds of errors of misidentification. Aside from Wittgenstein (whose views we also know of from Moore[47]), Lichtenberg and Schlick[48] are usually included among no-subject theorists, but Anscombe's paper from which we took the objection to Descartes, provides the most explicit early articulation and defense of a no-subject view that we have. The paper can be separated into two parts. The first is a defense of the Wittgensteinian inference from immunity to error ("it is impossible that in making the statement 'I have a toothache' I should have mistaken another person for myself") to no reference ("To say, 'I have pain' is no more a statement *about* a particular person than moaning is"). The second is a positive account—wholly original, I believe, with her—of the cognitive significance of 'I'-thoughts.

Anscombe begins by distinguishing two senses in which 'I' is immune to error: (1) the object it refers to is guaranteed to exist, and (2) its user cannot be wrong about what that object *is*, in the sense that it can't be present without her knowing it; she can't fail to pick it out of a crowd. "If "I" is a 'referring expression' at all", she writes

> it has both kinds of guaranteed reference. The object an "I"-user means by it must exist so long as he is using "I", nor can he take the wrong object to be the object he means by "I."[49]

46. Ibid., 67.

47. Moore reports: "The point on which [Wittgenstein] seemed most anxious to insist what that what we call "having toothache" is what he called a primary experience..."; and he said that what characterizes 'primary experience' is that in its case, " 'I' does not denote a possessor." In order to make clear what he meant by this he compared "I have a toothache" with "I see a red patch"; and said of what he called "visual sensations" generally ... that "the idea of a person does not enter into the description of it, just as a (physical) eye does not enter into the description of what is seen" ' and he said that similarly "the idea of a person" does not enter into the description of "having toothache"; and he quoted, with apparent approval, Lichtenberg's saying, "Instead of 'I think' we ought to say 'It thinks' " (302-3).

48. Schlick, "Meaning and Verification," writes: "thus we see that unless we choose to call our body the owner or bearer of the data [the immediate data of experience]—which seems to be a rather misleading expression—we have to say that the data have no owner or bearer" (45).

49. See Anscombe, "The First Person," 77.

Then she argues that there is no sense that can mediate thought and reference while providing the guarantees thought about the self exhibits.

> We seem to need a sense to be specified for this quasiname
> "I".... We haven't got this sense simply by being told which object
> a man will be speaking of, whether he knows it or not, when he
> says "I" ... his use of "I" guarantees that he does know it. But we
> have a right to ask what he knows; if "I" expresses a way its object is
> reached by him, what Frege called an "*Art des Gegebenseins*," we
> want to know what that way is and how it comes about that
> the only object reached in that way by anyone is identical with
> himself.[50]

The fundamental problem is that if to self-ascribe a thought or experience is to make a substantive claim about a relation between a pair of distinct existences—a self, on the one hand, and a psychological state, on the other—there ought to be *logical* room for mistake. Even if we are very *good* at recognizing our own experiences, we ought to be able to *conceive* of mistakes, we ought to know what a mistake would look like. But not even Descartes could conceive skepticism about the owner of his thoughts. There is no way, on the Fregean Model, barring the kind of drastic measure to which Frege himself resorted (i.e., of postulating infallibly present, unassailably accurate, necessarily private self-conceptions), that 'I' could secure reference in a nonmagical way and exhibit the kinds of immunity to error that it does. If there is mediation by senses, the ontological gap between senses and their extensions means there is always logical room for mistake about what it applies to, logical room for having the sense in mind even though there's nothing it refers to or, if there is something it refers to, logical room for being mistaken about *what* that is. If the 'I' in an 'I'-thought genuinely refers, that is, if it genuinely picks out an item in the world, there ought to be, on a Fregean Model, the possibility of both kinds of error. As Anscombe remarks, the only concept through which 'I' could be identified that would guarantee reference in both senses would be 'the thinking of the "I"-thought which secures this guarantee'[51]. But then there would be no way for two 'I'-occurrences to refer to the *same* thing. Anscombe's reaction, like Wittgenstein's, is to reject the imputation of reference. The reasoning is predicated on a Fregeanism that is quite explicit in Anscombe's paper. No reference without sense. No sense. Therefore, no reference. As she says,

> Our questions were a combined *reductio ad absurdum* of the idea of
> "I" as a word whose role is to 'make a singular reference' ... "I" is

50. Ibid., 69.
51. Ibid., 55.

neither a name nor another kind of expression whose logical role is to make a reference *at all*.[52]

The conclusion leaves Anscombe with the problem of saying what the cognitive significance of 'I'-thoughts is. If they don't really ascribe a property to a distinctly conceived particular, what do they do? Her answer is that there are three broad classes of 'I'-thoughts: self-ascription of corporeal predicates (e.g., 'I am standing'), self-ascription of mental predicates (e.g., 'I am in pain'), and 'I'-thoughts with the grammatical form of identity statements (e.g., 'I am Jenann Ismael'). Self-ascriptions of corporeal properties are just ordinary Fregean thoughts about bodies: 'I am standing' has the form F(a) and is true *if* Jenann Ismael is standing. Mental self-ascriptions, by contrast, don't have subject-predicate form; there is no ascription of a property to an independently conceived object. The statement 'I am in pain' is either an expression of pain akin to a groan, or a statement with the grammatical form of 'It is raining'. It is made true if a certain kind of experience obtains, but there is no genuine subject, nothing that is being said to have the property of being in pain any more than there is, in the case of 'it is raining', an object that is being said to rain. As Anscombe says:

> These I-thoughts are examples of reflective consciousness of states, actions, motions, etc., not of an object I mean by "I," but of this body.... [They] are unmediated conceptions (knowledge or belief, true or false) of states, motions, etc., of this object here.[53]

As for the indexical identity sentence 'I = Jenann Ismael', it identifies the human being about whose states these "unmediated awarenesses of conceptions, actions" provide information, the thing in the world that moves when I move, the thing in the world that is being pinched when I feel pinchings, the thing in the world that is situated near the foot of the Eiffel Tower when that is what I see, and so on. So thoughts of the form 'I am Jenann Ismael', for Anscombe, if I understand her, have the same function they do on my account. They provide semantic bridges between experience and thought; they determine how experience feeds into thought and vice versa. Anscombe doesn't elaborate, and one has to interpolate to get the accounts to coincide, but I think this is a fair reading. The central point of difference between Anscombe and the Pure Lockean, so understood, is that thoughts like 'I have a toothache' or the Cartesian 'I think' do for the Lockean, and do not for Anscombe, have the subject as a semantically articulated component.

52. Ibid., 77–78.
53. See Anscombe, "The First Person," 79.

Strawson, reacting most directly to Wittgenstein and Anscombe, advanced an objection to this class of views that is (with a qualification I'll make below) decisive. The no-subject theorist holds that we associate experience with a particular body because of the distinguished role that the body plays in experience and in that sense it makes sense to think of experience as being owned by a particular thing. But he insists that there is nothing to which experience can be ascribed in any other sense, that is, nothing that plays the traditional role of the subject. Against this, Strawson points out quite rightly that it is simply not true that my body plays a distinguished role in experience unless we tacitly restrict the class of relevant experiences to *mine*. The reference to the subject is ineliminable in proscribing the class of experiences in which it can be truly said that this or that body plays a distinguished role. In general terms, experiences have to be divided into equivalence classes of same-subject related events before any association of the sort Anscombe describes between experience and bodies can be made. But no-subject theories are characterized precisely by the denial that there are selves in a sense that would support this division. The question to which no-subject theorists need to provide an answer in order to make sense of their own position, but *cannot* with the materials they've allowed themselves, is: what is that in virtue of which distinct experiences are experiences of the same subject? In Strawson's words:

> I think it must be clear that [a no-subject view] is not coherent. It
> is not coherent, in that one who holds it is forced to make use of
> that sense of possession of which he denies the existence, in pre-
> senting his case for the denial. When he tries to state the contingent
> fact, which he thinks gives rise to the illusion of the 'ego', he has
> to state it in some such form as 'All my experiences are had by (i.e.,
> uniquely dependent on the state of) body B.' For any attempt to
> eliminate the 'my', or any expression with a similar possessive force,
> would yield something that was not a contingent fact at all.[54]

If it is a discovery that Anscombe's unmediated conceptions of states, motions, and so on bear a distinguished relation to *this* body, if relations to her body are not constitutive of their being hers, then something needs to be added into the picture that will provide the unifying principle for her states, something that the no-subject theorist explicitly fails to recognize.

There is one qualification to this: one can consistently hold a no-subject position if one is a solipsist of a very particular sort, that is, if one doesn't recognize any sense in which there can be thoughts and experiences that

54. See Strawson, *Individuals*, 97.

are not one's own (and hence, of course, doesn't recognize any sense in which they can be one's own). To be a consistent Anscombian is not to assert the truth of solipsism, it is to be unable to make sense of the position itself. But, as soon as it becomes conceivable that there are thoughts and experiences that are not one's own, the 'I' in self-ascriptions acquires the status of a semantically significant constituent. If you're not this brand of solipsist and you accept Anscombe's characterization of the cognitive significance of 'I am Jenann Ismael' thoughts (viz., Jenann Ismael is the person of whose actions, states, etc. these are unmediated conceptions), and deny that 'I'-thoughts have any referential role, then Strawson's objections bite. The real question here, the one that engaged Strawson—and even more pointedly, Evans—is how does one go from a term like the Anscombian 'I' (that is, one that is not functioning in the internal grammar as a singular term) to one that makes reference (that is, one that can be quantified over, permits existential generalization, and has all of the ordinary logical implications of referential purport)? How does one go, in short, from being an Anscombian solipsist to having a genuine conception of oneself, and a conception of oneself as a thing among things?[55]

On the Pure Lockean view, 'I'-occurrences are special cases of indexical identification. Indexical identification is a perfectly good kind of identification, and indexical identity statements are (*contra* Anscombe) still statements of identity. They have the logical form $A = B$ and the internal role of establishing links between cognitive paths that converge on the same object outside the mind. What distinguishes them from ordinary identity statements, the kind for which a Fregean treatment is apt, is that one of the cognitive paths is an architectural, non-conceptual one. 'I' shares the semantic peculiarities of other indexicals; cognitive significance is not preserved when intersubstituted with coreferential, nonindexical terms, and reference is not invariant under transport. 'I' also shares immunity to failure of reference in the first of Anscombe's senses (the assured, albeit contingent, existence of its referent) with nonindexical expressions that refer to themselves, and it shares immunity to failure in Anscombe's second sense (unsusceptibility to misdirected reference in virtue of having mistaken ideas) with other indexicals. It is the combination of these features that distinguishes it.

Once the Fregeanism is abandoned, however, or once it is embedded in a view that recognizes the role of architectural links in securing reference, the Wittgensteinian inference (if there is no possibility of failure, then no reference has been made) fails to go through and we no longer

55. Using 'thing' loosely.

have a basis for the negative conclusion. So, the Pure Lockean response to Anscombe is that if the Fregean Model of thought entails that immunity to failure of reference implies that no reference has been made, it is equally the case that immunity to failure of reference together with the recognition that reference has been made implies the falsity of the Fregean Model of thought. And Anscombe's reasoning can be seen as support for an anti-Fregean account. She is right to deny reference to the *expression* 'I', for reasons given in preceding sections, but wrong to deny it to situated tokens of the expression. Those refer, just not in the ordinary Fregean manner, that is, not by fixed association with an individuating sense. There is no possibility of error, and no criteria are employed in securing reference, because reference, in those very special cases, is not mediated by a sense.

11.11 CONCLUSION

I have argued that identification of oneself in thought in a manner that supports reidentification is just indexical identification, characterized by the very special feature that identification is made without any conceptualization. No sortals are employed. There is no explicit identification of intersubstitutability context. No criteria of identity are invoked at any stage in identification or reidentification. We have a term in the language of thought that is introduced by the mechanical procedure (attach indiscriminately to mental states, intersubstitute freely) and functions like a singular term. And if we let the procedure implicitly define the intersubstitutability context, we end up saying that particular tokens of the expression refer to connected streams of world-representing structure in which they are situated. What makes two occurrences of 'I' coreferential is just that they occur in the same stream. How much internal integration and isolation from the environment are required before we stop saying there is a self there or start saying there is more than one? How much unraveling around the edges, or permeability of boundaries can be tolerated without disintegration? How much internal structure, and what sort, is required before we call a self a *person*? Maybe these questions have answers; maybe they remain to be decided.

When a term is applied in this way without application of criteria of identity, any association with criteria of identity will show epistemic signs of contingency. The fact that we identify and reidentify ourselves in a way that leaves it entirely open what *sorts* of things we are creates the powerful sense of separability from any particular properties of the self. If no properties are used in the identification, then for any property P, it is an open question whether P(me) and I can imagine/conceive/coherently entertain the possibility that ∼P(me). These facts can be used as premises in arguments of the sort that we saw instances of in section 2 for the nonidentity of the self with any object for which criteria of identity can be provided. The conclusion that our selves are special, private objects, of which each of us has an exclusive and inalienable grasp, and that are only contingently associated with immanent things, will seem inescapable. The most famous argument of this form is, of course, the one put forward by Descartes in the Second Meditation in his *Meditations on First Philosophy*. And since I have defended him against Anscombe's charge that the argument fails because the purely reflexive notion of the self (to which his implicit definition of the self as that whose existence is made known in the act of trying to deny that it exists commits him) cannot support reidentification, it is worth returning to see where his argument goes wrong.

Descartes begins the argument with the observation that we have a way of referring to ourselves that is guaranteed reference and that leaves our nature entirely open. In his words:

> I who am certain that I am, do not yet know clearly enough what I am; so that henceforth I must take great care not imprudently to take some other object for myself.[56]

And it turns on the thesis that nothing can be true of my self that is not made known to me in the act of thinking

> Now it is very certain that this notion, thus precisely understood, does not depend on things whose existence is not yet known to me.[57]

Schematically, the reasoning seems to be this:

1. I=$_{def}$ that thing whose existence cannot be doubted (i.e., that thing whose existence is made known in the act of doubting that it exists).
2. I can't be identical to anything whose existence can be doubted.
3. I can doubt the existence of anything for which objective criteria of identity can be provided. (Give me a description and I can coherently doubt that it is satisfied.)
4. Hence, I can not be identical with anything for which objective criteria of identity can be provided.[58]

The crucial premise for our purposes is 2. In Augustine's version of the argument, the premise takes the form of the claim that the mind "is

---

56. See Descartes, *Meditations on First Philosophy*, 103.

57. Ibid., 103.

58. See Nagel, *The View from Nowhere*, 35. Nagel is expressing but not endorsing the view in this passage.

certain of being that alone, which alone it is certain of being."[59] The Tree-landers gave us a concrete understanding of example of a case in which this premise fails. It showed us how it *could* be possible to form thoughts about oneself, without having any conception of what kind of thing one is, that is, how we manage to refer in thought to an object of whose existence we are assured, and *know* that we are assured, but of whose nature we are *entirely* and *completely* ignorant. And all of this without the self being anything but a perfectly mundane sort of object.

59. See Augustine, *De Trinitate*, Book X.

12

The Unified Self

> [W]e are virtuoso novelists, who find ourselves engaged in all
> sorts of behavior, more or less unified, but sometimes dis-
> unified, and we always put the best "faces" on it we can. We try
> to make all of our material cohere into a single good story. And
> that story is our autobiography. The chief fictional character at
> the center of that autobiography is one's self. And if you still
> want to know what the self really is, you are making a category
> mistake.
>
> —D. C. Dennett, *Self and Consciousness*, 114.

There is one final challenge to be addressed that I've left until last because
it brings us back full circle to the themes of part I. We've come a long way
from the view of the self as a simple substance lodged in the mind in favor
of a view of the mind as a mapkeeper that stores the information coming
through the senses in an internal model of self and situation that it uses to
steer the body through a complex and changing environment. This view of
the mind makes self-representation one of its principle tasks and accords
it a central role in the intrinsic dynamics of the body. Dennett, inspired
by the increasingly decentralized models of cognition coming out of
cognitive science and by our growing understanding of how apparently
intelligent behavior can emerge from the uncoordinated activity of autonomous components, has taken a rather different view of self-representation. In his view, there are no selves, and although he recognizes the
time and energy that we devote to self-representation, he regards self-
representation as propaganda meant to encourage an external audience in
the fiction of a central controller. In his words:

> Our fundamental tactic of self-protection, self-control, and self-
> definition is not spinning webs or building dams, but telling stories;
> and more particularly concocting and controlling the story we tell
> others—and ourselves—about who we are.... These strings or

streams of narrative issue forth as if from a single source—not just in the obvious physical sense of flowing from just one mouth, or one pencil or pen, but in a more subtle sense: their effect on any audience is to encourage them to (try to) posit a unified agent whose words they are, about whom they are.[1]

There is a genuinely new and interesting form of antirealism here, one that forces a confrontation between the increasingly decentralized view of the mind coming out of cognitive neuroscience and the centralization suggested by talk of an inner self. *You*, after all, are supposed to be the proper subject of thought, experience, and action; and if it turns out that there is no central informational hub or locus of control for your behavior, that will look like a reason to deny that there is a self.

12.1   DENNETT

According to Dennett,[2] if we look to the scientific image of the mind, we find nothing in the head for the 'I' of the internal monologue to refer to. There is no "brain pearl", "Oval Office" or "Central Command" in the brain where the information coming in through the senses is collected and brought to bear on behavior. There is nothing but multiple processing streams, a collection of autonomous sensorimotor subsystems, and nonintersecting causal and informational pathways leading from the sensory surfaces directly into the motor pathways, a motley 'bag of tricks' that neither requires nor supports talk of an inner self. Dennett writes:

> On my first trip to London many years ago I found myself looking for the nearest Underground station. I noticed a stairway in the sidewalk labeled "Subway," which in my version of English meant subway train, so I confidently descended the stairs and marched forth looking for the trains. After wandering around in various corridors, . . . [i]t finally dawned on me that a subway in London is just a way of crossing the street underground. Searching for the self can be somewhat like that. You enter the brain through the eye, march up the optic nerve, round and round in the cortex, looking behind every neuron, and then, before you know it, you emerge into daylight on the spike of a motor nerve impulse, scratching your head and wondering where the self is.[3]

1. See Dennett, "The Reality of Selves," in *Consciousness Explained*, 418.
2. Dennett's views are vividly rendered in a number of places. The penultimate chapter in *Consciousness Explained* entitled "Reality of Selves."
3. See Dennett, "The Origin of Selves," 1.

Dennett tends to put his case by analogy with the self-organizing systems mentioned in chapter 7, systems in which apparently coordinated activity arises from the joint operation of autonomous subcomponents. Just as Evolution eliminated God from the natural world by providing a self-organizing explanation of biological design, neuroscience eliminates the self by providing an account of how separate subsystems in the brain generate coordinated behavior without central supervision.[4]

> The revisionist case is that there really is no proper-self: none of the fictive selves—including one's own firsthand version—corresponds to anything that actually exists in one's head.
>
> At first sight this might not seem reasonable. Granted that whatever is inside the head might be difficult to observe, and granted that it might also be a mistake to talk about a "ghostly supervisor," nonetheless there surely has to be some kind of a supervisor in there: a supervisory brain program, a central controller, or what-ever. How else could anybody function—as most people clearly do function—as a purposeful and relatively well-integrated agent.
>
> The answer that is emerging from both biology and Artificial Intelligence is that complex systems can in fact function in what seems to be a thoroughly "purposeful and integrated" way simply by having lots of subsystems doing their own thing without any central supervision. Indeed most systems on earth that appear to have central controllers (and are usefully described as having them) do not. The behavior of a termite colony provides a wonderful example of it. The colony as a whole builds elaborate mounds, gets to know its territory, organizes foraging expeditions, sends out raiding parties against other colonies, and so on. . . . Yet, in fact, all this group wisdom results from nothing other than myriads of individual termites, spe-cialized as different castes, going about their individual business—influenced by each other, but quite uninfluenced by any master-plan.[5]

We do know that nature is full of systems in which the impression of centralized control is misleading, and we have detailed models of how some instances of these systems work. The jury is still out on whether there is a fully general, abstract characterization of the general phenom-enon of self-organization,[6] but the practice has taken hold nevertheless in fields that range from physics through the social sciences of treating any complex dynamical system (i.e., any system that has parts and whose state changes with time) as self-organizing. Dennett's attack on the self is an

4. "The Origin of Selves" is self-consciously titled to evoke Darwin's *Origin of the Species*.
5. Ibid., 39–40.
6. See my "Selves and Self-organization."

extension of this view to the mind.[7] The mind, on this view, decomposes into functionally autonomous components whose apparently choreographed activity is not the product of a controlling intelligence, but a clever system of feedback and feed-forward cycles that lock components into co-ordinated patterns of behavior. We talk of the inner 'I', on this view, for the same reason that we give centralized explanations of the behavior of termite colonies and schools of fish, namely, because it's a useful fiction that faithfully tracks the gross movements of the body and that abstracts from microfacts that introduce irrelevant mathematical complexity. We tell it to others, and get wrapped up in it ourselves, spinning it in blissful unconsciousness of the complex interactions that actually regulate behavior.

There is much in what Dennett says—both in substance and detail—that we can, and should, agree with. First, there is no question, as I said, that there are systems that look as though they are controlled by a central intelligence, but in which the collective behavior is emergent from the unchoreographed dynamics of autonomous components. And certainly a lot of what the mind does is self-organizing in this way. Second, we should ruthlessly excise the Cartesian bathwater in our conceptions of the mind, and stop thinking of the stream of consciousness as a description of the parade of ideas across a central stage. The brain is a storehouse of information brought in through different sensory pathways, and acquired at different times and places. Information contained in occurrent sensory states that has a fixed bearing on behavior is used by sensorimotor subsystems without conscious•registration. The special narrative module charged with production of an autobiography—which Dennett calls, evocatively, the 'Joycean Machine'—selectively culls information from this cacophony of nonconscious, nonintersecting causal and informational pathways and transforms it into a first-personal portrait of the world that casts its narrator and protagonist in the role of agent. The monologue is pieced together in a highly constructive process that draws information from different parts of the brain and goes through multiple drafts.[8] I

---

7. Termite colonies decompose along more easily visible lines than minds, but it's really the possibility of decomposition into functionally autonomous components that is in question.

8. "Visual stimuli evoke trains of events in the cortex that gradually yield discriminations of greater and greater specificity.... As soon as any such discrimination has been accomplished, it becomes available for eliciting some behavior.... This multitrack process occurs over hundreds of milliseconds, during which time various additions, incorporations, emendations, and overwritings of content can occur, in various orders. These yield, over the course of time, something rather like a narrative stream or sequence.... The narrative stream can be thought of as subject to continual editing by many processes distributed around in the brain, and continuing indefinitely into the future. Contents arise, get revised, contribute to other contents or to the modulation of behavior (verbal and otherwise), and in the process leave their traces in memory, which then eventually decay or get incorporated into or overwritten by later contents, wholly or in part" (Dennett, *Consciousness Explained*, 135).

believe that there is an important and deeply anti-Cartesian revolution in replacing the internal humunculus with the Joycean Machine, and that Dennett is absolutely correct that if we really want to understand what selves are, we should be looking not for an inner self to serve as subject for our self-portraits, but at how a self-centered portrait of the world is pieced together by the Joycean Machine from a set of autonomous informational streams. But I strongly dispute the suggestion that the resulting monologue is a just-so story fabricated for an external audience with no role in the intrinsic dynamics of the body. I'm not interested in reviving the Cartesian picture, but I believe that the denial that there are any selves and the assimilation of human minds to self-organizing systems is at least as misleading. The denial that there are selves is misleading because it mistakes a self-centered portrait for a portrait of a central, substantial self, and the assimilation to self-organizing systems misses the important unifying role that a self-centered portrait can play.

12.2   THE INNER MONOLOGUE

To get a better sense of the content of the Joycean stream and the role that it plays in the intrinsic dynamics of a system, let's return again to our favored example of a self-representation—a map with a red dot—and embed it in a system that Dennett himself suggests, not unfacetiously, as a model of self-representation: a ship that uses a map to navigate.[9] By 'ship' I don't mean just the physical vessel, I mean the whole complex system including the crew and the instruments and the computer networks that support it. I will suppose that navigation goes in cycles; sightings are made and instrument readings are taken; these are transformed—by a potentially attenuated chain of representation and re-representation—into a fix on the ship's coordinates. Those coordinates are fed to a mapkeeping subsystem contained in the main cabin of the ship, where they are plotted together with the ship's targeted destination. A passable route is identified, and commands of the form "head due north at ninety-eight knots" are issued from the main cabin, transformed by the crew into operational procedures that are translated by the ship, in cooperation with its environment, into motion. The cycle then begins again. New measurements are taken, the ship's coordinates are computed and fed to the main cabin where they are plotted against a targeted destination, commands are

9. For a realistic account of navigation from a computational perspective, see Hutchins's *Cognition in the Wild*.

issued and carried out, and if all goes well the ship moves in its intended direction.

Focus on the mapkeeping subsystem, and suppose that everything that goes on outside is invisible to it. The mapkeeping subsystem might comprise anything from a captain with a tabletop map and a ruler to a team of experts with a digital map and a battery of peripheral instruments.[10] Its job in the dynamical economy of the ship is to transform the self-locating information passed to it by the crew into prescriptions for action. The computation it carries out involves explicit representation of its location and a targeted destination of the ship against the background of an objectively rendered landscape, and instrumental reasoning about how to get from the one to the other. A report of that computation would read: here I am now, here's where I want to go. How should I get from one to the other? What routes are open to me? What do I know that is relevant? This computational cycle has roughly the form:

self-location $\rightarrow$ representation of ends $\rightarrow$ instrumental reasoning $\rightarrow$ action

We can increase the complexity of the computation in ways that make it look more like our own deliberative processes by allowing flexibility in destination, balancing of multiple competing ends, and so on.

The first thing to notice is that the 'I' as it figures in the computation is reflexive; it refers to the system on which the map is centered. That will be the ship, the mapkeeping subsystem, or the map itself, depending on the resolution of the map. The second thing to notice is that there's little temptation to view the mapkeeping subsystem as an idle wheel. It is connected in the ship's dynamical organization on both ends, fed on one by subsystems leading from instrument readings and sightings taken at the ship's periphery, and feeding on the other into subsystems that govern locomotion. In the dynamical economy of the ship, the mapkeeping subsystem occupies a central position acting simultaneously as locus of information and control. Its job is to provide the rich representational environment within which the computation that guides ship's motion takes place.

We, too, steer by self-centered maps. Ours are more complex and richer in content than those of most ships, but they have the same form. They are not fictional portraits of an inner subject, but portraits of the world, like maps with red dots, centered reflexively on the body, and—in

---

10. It might even include a computer, for all that's been said, with a virtual map stored in its database. Although there are important differences, we don't need to distinguish here between human machinery and the rest of the physical apparatus. From the perspective of the main cabin, crew members are part of the machinery of the ship.

more articulated versions—on the mind. And they play the same role in the dynamics of bodies that centered maps play in ship dynamics. Consider your own stream of consciousness, or, if you prefer, lift a passage from Faulkner or Joyce. The stream will contain a jumble of ideas, impressions, beliefs, self-ascribed and woven into a developing self-centered portrait of the world. There is a lot of looking around, idle curiosity and voyeurism. We are not particularly discriminate informational scavengers, reading the paper on the subway, picking up *People* magazine in the doctor's office, listening to conversations between strangers in coffee shops, gossiping at work. What doesn't get forgotten gets woven into our conception of history and our place in it, our conception of what's happening in the world and how those events relate to the here and now. There is constant rehashing, reorganization, and reflection. While biking to class you think about a fight with your spouse or an unexpected remark from a colleague, you reflect on the history of the relationship, you reassess your understanding of it. Perhaps a smell or a song evokes a memory that you replay in your mind. You anticipate things to come, think about what you want to do, and how you plan to do it. Maybe you change your mind about reconnecting with an old friend, or reaffirm a resolution not to let work overtake your personal life. All of this is part of the Joycean stream. It's all organized into a coherent picture of a developing world as seen through your eyes, from your changing position in space and time.

The focus is usually outward ("That last bout of turbulence felt funny"), but it can also be reflective or focused on itself ("Why do I worry so much?"). It has both quality and content, and to capture its qualitative aspects, we need to widen our view of phenomenology beyond the sensory qualities that tend to dominate philosophical discussion to include the less clearly defined conative and emotional components that contribute to the full, felt quality of a life. Even Joyce or Faulkner evokes only a fraction of the phenomenological and psychological complexity embodied in a single temporal cross section of a human consciousness. Their genius is to capture in language—a medium that has a dramatically decreased bandwidth relative to experience itself, and a medium that, we have seen, can convey the content and structure, but not the quality of experience—some glimmer of that complexity.[11]

11. Joyce himself gives us an especially vivid illustration of the inability to convey quality. Think of how empty the last few pages of *Ulysses* would be to a ten-year-old. The problem has nothing to do with the difficulty of the language, the child would lack the exemplars needed to infuse the words with the necessary quality.

There is a heavy preoccupation with purely epistemic matters. We spend a lot of time adding to, reorganizing, and revising our maps, broadening their scope and filling in details. And we also spend a lot of time engaging in evaluative reasoning, reconsidering our ends, recognizing new sources of value, and changing our priorities. But woven into the stream of consciousness, in a more or less explicit form, there is the business of deciding what to do, and it is in the business of deciding what to do that our maps are put to use. I didn't include analogues of the epistemic and evaluative components of conscious thought in the example of the ship because I wanted to bring the practical role of self-representation into relief, but these aspects are easily incorporated. They are just part and parcel of the general business of producing and maintaining a self-centered portrait of the world. The Joycean Machine isn't there just to paint a pretty picture for an external audience, it creates a representational environment in which we can bring all of the information accumulated over a history of experience to bear on the here and now.

I mentioned Ramsey's suggestion earlier that representations are maps that we steer by, and I've been using the image of a map with a red dot to convey the content of a self-centered representation. If we fill such a map out with qualitative and temporal dimensions, adding reflexive elements on every dimension, and let it evolve in real time, we have something that more closely approximates the content of the stream of consciousness. But even that isn't enough. What's missing is causal structure. Bodies collide, one thing brings about another, information and energy are exchanged. The mind represents the world as a richly interconnected causal fabric, and represents itself as a nexus of incoming and outgoing causal pathways converging on the body. It keeps track of the changing properties of the environment by monitoring its own causal states, treating them as pointer observables in measurements of external quantities, and makes its contribution to the causal order by feeding the motor pathways that exercise control over the body.

We've talked up to this point about the epistemic components of perspective: spatial, temporal, sensory. We see now the need for a fourth, what we might call the mind's effective perspective. The effective perspective of a representational system tells it how changes in its own state propagate into the landscape. Activity directed at ends demands an explicit understanding of how internally controlled changes of state feed into the landscape. Keeping track of the four components of perspective is simplified greatly by the fact that the body mediates causal interaction with the environment, all that the mind has to do is locate itself in the sensory and motor pathways of a particular body and then track that body's movements through space. The body coordinates the four components of perspective with one another by tying them into a relatively fixed configuration and using subpersonal processing of proprioceptive information to take up the slack. If we changed bodies regularly, or if the connections between skin and skull were not fixed, things would be more complicated.[12] It's an open question just how fixed the architectural links between the parts of the body have to be in order for the brain to be able to extract enough information from its causal states to self-locate. As it is, the fact that incoming and outgoing pathways converge on a body and that bodies travel continuous paths through space places enough constraints on the computation that it is soluble.

It has been held by some, following Kant's lead, that the unity of the self is the unity of a point of view. What we've discovered here is some internal complexity in the notion of a point of view. We're not generally aware of that complexity, because the connection between the incoming and outgoing pathways is part of the fixed architectural background of thought. But we can separate these components of perspective in imagination. We can imagine, for example, having bodies that come apart and move through space independently of one another: e.g., hands and ears that we can remove and send off as mobile explorers or limbs that we keep in different parts of space and control by remote. And we are all adept at the quick imaginative transformations that take us momentarily into perspectives other than our own. While we watch a baseball game, we can jump from the perspective of the sportscaster broadcasting from the booth above—"there's the throw, there's the play at the plate; it's looking like he might make it . . ."—to those of the various players: the outfielder making the throw, the catcher at the plate, the runner rounding the bases, each in his own world of suspended tension, absorbing the actions of others and injecting his contribution where, when, and how he can. Each is mapping a distinct set of experiences and potential actions into a more or less shared conception of a causally structured landscape. Each mind sees its own activity as part of that landscape, and its activity is structured by that self-conception. Of course, really getting into the head of another is much more complicated than simply projecting oneself into his or her momentary spatial, temporal, and effective perspective. Really imagining what it is like to be so and so, and to act in his shoes, even for a moment, is a feat that we learn by degree and with only limited success, for the reasons that I said above. The emotional and psychological complexity built up over a history of reflective experience is so highly individual that it

---

12. Some of these complexities are explored in Ismael, "The Self, the Body, and Space," where the themes of the next couple of paragraphs are taken up. See also, Ismael and Pollock, "So You Think You Exist;" and Dennett, "Where Am I?". Dennett's paper initiated these kinds of thought experiments.

makes us penetrable only to those who have known us for some time, and only, for the most part, at only a relatively shallow level.

12.3 DELIBERATION

I suggested that if we squint in the right way, we can discern steps in the jumbled progression of impressions and ideas that correspond to the stages of deliberation. When you're deciding how to act, you take stock of what you know about the world and your situation in it, and you compare that with the way you would like it to be. You think to yourself "this is the way the world is; here is the path that I have traced through it; and this is the juncture at which I find myself. These are the commitments I have accumulated and the entitlements I have earned. Here are my desires and ends." Perhaps you do a bit of evaluative reassessment: "Are these the right ends to have? Are they weighted properly? Am I entitled to pursue them? Do they fulfill my commitments?" Then you do some instrumental reasoning. You find the causal routes open to you, do some weighing and balancing, form an intention, and act.[13] There is debate about the proper way to understand the volitional acts in which deliberation terminates. These parallel some of the issues about how to understand the content of experience. For our purposes, we can treat them as conscious mental events that, from the perspective of the mind, exercise immediate control over bodily movement.[14]

There are limits to how much we know about the world, and not just because our sensory powers are limited. We're not fixed points moving across a static landscape; our actions are part of the landscape. They change both the landscape and our constellations of cognitive and conative commitments in ways too complex to take full account of beforehand. We have to be what John Pollock calls 'evolutionary planners'. We have to reason by forming partial, defensible plans that are carried out in stages, stopping often to reconsider and reevaluate. The cycle of deliberation is ongoing and simultaneous with the epistemic activity of adding to, refining, and revising the objective content of our maps. And it all goes on inside the rich representational environment provided by the map.

---

13. This can all be modeled formally in ways that reflect both degrees of belief and strength of desire, as measures over sets of centered worlds. It's a common complaint that formal models of decision making have a limited applicability to the real, day-to-day thought that governs everyday activity. That may be. We only need enough regimentation here to recognize that at least some behavior is guided by reasoning that confirms schematically to a self-representational loop.

14. See my "Causation, Participation, and Perspective."

To review, then, on my view, our self-portraits are not portraits of an inner self, but self-centered portraits of an objective world, evolving in tandem with that world, and retaining a record of their own history. These maps provide the representational setting for a computation that steers the body. The result is a system that, viewed from the outside, really does contain an internal locus of information and control, contrasting sharply with the dynamical organization in the self-organizing systems Dennett suggests as comparison. We can do away with the Cartesian Theater, embrace the constructive account of how brains 'grow self-representations', and still salvage an inner hub of information and locus of control. Compare these types of dynamical organization as models for human selves.

Self-organizing system: Informational streams leading from disparate peripheral sources feed directly into separate motor systems. The apparently coordinated behavior of the system is emergent from the collective activity of autonomous sensorimotor components.

System that steers by a self-centered map: Information from disparate peripheral sources is transformed into a unified, self-centered informational stream and passed through a deliberative cycle before being fed into the motor pathways that govern the movements of the body.

Dennettian system: Information from disparate peripheral sources is transformed into a unified informational stream, but the stream empties into the environment. Behavior is controlled by subsystems that bypass the deliberative processes occurring in the self-representing stream.

Dennett's model occupies an uncomfortable, intermediate position between the first two. It recognizes the Joycean Machinery that unifies the informational streams leading from the sensory into the motor pathways, and even goes through the stages of deliberation, giving reasons for behavior, generating prescriptions for action, and representing those prescriptions as causally implicated in the production of motion. But Dennett makes it an idle wheel in the internal dynamics.

12.4   THE MANY VOICES OF DENNETT

Does the Joycean Machine really empty into the environment, or are the contents of the unified stream it generates fed back eventually into the motor pathways and used to regulate motion? Do the mechanisms that govern behavior—not just the beating of the heart, but the voluntary behaviors we regard as our own, those for which we give reasons and accept responsibility—bypass the self-representational loop? I don't think Dennett believes unequivocally that they do. It's an artifact of the richness and the sheer volume of his work that one can find multiple argumentative streams, and it's not always easy to reconcile them. I have followed one of these streams here, the one that advocates the analogy with self-organizing systems, insists that information and control are both thoroughly distributed, speaks as though the inner rehearsal of reason-giving and choice that plays out in the Joycean monologue is a charade, and seems to deny that the monologue plays a role in the dynamical economy of the body. I don't want to play the role of Joycean Machine to the many voices of Dennett, but if I were trying to weave a consistent narrative, this would strike me as a rather discordant stream. When Dennett is speaking in other voices, he assigns the Joycean Machine a central and quite substantial role. It becomes the repository for information, the global workspace in which information is deposited for systemwide use, and the place where opportunistic coalitions are formed by separable subsystems. He writes, for example,

> one of the fundamental tasks performed by the activities of the Joycean Machine is to adjudicate disputes, smooth out transitions between regimes, and prevent untimely *coups d'etat* by marshalling the 'right' forces. Simple or overlearned tasks without serious competition can be routinely executed without the enlistment of extra forces, and hence unconsciously, but when a task is difficult...we accomplish it...[with self-manipulations].
>
> These techniques of representing things to ourselves permit us to be self-governors or executives in ways no other creature approaches. We can work out policies well in advance, thanks to our capacity for hypothetical thinking and scenario-spinning; we can stiffen our own resolve to engage in unpleasant or long-term projects by habits of self-reminding, and by rehearsing the expected benefits and costs of the policies we have adopted[15]

And later,

> the broadcasting effect...creates an open forum of sorts, permitting any of the things one has learned to make a contribution to any current problem.[16]

He even refers to the Joycean Machine at times as the 'control center' of the human organism.

15. See Dennett, *Consciousness Explained*, 277–78.
16. Ibid., 278.

Anyone or anything that has [a Joycean Machine] as its control system is conscious in the fullest sense.

There are passages like the following, close to the end of *Consciousness Explained*, that are in almost full agreement with the role that I have assigned to self-representation:

> Thus do we build up a defining story about ourselves, organized around a sort of basic blip of self-representation. The blip isn't a self, of course; it's a representation of a self... it gathers and organizes the information on the topic of me in the same way other structures in my brain keep track of information on Boston, or Reagan, or ice cream.... The task of constructing a self that can take responsibility is a major social and educational project, and you are right to be concerned about threats to its integrity. But a brain-pearl, a real, "intrinsically responsible" whatever-it-is, is a pathetic bauble to brandish like a lucky charm in the face of this threat. The only hope, and not at all a forlorn one, is to come to understand, naturalistically, the ways in which brains grow self-representations, thereby equipping the bodies they control with responsible selves when all goes well.[17]

Dennett has described better than anybody else the bootstrapping process of self-regulation and internal control that leads to the person-making qualities that distinguish us from other creatures. But, as he himself emphasizes, it's only within the context of an explicit representation of self against the background of an objectively rendered world that the ability to take oneself and one's relation to the world as intentional objects arises. The stream of consciousness is in Dennett's view, as on mine, the space within which self-reflection and self-evaluation are possible, and the Joycean Machine creates that space.

> The aspirant to a high order of self-control must have the capacity to represent his current beliefs, desires, intentions, and policies in a detached way, as objects for evaluation.[18]

I don't know how to reconcile the tension between these remarks and the remarks that advocate the analogy with self-organizing systems. It's closely related to a tension that Clark has diagnosed between Dennett's tendency to insist, on one hand, that human minds are entirely continuous with the minds of other adaptive creatures, and, on the other hand, to recognize that there is something special about the human mind, something that underwrites the matrix of quite specialized capacities

17. Ibid., 429–30.
18. Dennett, *Elbow Room*, 86.

that accrue to specifically *human* intelligence.[19] Dennett identifies language as the source of these capacities. In his view, it is language that *gives* us labels for states of ourselves and of the world and allows us to take the relationship between the two as intentional objects. But there are indications, noted here by Clark, that there is a deeper architectural difference that makes language apparently specifically available to the human mind.

> The rats, hamsters and snakes of the world cannot seem to acquire the [capacity to use words to label states of themselves and of the world] to any significant degree, no matter how hard we humans try to inculcate it. Chimps and dolphins, it seems, do significantly better. But no other animal looks capable of acquiring a linguistic framework comparable in depth, breadth, and expressiveness to our own. Doesn't this suggest, rather strongly, that the crucial cognitive innovation (that special something) actually precedes, and in fact makes possible, the acquisition of human-style language and the subsequent cascade of designer mind-tools?[20]

The tension is resolved if we can see language as rooted in the development of explicit self-representation, not simply representation of the movements of our bodies through a spatially extended landscape, but representation of ourselves and our states in a causally structured network. This much richer representational environment is the context within which the conception of ourselves as perceivers and agents, effecting and effected by events in our surroundings, arises. It is the one within which the distinction between our own states and states of the environment, and between our own actions and events in our surroundings, can be made. And it is the one that is required for the bootstrapping process of self-regulation and self-control that Dennett identifies as the source of the qualities that constitute us as persons. This accords the Joycean monologue a position of quite central importance: information hub, seat of reasoning, locus of control. Full-blown personhood arises, by Dennett's own account, just as it does on mine, out of the process of self-representation.

What led Dennett to deny—in at least one voice—that there really was any central locus of control? The example of self-organizing systems, the insights of embodied cognition, and the success of cybernetics in deploying those insights in designing systems that negotiate complex environments successfully without explicit mapkeeping. These systems use clever systems of direct informational links between sensory and motor pathways to

---

19. See Clark, "That Special Something."
20. Ibid., 10.

generate emergent patterns of behavior that mimic some of the characteristics of mapkeepers. They have limits, however, that emerge when we look not at their first-order responses to stimuli, but at how those responses to stimuli change with changes in situation. The dynamical advantages of self-modeling can be put in a nutshell, and are quite nicely illustrated with the example of the ship. Explicit representation of the situated self allows us to bring the full body of explicitly stored information to bear on action in a manner that depends immediately and directly on the values of self-locating parameters.[21] It adds degrees of freedom that allow a system to adjust its responses to stimuli spontaneously to changes in its situation.

We need to steer a careful path between the inner theater and the ant colony. It is important that we can view the central, self-representing subsystem in the mind as a late addition to cognitive architecture that is self-organizing at the foundation. If we want to view ourselves as naturally evolved creatures, we need to see a line of development that leads from simpler systems to Joycean autobiographers. And we don't want to *un*learn what we've learned from designing robots and studying termite colonies about how much can be done *without* explicit representation. What practical role the self-representing subsystem has is commandeered by diverting causal pathways from other subsystems, and only behavior that can't be effectively controlled by subpersonal mechanisms is usefully diverted. But we shouldn't lose sight of the virtues of steering by explicit self-centered world models. We can find a place for guidance by a mapkeeping subsystem without relinquishing these lessons.[22]

12.5 SELF-PRESENTATION, PHENOMENOLOGY, AND CONSCIOUSNESS

Returning now to tie up some loose ends. Recall the lesson of part I: we steer by maps because it brings all of the information accumulated over a lifetime—not just what we can glean about the world from our own sensory experience, but everything we learn from one another, and from

---

21. For development of this point, see my, "Selves and Self-organization."

22. This is not to say that Dennett isn't right that there is some self-deception—probably a good deal of it—in representing past behaviors as though they were the product of deliberation. Although I think perhaps Dennett is not sensitive enough to the fact that when we give reasons for past behaviors, we are not always presenting the reasons as causal history. Sometimes we are simply satisfying ourselves that there are reasons to act as we did, i.e, that whatever led us to do it, we *did* right. Psychological research shows that people spend more time on average doing comparison shopping, reading consumer reports, and price checking after they make a large purchase like a car than before.

books—into the path between perception and response. The full power of objective representation is exploited when we begin to stockpile information at the cultural level and bend our collective efforts over time on processing and organizing it. It's this whole fund of 'culturally incubated' information, supplemented with the knowledge of our personal histories, that is made available to us in deliberation. The process by which it is brought to bear on behavior—what I referred to in part I as the self-representational loop—involves explicit representation of current situation and targeted destination against the background of an objectively rendered world. It begins with self-locating perception and terminates in volition. From an external, dynamical perspective, we get a smooth picture of the propagation of information through the sensory pathways, into the map-keeping subsystem, and back out through the motor pathways. From that perspective, the transitions are just transformations of physical state. But there is a real question about how exactly we are to understand the interfaces from the perspective of the conscious mind. What form does the external input to consciousness have, that is, how are we to understand the contents of perceptual states? It is widely recognized that conscious experience isn't just an unprocessed phenomenal array, but there is no general agreement about how to characterize its content. And what about the outputs, how are we to understand the contents of volitional acts?

This is more of an in-house matter than others. Readers less interested in the details can move to the Reprise. My conclusion is going to be that we should understand the contents of perceptual states and acts of will as self-locating and self-descriptive. The content of a taste or sound or visual experience, for example, relates the experience *itself* defeasibly to its presumed causal source, and the content of an act of will relates the act *itself* defeasibly to expected causal effect. To arrive at this conclusion, we will need to recall some of the machinery of part I. In chapter 5, self-description was introduced as the descriptive analogue of self-location. Examples of self-description were drawn from written and spoken media included the spoken sentence "My voice on that night was as you hear it now," or the inscription "Her eyes were as black as this ink". We introduced the Strawsonian definition that linked objectivity to the capacity for self-description. A medium is objective just in case the distinction between its own representational states and what those states represent is one that it makes itself, or (paraphrasing) just in case its states have, from their own perspective, both a quality and content. The capacity for self-description is not necessary for using information contained in a causal state to regulate behavior. Nor is it necessary for spatial self-location. Both of these are formal points, easily illustrated with languages. There are many languages that contain no reflexive exemplifying expressions, including some that contain spatial indexicals.[23] Both self-locating and self-describing expressions are, however, needed to be able to put information contained in informational states to *flexible* use, that is, to adjust their interpretation or dynamical role, to content-relevant changes in situation.

Against this background, it's quite natural to view of the contents of conscious experience as both self-locating and self-describing. To have a dog-gish experience is to self-ascribe a causal state that, under ordinary conditions, indicates the presence of dogs. To have a reddish experience is to self-ascribe a causal state that, under ordinary conditions, indicates the presence of red things. The reddishness of the experience is, literally, a part of the content of the experience. It is at once distinguished from and related to the reddishness of the object, and this dual character is what allows it to satisfy the otherwise cryptic-sounding requirement Strawson places on objectivity.

> The point of the objectivity condition is that it provides room...on the one hand, for "Thus and so is how things objectively are" and, on the other, for "this is how things are experienced as being"; and it provides room for the second thought because it provides room for the first.... What is necessary is that there be a distinction...implicit in the concepts employed in experience, between how things are in the world which experience is of and how they are experienced as being, between the order of the world and the order of experience.[24]

The complexities here are tremendous, and there is no hope of addressing them properly. I believe this is the form that the contents of experiences have to have to play the role they do in thought. It speaks to the epistemic role of conscious experience; experience has to be belieflike because it has to act as input to an inferentially articulated worldview. It also speaks to the logical form of the content; the content of experience has to have a reflexive structure to play a self-locating role. It explains the notorious theory-ladenness of perception by entailing that the conscious contents of experience vary with our ideas about the causal structure of the world. It doesn't require any self-conscious interpretation of experience (no inference is needed to generate a content from a phenomenal array), but makes logical room for conditions that defeat the inference to any objective state of the world. It explains why we can't be wrong about the presence of an experience, though its content can misrepresent. And finally, it

---

23. This emphasizes in a different way that there was no imputation of consciousness to the difference minimizing computation described in Evans's Simple Theory of Perception. That was just meant to illustrate the kind of computation that separates the objective and reflexive components of content.

24. See Strawson, *The Bounds of Sense*, 105.

gives us a nice theoretical symmetry: self-description plays the role for descriptive vocabulary that self-location plays for singular vocabulary.

Similar points can be made about willful action. Deliberate activity is, by its nature, activity directed at ends. The content of a willful act has to give its coordinates in the causal order where it can be related to the ends at which it is directed. Just as an experience presents itself *as* the taste of cardamom, the sound of tires on gravel, or a pain in the foot, a willful act is conceived *as* the movement of an arm, the turning of a head, or the arching of a back.

The self-representational loop is the process described in this schema:

$$\text{experience} \rightarrow \text{deliberation} \rightarrow \text{volition}$$

We understand now that the input (experience) and the output (volition) are to be understood as self-centered representational states with both self-descriptive and self-locating contents, and that the deliberative process can be literally and accurately modeled as involving navigation by a map. Now that we have an explicit understanding of what is involved in navigation and a suitably general notion of map, any earlier suspicion that we were working with a metaphor should have been removed.

Let's say that a representational state has a *phenomenology* if its content is self-presenting, that is, if its intrinsic properties are part of its intentional foreground. We can then say that the representational states of an objective medium have a kind of phenomenology that is brought into the foreground in self-description. Since the content of a conscious experience is self-describing, conscious experiences necessarily have a phenomenology; their quality is always part of their content. Likewise, willful action. Although the phenomenology of willful action can be transparent to the mind, any activity that we can bring under voluntary control does have an associated phenomenology. I can feel my arm moving or my back arching, but I can't feel my immune system marshaling its forces against infection, or my kidneys removing waste. Having a phenomenology is not sufficient for being deliberately controllable (I can feel but not control the beating of my heart, for example), but it does seem necessary. We have to both feel our internal muscles flexing and be able to locate them in the causal order before we can use them to effect ends.

We can separate the computation occurring in the intentional foreground of thought from processes that are part of the architectural background. This includes the unconscious processing that mediates sensory stimulation and experience and the processes that transform volition into motion. From the perspective of thought, the effect of sensory stimulation on experience and the effect of will on bodily motions are immediate. The wiring and connections inside the body that mediate those events causally are part of the fixed environment of thought and ordinarily remain, for the most part, invisible to it. The brain transforms sensory information into experience, and feeds it into thought where it is passed through a deliberative loop that terminates in volition, and the baton is passed back to the body where, if all goes well, it is translated into motion.

$$\text{Sensory stimulation} \rightarrow \text{experience} \rightarrow \text{self-representational loop}$$
$$\rightarrow \text{willful act} \rightarrow \text{behavior}$$

There is one more important addition we need to make to this schema. We need to recognize a space for the kind of self-conscious epistemic reasoning involved in scientific theorizing which refines our understanding of the causal structure of the world. Perception gives us self-centered belief, but we reprocess it after the fact to yield the more fully considered, more articulated beliefs. These are the ones that get fed into the self-representational loop we actually steer by.

$$\text{Sensory stimulation} \rightarrow \text{experience} \rightarrow \{\text{epistemic theorizing}\}$$
$$\rightarrow \text{self-representational loop} \rightarrow \text{willful act} \rightarrow \text{behavior}$$

Thought can be characterized in all of this abstractly as the medium in which the self-representational loop is computed. The line between processing done in thought and processing that is part of the architectural background to thought has a dynamical import, but no ontological significance. Everything whose bearing on behavior has to be flexible, and everything to which flexible behaviors have to be sensitive, has to be explicitly represented in thought, so we can expect everything that needs to be deliberately controlled, or is usefully taken into account in deliberation, to be introspectively accessible. That leaves alot of room for processes regulated by mechanisms that bypass the self-representational loop. The body, like any complex bureaucracy, has to find a balance between processes that are monitored by central intelligence and those that are regulated by autonomous subsystems.

I have focused on the capacity of thought for self-presentation, i.e., the fact that its intrinsic properties are introspectively available to it, and the flexibility that a pass through a medium that has this property adds to the dynamical profile of a system. But there is a question about the relationship between this formal property, which we might call 'self-consciousness', and *consciousness*.[25] Is self-consciousness *consciousness*? No.

---

25. Frankfurt tellingly uses the term. He writes: "What I am here referring to as 'self-consciousness' is neither consciousness of a self—a subject or ego . . . the reflexivity in question is merely consciousness's awareness of itself. To hear a sound consciously, rather than to respond to it unconsciously, involves being aware of hearing it or being aware of the sound as heard" (*The Importance of What We Care About*, 162). The remarks occur in the context of discussion of necessary conditions for consciousness. Frankfurt is not himself offering a purely reflexive account of consciousness.

Self-consciousness is a formal, relational property. A medium is self-conscious just in case it can take its own states as reflexive objects and distinguish between their quality and content. Consciousness, on the other hand, in the way it is understood in the literature by people like Chalmers and Levine, is characterized as an intrinsic quality that doesn't supervene on the formal properties of a medium. I remain officially neutral on the nature of consciousness, but we might think of its formal connection to self-consciousness as follows. Consciousness is an implicitly relativized kind of self-consciousness—self-consciousness with the parameter that represents the medium in which it is expressed is suppressed. Every self-conscious stream has its own special generic quality, definable only reflexively. 'Consciousness' in my mouth refers to the generic property of *being mine*, or being *for me*. This doesn't mean that Jenann and Zombie Jenann are both conscious.[26] It means that we both speak the truth when we self-ascribe consciousness, but 'conscious' in Zombie Jenann's mouth means something quite different than it does in mine. When we remove all particular qualitative content, and de-relativize, so that we try to entertain thoughts about the generic quality of being conscious, I'm not certain that we don't lose all content. I'm not sure that what we're left with is not something like the spatial quality 'here-ness' or the temporal quality 'now-ness'.

12.6 UNITY

The real issue just under the surface of Dennett's challenge to the reality of the self had to do with the synchronic unity of the self. His claim was, in effect, that the unity implicit in the notion of the thinking/perceiving subject dissolves on close inspection, as the mind separates into a collection of autonomous subsystems, none of which deserve the title on its own. It should not be surprising that looking closely reveals complexity on the fundamental level. If selves are not to be added to our ontologies as primitive, nonphysical whatnots, they have to be constituted, like everything else, out of more basic building blocks. What we need to understand, if we want to understand the synchronic unity of the self, is what kinds of unity are possible for complex systems in a material world. And which of these does the self exhibit? When it comes to talking about the relations between simple and complex, philosophy has tended to think in

---

26. Zombies have come to play an important role in the literature on consciousness. Zombie Jenann is supposed to be the unconscious physical duplicate of Jenann.

terms of building blocks. Big things are conceived as bundles of little things, and mereology gives us the logic of part and whole. Combine microphysics with mereology and you've got the physics of the macroscopic world.

In fact, this is much too easy. As it turns out, mereology is almost useless for talking about the relations between parts and wholes in dynamically interesting macroscopic things. The reason is that persistence conditions for mereological sums crosscut those for dynamically separable units on the macroscopic level. Such units gain and lose parts, maintaining their structural integrity sometimes by mechanical bonds, sometimes by dynamical bonds that tie them into fixed configurations, moving themselves around and resisting onslaughts by metabolizing energy from the environment. In some cases, the identity conditions for the whole are completely independent of those of their parts. Waves provide an example of a dynamically interesting object that maintains its structural integrity and can be tracked over time, but is by its nature composed of different parts at *every* point in its history. Most physical systems have more mereological continence than waves, but they are wavelike in that the properties that make them interesting dynamical units at the macroscopic level are independent of identity of their components over time.[27] This goes for tables and chairs and rocks as surely as it does for roses and orangutans. If we want to understand how systems like these—real complex macroscopic systems with interesting dynamical properties—relate to their microscopic constituents, we're going to need something more than mereology. The attention to self-organizing systems has given science a new and quite revolutionary way of understanding complexity. This has led to talk of levels of organization and an appreciation of the intricacy of the relationship between 'objects' at different levels. I believe that this is the right framework for understanding the kinds of unity we should look for in selves, but the scope has been restricted by the focus of examples of self-organization. The example of complex systems that steer by maps reveals new types of unity, types of unity that distinguish them from primitive loci of mental life, on the one hand, and from the termite colonies, and schools of fish that have been the focal point of research on complex systems, on the other. I want to say briefly what they are.

A mapkeeping subsystem plays an important unifying role. Its job is to recombine informational streams that were separated by passage through

27. The issue is independent of the challenge to the atomic model presented by quantum mechanics. Even if matter were composed of microscopic constituents of the sort that Newton supposed, the persistence conditions for ordinary everyday bodies would crosscut those of mereological sums of constituents.

the body by mapping them into an internal reconstruction of the external environment. That internal reconstruction provides the representational context within which a self-representational loops is computed. We saw the benefits, in terms of versatility and flexibility of response on the global level, that this unification afforded. There are three related types of unity that emerge from this arrangement. The first is what I will call the synthetic unity attained when information drawn from incommensurate sources are mapped into a common frame of spatiotemporal and descriptive reference. The second is the univocity attained when a set of separate, potentially conflicting informational streams is united into a single, collective voice. The third is the dynamical unity achieved when the parts of the system operate under the command of this single voice.

Synthetic Unity

One doesn't combine informational streams by just having them dump into a common bin. The information has to be sorted, organized, and plotted in a common frame of spatiotemporal and descriptive reference that identifies overlap in content. The information coming in through the eyes has to be rendered in a commensurate form with information coming through the fingertips and ears. Information coming from the past has to be rendered in a commensurate form with information contained in current sensory states. Just as a manifold of sensory qualities (visual representations, kinesthetic sensations, smells, sounds, tastes) is united in the instantaneous conception of a common object, so the whole manifold of experiences is united in the concept of an abiding world viewed through the eyes, ears, nose, and so forth of a traveling body. When informational streams are unified in this way, there is an overall reduction in the number of degrees of freedom. The place about which one is getting information at one time is regarded as the *same* place about which one is getting information at another time. The object about which one is getting information on one occasion is regarded as the *same* as the one about which one is getting information on another. The properties about which one is getting information visually are regarded as the *same* as those about which one is getting information kinesthetically. These identifications place tight constraints on relations between properties associated with different modalities and experience acquired at different times and places, imposing order on the 'bloomin, buzzin confusion' and allowing information to be passed cross-modally and carried across space and time. The phenomenal array is regarded as massively redundant, affording multiple distinct sensory representations of the same information. Once the redundancy is recognized, we can combine information drawn from different modalities, use it to generate expectations (a very vivid illustration of this is provided by the reflection that to a blind man, the sighted person is gifted with fore-sight; she can tell him what he will encounter if he reaches out his hand, that he will stumble if he walks three steps, and so on), and as a check against misinformation (you don't trust your eyes in the dark, so you reach out with your foot or a cane to make sure of the ground in front of you). The objective conception of the world serves as a grand, multi-dimensional filing cabinet where information about a common external source is stored at a common internal location regardless of the time and place at which it was obtained and the internal pathway through which it passed. The fund of information contained in this cabinet is continuously undergoing re-vision and rearrangement; new files are formed, old ones are merged, redundancy and misinformation are identified and weeded out, and the whole thing is organized and re-organized for ease of use.[28]

Something like this integration of information is effected by a detective weaving a coherent narrative out if the partially overlapping testimony of witnesses. Personal time lines and spatial movements are plotted jointly in an objective frame of reference to identify points of contact. The time at which one witness was watching the late show is identified with the moment another saw a stranger in the alley, a bang heard by one is connected to a flash seen by another, and a glove reported missing by one witness is identified with one found later at the scene. The story goes through multiple drafts, information is added where narrative holes emerge, trajectories are contin-ued when they pass out of sight, and choices are made to resolve conflicting accounts. The integrated story doesn't report something seen by any one witness. That's not its role. It is rather a compilation of their contents. Our objective conception of the world is a product of this kind of reconstruction; it is not *given*, but reconstructed by the mind in largely unconscious processes that integrate sensory information. To say that the inner world is a product of construction is not to say, obviously, that there is no outer world. The world of experience is a self-centered reflection of the material world in which the body lives, constructed to guide the body through that world.

Univocity

This process of integration resolves the cacophony of voices in the brain into a single coherent stream. When you resolve a collection of potentially

---

28. And of course, not all of the information that makes it through the senses is passed on to the mapkeeping subsystem and incorporated into the world-model. Some of it is used by subpersonal pro-cesses and never registered consciously. Only information that is usefully combined and specifically relevant to purposeful behavior is selected for inclusion.

competing informational streams into a single coherent stream, I will say you give them a collective voice. The importance of this resolution is easily seen by looking at other examples. Consider the way that elections and referenda turn the cacophony of competing individual voices in a population into a univocal coherent stream. A population is officially polled for answers to questions on matters of public importance and the results of polls act in an official capacity as the collective voice of the people. The electoral process *gives* the community a collective voice. We can speak in a loose and metaphorical way of the voice of the people, but without the electoral machinery that resolves the collection of individual opinions into a collective 'yes' or 'no', there is no truly *collective* opinion. Or consider the procedures that turn the opinions of Supreme Court judges into a single collective opinion, expressed in the form of written or spoken pronouncement issued by the collective. Without a collective voice, there is no collective opinion.

When we say "The people have chosen so and so as their new president" or "The court has decided that the amendment to the law is unconstitutional" we attribute these attitudes to the collective, and we all recognize that the collective attitude bears a complex relationship to attitudes properly attributed to its members. The choices of the people are not mine or yours; they are *ours*. The opinions of the court are not the opinions of Souter or Roberts, they are opinions of the group.[29] Collective opinion need not be any simple function of the opinions of its members. Indeed, in the typical case the process that generates the collective opinion—the back and forth of debate leading up to an election or a ruling—has a complex dynamics involving feedback and feedforward that changes the opinions of the group in a manner that makes it effectively unpredictable. When it is given a collective voice, a complex system constitutes an intentional system in its own right.

The Joycean Machine is the mind's voice-piece. It gives the mind a collective voice. Without it, there is a collection of informational streams leading from the sensory surfaces into the motor pathways, but no whole to which representational states are properly ascribed in anything but a derivative, metaphorical sense. With it, the mind is a unified representational system with a voice of its own. The attitudes self-ascribed in the Joycean monologue belong to the unified system as surely as the attitudes self-ascribed by the spokesperson for the Supreme Court belong to the collective. Does a voice-piece report? I would rather say it asserts, with an

29. Individual members may share the opinions of the group, just as you and I may share opinions, but the opinion of the group is distinct from the opinion of any one or subset of its members.

emphasis on the performative character of assertion. Reportage carries the implication of a subject matter that obtains independently of its pronouncement. A voice-piece *makes* true what it reports *by* pronouncing it. The people haven't spoken until election results are in, and the Supreme Court hasn't made a decision until that decision is self-attributed on behalf of the collective by its spokesperson. Performances of this sort are truth bearing but self-fulfilling. Dennett treats the Joycean Machine as a propaganda artist, like a White House crony that misrepresents leaderless government as a unified agent. The 'I' of the mind isn't a brain pearl lodged in the wetware, any more than 'we, the people' is a controlling agent lurking among the populace. Looking in the population for an owner of the collective voice, or searching on the bench for the one who makes the court's decisions, one will find oneself as bereft as Dennett looking in the brain for a self (or, for that matter, Hume searching through his impressions for an impression of the self).

The lesson of all of this is that there doesn't have to be a controlling intelligence *in* a system to support the attribution of intentional attitudes to it. And if selves aren't added into the world as primitive loci of mental life, this is going to have to be the case. If there are subjects of intentional attitudes, and they are not put into the world by hand at the fundamental level, they are going to have to be composed somehow out of other systems. The kind of unity that is possessed by subjects of intentional attitudes is not given, but achieved. And the suggestion here is that it is achieved by forging a collective voice. In our own case, it is not just the informational streams leading from the various sensory surfaces and from experiential memory that need to be unified, but also the many voices of past selves, each with its own constellation of conative and doxastic commitments. Integration of the informational streams leading from sensory surfaces and experiential memory is something the brain does for us; integration of the voices of past selves, by contrast, is the hard-won product of self-conscious discipline and work.[30]

I think this properly captures both the sense in which I—that is, the subject of *these* self-attributed thoughts and impressions, the thing that thinks when I think and acts when I act—am simple, and the sense in which I am complex. I am complex because I am composed of a collection of subpersonal components, but I am simple because I speak to the world in a unified voice, and the attitudes self-attributed in my personal voice

---

30. The benefits have been emphasized in the literature on moral psychology. We have to be able to trust our future selves to carry out present intentions if we are going to embark on extended plans, and we can only enter into social contracts and relationships if we regard our present commitments as binding on our future selves.

belong to me and not my parts.[31] Voices are not made of voice-parts, and the attitudes self-attributed by voices aren't attributed to any part of the system that produces them. One way of putting this is to say that mereology might give the compositional logic of material systems, but it does not give the compositional logic of voices. A community is a collection of people, but a collective voice is not a collection of voices.[32]

The fact that we treat self-attribution in the Joycean Monologue as criterial for a representational state's being properly attributed to the subject and (implicitly) being controlled by the Joycean Monologue as criterial for an action's being properly attributed to the subject, together with the fact that the Joycean Machine is the place from which the monologue issues, make it tempting to identify the self with the Joycean Machine. That temptation should be resisted. The Joycean Machine is a voice-piece that plays a central unifying role for a collective. But the voice is the voice *of* the collective. To identify the self with the Joycean Machine would be like identifying the 'we' of the people with the electoral machinery through which it speaks, or the 'we' of the court with its spokesperson.

Dynamical Unity

The importance of integrating informational streams emerges from a dynamical perspective. A voice is a channel for the propagation of information. It can mediate interaction with other systems. In a social setting, a complex system with a voice-piece making public assertions on its behalf can acquire the normative status of agent, with all of the public commitments and entitlements that entails.[33] This goes for companies and cor-

31. This leaves us with a vagueness that I'm happy to acknowledge. What exactly are the contributors to my voice? The informational streams that it unifies originate in the environment, and the distinction between body and environment is soft in ways emphasized nicely in Dennett (*Kinds of Minds*) and Clark (*Being There*). We can say the same thing about populations. Who, exactly, is the we of the people? The informational streams that get resolved into the collective voice are attenuated and there is no obvious terminus. There are the voters, of course, but also the people who voters talk to, and the news media and informal channels through which they get information, and so on.... And then there is the question of the collection of parts that is controlled by the government; there are the citizens, of course—the polis, or body politic—but there is a much wider circle of influence affected by more attenuated links, and only arbitrary or 'legislative' boundaries. I think all of these sources of vagueness are present, though largely unacknowledged, in the case of the self.

32. We need to expand our vocabulary for the relations between parts and wholes to make room for collectives in addition to collections and in a way that interfaces with our criteria for individuating objects. There is no uniform usage here. Do we want to say you have new *objects* at the higher level? Or new *agents* but no new *objects*? Or is there some other way of describing these cases?

33. Of course that status can be revoked. Entitlements are hostage to fulfillment of commitments, and who knows what it takes to acquire the status in the first place. Maybe it has to be earned, maybe it's extended on promise to all members of the species.

porations as surely as it does for persons and governments. And when we have a system of collectives communicating through public voices we get an emergent dynamics at the intercollective level: special patterns of interaction that are often not predictable from the laws that govern their components.[34] Again, political communities provide a nice example. Populations band together into national units with governments acting as voice-pieces, giving rise to a dynamics at the international level. Complex interactions involving feedback and feedforward can make the dynamics at the intercollective level effectively irreducible. A collective voice can also have an internal role, feeding back into the lower level organization of the system, guiding the behavior of its components. Think of a committee that comes together to decide its collective activities and then disbands, leaving each member to carry out its part of the collective plan. The parts of a complex system under the command of a collective voice act with a singleness and flexibility of intent and purpose that is impossible for the collection of components acting alone. As a general phenomenon, a dynamical link from a higher level of organization to a lower one is probably the source of most macroscopic order. There are channels for the propagation of information between levels also in self-organizing systems, that is, systems that don't have voices in the sense implied, namely, voices that self-ascribe intentional attitudes. What is special about systems that have voices in this sense is that the interaction between the collective and its components is mediated by a self-representational loop, and hence there are degrees of freedom that there aren't present in systems that don't self-represent. This is just a reiteration of the point from chapter 6.

The unified voice of the internal monologue does both of these things: it allows selves to act as unified agents interacting with other selves, and it also, to the extent that it exercises control over its 'constituency', allows selves to act as a team, making a coordinated effort in pursuit of a common goal. There is a new and rapidly growing literature on the dynamics of complex systems, and I have simplified things greatly to highlight the important ideas. But I think there's a real opportunity here for cross-fertilization between science and philosophy. It is worth remarking in this connection that I have stayed away from issues of social embeddedness, but I am increasingly convinced that it is part of the necessary background of normative intentionality.[35]

34. There is a proliferating popular and scientific literature exploring these themes. For some nice popular discussions, see S. Johnson, *Emergence: The Connected Lives of Ants, Brains, Cities, and Software*; P. Ball, *Critical Mass: How One Thing Leads to Another*; or A. S. Mikhailov, *From Cells to Societies*.

35. Of course that status can be revoked; entitlements are hostage to fulfillment of commitments, and who knows what it takes to acquire the status in the first place. Maybe it has to be earned, maybe it's extended on promise to all members of the species.

When you give a system a public voice you create a space within which epistemic norms operate. Assertions in a public voice carry cognitive and practical commitments that get their meaning in the social setting. It may well be that this public space is the originary source of notions like truth, accuracy, and warrant.[36]

12.7 CONCLUSION

In sum, the synchronic unity of the thinking subject is the unity of voice and agency wrought by the unifying activity of the Joycean Machine. In dynamical terms, the collective voice can have a causal role. Turned outward, it can mediate the communication between systems, allowing them to act as unified agents in interaction with one another. Turned inward, it can govern the activity of the components. There is a lot that is undeveloped here. I've been skirting Kantian territory throughout the book, but here we come right up against it.

---

36. Davidson, Brandom, McDowell, Sellars, Kant, and Wittgenstein held views suggestive of this. The qualification at the end of chapter 4 was a concession to the idea that it might be here, in the social space in which norms arise, that talk of an intended interpretation for thought can be made out.

13

Reprise

"The I, the I, is what is deeply mysterious."

—Wittgenstein, *Notebooks*, 82

Naomi Eilan, at the end of a discussion of the role of the subject in thought that develops the Wittgensteinian analogy with the role of the eye in the visual field, remarks:

> the essence of the account . . . makes the way you figure in the account, as the focal point of your experiences, representationally silent. There is a yawning chasm between your detached represen-tation of yourself as an object and your representationally silent occurrence as an extended point of view. . . . This, I venture, is at least part of the source of the sense of a deep elusiveness of the self.[1]

The remark captures nicely the central problem: how to bring the view from within, on which I am the frame of the world, the unrepresented representer who contains the whole of it, together with the view from without, on which the world is the frame, and I am somewhere inside the picture, an undistinguished thing among things. In the first, the world is in *me*; my consciousness is the canvas on which it is painted, everything from the sun and moon to the most distant stars and the smallest insect. The Wittgenstein of the *Notebooks*, with his frequently incanted "I am my world," was especially good at evoking this part of the picture.[2] This view is also poignantly expressed by the solipsistic worry that there is nothing external to me. In the second view, I am a tiny, transitory center of a universe that extends beyond me on every side. Both pictures are

---

1. See Eilan, "Consciousness and the Self," 355.
2. See Wittgenstein, *Notebooks*, 82.

internally consistent, but together they seem to present an impossible Escheresque construction, each containing the other, confounding attempts to get a unified, overall vision of reality. They seem, that is, to present a pair of incompatible pictures, one superimposed on the other, with the self playing the role played in Escher pictures by the crucial ambiguity (the corner that has to be convex in the context of one picture and concave in the context of the other, or the step that has to go up in the context of one picture, down in the context of another). When we are not capable of systematic doublethink, we resort to an image of two worlds evolving in parallel: the internal world of thoughts, images, experience, and so on, that constitute the living history of the subject, on the one hand, and the external space that those thoughts, images, experiences are *of*, on the other. The history of philosophy, with its swings between solipsism and brute materialism, has been a continuous series of failed attempts to reconstruct one in the other.

The key to reconciliation, in my view, is the reflexive structure embodied in microcosm in a sentence that says "I am —" where the blank is filled by its own Godel number (its position in an enumeration that relates it implicitly to all other expressions in the same language), or a map with a red dot. It is because there is no way of reproducing the reflexive structure in a purely pictorial way that the Escher pictures that come so close to capturing the relationship make essential use of a visual ambiguity (e.g., the corner that goes both in and out, the step that goes both up and down). The self is contained in the world in the way a map of SS213 (the philosophy department office on the campus of the University of Arizona) might be contained in SS213, and it contains the world, in its turn, in the way that SS213 is contained in the map. There are two distinct senses of containment here that the mind relates to each other when it self-locates.

For simple models of the reflexive structure, maps and self-locating sentences serve well enough, but to get something with the complexity of thought, we need to add qualitative dimensions of representation. In symbolic media, we make little representational use of the qualitative properties of the medium. Even when we are constructing maps, instead of using color or texture to represent intrinsic features of the landscape, it is often more convenient to use mathematical objects. We use real-valued functions, for example, to represent continuously varying quantities. The mind, by contrast, makes very heavy representational use of the qualitative features of its states. And it uses self-description to bridge the gap between its properties and what they represent in precisely the way a map uses self-location to bridge the gap between its parts and what they stand for.

The pressures that lead us to view the self, or the individual consciousness, as something outside of the natural order are many and deep, but a surprising number hinge in one way or another, on misunderstandings about reflexivity. There has been too much focus in the philosophical literature on questions about whether phenomenal properties, or consciousness and intentionality are reducible to physics. If we're not looking for reduction, but trying to understand whether we can integrate our mental lives into the closed causal order described by physics, the prospects are not so bad as they have been made to seem. This is a big picture, painted in very broad strokes. More careful development of some particular themes has been relegated to peripheral papers where they can be treated at a closer level of detail, but the full wealth of detail needed to bring the picture into focus will require contributions from many hands.

Bibliography

Anscombe, G. E. M. "The First Person." In *Mind and Language*. Edited by Guttenplan. Oxford: Oxford University Press, 1975.

Augustine. *De Trinitate*. City: New City Press, 1998.

Ball, Philip. *Critical Mass: How One Thing Leads to Another*. New York: Farrar, Strauss, and Giroux, 2004.

Barbour, J. B. *The End of Time: The Next Revolution in Physics*. Oxford: Oxford University Press, 1999.

Bennett, J. *Kant's Dialectic*. Cambridge: Cambridge University Press, 1974.

Brandom, R. *Articulating Reasons: An Introduction to Inferentialis*. Cambridge, MA: Harvard University Press, 2000.

————. *Making it Explicit: Reasoning, Representing, and Discursive Commitment*. Cambridge, Mass.: Harvard University Press, 1994.

Brook, Andrew. "Kant's View of the Mind and Consciousness of Self." In *The Stanford Encyclopedia of Philosophy* (Winter 2004). Edited by Edward N. Zalta <http://plato.stanford.edu/archives/win2004/entries/kant-mind/>.

Burge, T. "Belief De Re." *The Journal of Philosophy* 74 (June 1977): 338–62.

————. "Sinning against Frege." *The Philosophical Review* 88 (July 1979): 398–432.

Carnap, R. *Der logische aufbau der welt*. Berlin-Schlachtensee: Weltkreisverlag, 1928.

————. *The Logical Structure of the World: Pseudoproblems in Philosophy*. Berkeley: University of California Press, 1967.

Carruthers, P. "On Being Simple Minded." *American Philosophical Quarterly* 41 (2004), 205–20.

Chalmers, D. J. *The Conscious Mind: In Search of a Fundamental Theory.* Oxford: Oxford University Press, 1996.

———. "The Content and Epistemology of Phenomenal Belief." In *Consciousness: New Philosophical Perspectives.* Edited by Q. Smith and A. Jokic. New York: Oxford University Press, 2003.

———. "Phenomenal Concepts and the Explanatory Gap." In *Phenomenal Concepts and Phenomenal Knowledge: New Essays on Consciousness and Physicalism.* Edited by T. Alter, and S. Walter. Oxford: Oxford University Press, 2006.

Chalmers, D. J., and T. Bayne. "What Is the Unity of Consciousness?" In *The Unity of Consciousness: Binding, Integration, Dissociation.* Edited by Cleeremans. Oxford: Oxford University Press, 2003.

Chalmers, D. J., and F. Jackson. "Conceptual Analysis and Reductive Explanation." *Philosophical Review* (2001):110, 315–61.

Clark, A. *Being There: Putting Brain, Body and World Together Again.* Cambridge, Mass.: MIT Press, Bradford Books, 1997.

———. *Mindware: An Introduction to the Philosophy of Cognitive Science.* Oxford: Oxford University Press, 2001.

———. *Natural-Born Cyborgs: Minds, Technologies and the Future of Human Intelligence.* Oxford: Oxford University Press, 2003.

———. "That Special Something." In *Dennett and His Critics.* Edited by Dahlbom. Oxford: Blackwell; Cambridge, Mass., 1993. See also his Web site.

Cosmides, L., and J. Tooby. "Consider the Source: The Evolution of Adaptations for Decoupling and Metarepresentation." In *Metarepresentation: A Multidisciplinary Perspective.* Edited by D. Sperber. Oxford: Oxford University Press, 2000.

Davidson, D. *Inquiries into Truth and Interpretation: Philosophical Essays of Donald Davidson.* Oxford: Oxford University Press, 2001.

———. *Consciousness Explained.* Boston: Little Brown and Co, 1991.

———. *Freedom Evolves.* New York: Viking, 2003.

———. *Kinds of Minds.* New York: Basic Books, 1996.

Dennett, D. C. "The Origin of Selves." *Cogito* 3, 163–73.

———. "The Self as a Center of Narrative Gravity." In *Self and Consciousness: Multiple Perspectives.* Edited by F. S. Kessel, P. M. Cole, and D. L. Johnson. Hillsdale, NJ: Lawrence Erlbaum, 1992.

———. "Ways of Establishing Harmony." In *Dretske and His Critics.* Edited by McLaughlin. Oxford; Cambridge, Mass.: Blackwell, 1991.

———. "Where Am I?" In *The Mind's I: Fantasies and Reflections on Self and Soul.* Edited by D. R. Hofstadter, and D. C. Dennett. New York: Basic, 2001.

Dennett, D. C. and D. R. Hofstadter. *The Mind's I: Fantasies and Reflections on Self and Soul.* New York: Basic, 2001.

Descartes, R. *Meditations on First Philosophy*. Translated by F. E. Sutcliffe. New York: Penguin, 1968.

Dretske, F. "Are Experiences Conscious?" In *Naturalizing the Mind*. Cambridge, Mass.: MIT Press, 1995.

———. *Explaining Behavior: Reasons in a World of Causes*. Cambridge, MA: MIT Press, 1988.

———. *Knowledge and the Flow of Information*. Cambridge, Mass.: MIT Press, 1981.

Eilan, N. "Consciousness and the Self." In *The Body and the Self*. Edited by J. Bermudez, A. Marcel, and N. Eilan. Cambridge, Mass.: MIT Press, 1995.

Evans, G. *Varieties of Reference*. Oxford: Oxford University Press, 1983.

Frankfurt, H. *The Importance of What We Care About*. New York: Cambridge University Press, 1988.

Frege, G. "On Sense and Reference." *Begriffsschrift*. In *Frege and Gödel*. Edited by van Heijenoort, Cambridge, Mass.: Harvard University Press, 1970.

Gardner, Martin. *The Ambidextrous Universe: Mirror Asymmetry and Time-Reversed Worlds*. Scribner, 1980.

Gendler, T., and J. Hawthorne, eds. *Conceivability and Possibility*. Oxford: Oxford University Press, 2002.

Haaken, H. *Information and Self-Organization: A Macroscopic Approach to Complex Systems*. Berlin: Springer-Verlag; New York, 2000.

Haslanger, S. "Persistence through Time." In *Oxford Handbook of Metaphysics*. Edited by M. J. Loux, and D. W. Zimmerman. Oxford: Oxford University Press, 2003.

Haugeland, J., ed., *Mind Design*. Cambridge, Mass.: MIT Press, 1981.

Hutchins, E. *Cognition in the Wild*. Cambridge, Mass.: MIT Press, 1995.

Ismael, J. T. "Causation, Perspective, and Participation," *Psyche: An Interdisciplinary Journal of Research on Consciousness*, Forthcoming.

———. "Doublethink: A Model for a Dual-Content Cognitive Architecture." *Psyche: An Interdisciplinary Journal of Research on Consciousness*, (July 2006): 1–11.

———. "How to Combine Chance and Determinism: Thinking about the Future in an Everett Universe." *Philosophy of Science* (October, 2003).

———. "Saving the Baby: Dennett on Autobiography." *Philosophical Psychology* (June 2006).

———. "Selves and Self-Organization" *Minds and Machines*, forthcoming.

Ismael, J. T., and J. L. Pollock. "So You Think You Exist? In Defense of Nolipsism." In *Knowledge and Reality: Essays in Honor of Alvin Plantinga* (Kluwer). Edited by T. Crisp, M. Davidson, and D. Vander Laan. Berlin; New York: Springer-Verlag, 2004.

Jackson, F. "Mind and Illusion." In *Minds and Persons*. Edited by A. O'Hear. Cambridge: Cambridge University Press, 2003.

———. "What Mary Didn't Know." *Journal of Philosophy* 83 1986: 291–95.

James, W. *The Principles of Psychology*, volume 1. New York: Dover, 1950.

Johnson, Steven. *Emergence: The Connected Lives of Ants, Brains, Cities, and Software*. New York: Touchstone, 2001.

Kaplan, D. "Demonstratives" and "Afterthoughts." In *Themes from Kaplan*. Edited by J. Almog et al. Oxford: Oxford University Press, 1989.

Kripke, S. *Wittgenstein on Rules and Private Language*. Cambridge, Mass.: Harvard University Press, 1984.

Leslie, A. "How to Acquire a Representational Theory of Mind." In *Meta-representations: A Multidisciplinary Perspective*. Oxford: Oxford University Press, 2000.

Levine, J. "Conscious Awareness and (Self-) Representation." Forthcoming, Kriegel.

———. *Purple Haze: The Puzzle of Consciousness*. Oxford: Oxford University Press, 2001.

———. "How to Define Theoretical Terms." Reprinted in Lewis, *Philosophical Papers*, vol. 1., Oxford: Oxford University Press, 1983.

———. "New Work for a Theory of Universals." *Australasian Journal of Philosophy* 61 (1983): 343–77.

Lewis, D. K. "Putnam's Paradox." In *Papers on Metaphysics and Epistemology*. Edited by 56–77. Cambridge: Cambridge University Press, [1984] 1999.

Locke, John. *Essay Concerning Human Understanding*. New York: Dutton, 1979.

Mcglaughlin, Brian, ed. *Dretske and His Critics*. Cambridge, Mass.: Blackwell, Oxford, 1991.

McTaggart, J. "The Reality of Time." *Mind* 18 (1908): 457–84.

Mellor, H. "McTaggart, Fixity and Coming True." In *Reduction, Time, and Reality*. Edited by R. Healey. Cambridge: Cambridge University Press, 1981.

Mikhailov, Alexander. *From Cells to Societies*. Berlin: Fritz-Haber Institut, 2002.

Moore, G. E. *Philosophical Papers*. New York: Macmillan, 1959.

Moran, R. *Authority and Estrangement: An Essay on Self-Knowledge*. Princeton, N.J.: Princeton University Press, 2001.

Nagel, T. *The Possibility of Altruism*. Princeton, N.J.: Princeton University Press, 1979.

———. *The View from Nowhere*. Oxford: Oxford University Press, 1986.

Nida-Rumelin, M. "What Mary Couldn't Know: Belief about Phenomenal States." In *Conscious Experience*. Edited by T. Metzinger. Paderborn: Ferdinand Schoningh, 1995.

Parfit, D. *Reasons and Persons*. Oxford: Oxford University Press, 1984.

———. *Identity, Personal Identity, and the Self*. Indianapolis: Hackett Publishing Company, 2002.

———. *Knowledge, Possibility, and Consciousness*. Cambridge, Mass.: MIT Press, 2001.

———. *Reference and Reflexivity*. Stanford, Calif.: CSLI, 2001.

————. *The Problem of the Essential Indexical and Other Essays*. Oxford: Oxford University Press, 1993.

Perry, J. "Thought without Representation." In *Problem of the Essential Indexical and Other Essays*. Oxford: Oxford University Press, 1993, 205–25.

Putnam, H. "Realism and Reason." In *Meaning and the Moral Sciences*. London: Routledge and Kegan Paul, 1978.

Quine, W. "Naturalizing Epistemology." In *Naturalizing Epistemology*. Edited by H. Kornblith. Cambridge, Mass.: MIT Press, 1994.

Schlick, M. "Meaning and Verification." In *Readings in Philosophical Analysis*. Edited by H. Feigl. Atascadero, Calif.: Ridgeview Pub. Co., 1982.

Sellars, W. "Empiricism and the Philosophy of Mind." *Minnesota Studies in the Philosophy of Science*. (1956): 1:253–329. Reprinted as *Empiricism and the Philosophy of Mind*. Cambridge, Mass.: Harvard University Press, 1997.

Shoemaker, S. *The First-Person Perspective and Other Essays*. Cambridge: Cambridge University Press, 1996.

————. *Self-Identity and Self-Knowledge*. Ithaca, NY: Cornell University Press, 1963.

Sider, T. *Four-Dimensionalism: An Ontology of Persistence and Time*. Oxford: Oxford University Press, 2003.

Sperber, D., ed.; *Metarepresentation: A Multidisciplinary Perspective*. Oxford: Oxford University Press, 2000.

Sterelny, K. *Thought in a Hostile World*. Cambridge, Mass.: Blackwell, Oxford, 2003.

Strawson, P. *Bounds of Sense: An Essay on Kant's Critique of Pure Reason*. New York; London: Methuen, 1975. Distributed by Harper & Row, Barnes & Noble Import Division.

————. *Individuals*. London: Routledge, 1990.

Velleman, D. "Identification and Identity." In *The Contours of Agency: Essays on Themes from Harry Frankfurt*. Edited by S. Buss, and L. Overton, Cambridge, Mass.: MIT Press, 2001.

————. *The Possibility of Practical Reason*. Oxford: Oxford University Press, 2001.

————. "Self to Self." *The Philosophical Review* 105, no. 1 (1996): 39–76.

Vendler, Zeno. *The Matter of Minds*. Oxford: Oxford University Press; Clarendon Press, 1985.

Weyl, A. *Philosophy of Mathematics and Natural Science*. New York: Atheneum, 1949.

Wittgenstein, L. *The Blue Book and Brown Books*. City: Blackwell, 1972. First published in 1958 by Blackwell.

————. *Notebooks*. New York: Harper & Row, [1914–1916] 1961. First published in 1914–1916 by Blackwell.

————. "Notes for Lectures on 'Private Experience' and 'Sense Data.'" *The Philosophical Review*, 77, no. 3 (1968): 275–320.

————. *Philosophical Investigations*. City: Blackwell 1974. First published in 1953 by Blackwell.

Index

blindsight, 79

body, 18–19, 26, 41–42, 52, 54, 55, 69, 70–71, 73, 76, 80, 89–90, 151–153, 196, 208–211

bootstrapping, 65, 72, 213

brain, 19, 30, 42, 52, 64, 76, 77–78, 89, 100, 151, 155, 201–209, 218, 225

brain state, 95–106, 130–132, 158–159

Brandom, Robert, 32 n.19, 108, 228 n.36

Brentano, Franz, 75

Brooks, Rodney, 19, 56, 88–89

Burge, Tyler, 13–17

calibration, 28–29, 71–72, 113

Carnap, Rudolph, 24 n.9

causal environment, 110–111

causal feedback, 53, 203, 211, 224

causal order, 26, 31, 55, 218

causal-informational pathways, 4–6, 27, 30–32, 54–55, 66, 77, 201–203, 209, 215

causal-informational relations, 25–26, 31–32, 60, 85, 182–191

causality, 38 n.4, 43, 54, 59, 71

centering, 7, 30, 52, 55, 85, 142–144, 168, 186, 205–208, 211, 215

ceteris paribus conditions, 43

Chalmers, David, 37 n.1, 110, 129–134, 152, 220

change, 85–87, 138–143

character, 68, 71, 130

chiral properties, 117–120, 127–128

CI accounts of intentionality, 27, 32–34, 40

CI links. See causal-informational relations

circumstances. See situation

Clark, Andy, 19, 213

clock tower, 157

cognition, 76, 87, 106, 165

cognitive capacity, 80

cognitive psychology, 19, 42, 52, 73, 87, 201 See also AI

coincidence. See fixed points

collective voice, 224–228 See also voice

color, 6, 60–68, 77–79, 93–105, 109–116, 120, 127, 155–157, 217

communication, 53, 67–70, 78, 91, 121, 131, 148, 172, 181–182, 228

community, 5, 69

compass, 39

competence, 67

complex properties, 62

complex systems, 38, 90, 203–204, 221, 224–227 See also complexity

complexity, 50, 203–209, 220–227 See also complex systems

computation, 52, 206, 209–211, 218

concepts 13–17, 21, 54–55, 60–66, 100–107, 119–121

application of, 60–62, 126–127, 187

development of, 59–66, 69, 98–108

conceptual network, 29, 33, 40, 47, 53, 61, 65, 78, 104, 176–177 See also web of ideas

conceptual relations, 57

conditions. See context, ambient conditions

confinement, 22–28, 34

argument from, 22–27, 34, 66, 104

conscious processing, 30, 41–42

conscious thought, 37, 52, 42, 79, 208

consciousness, 19, 82, 130–133, 151–153, 169–170, 178, 186, 207–208, 216, 219–220, 227–231

content, 6, 18, 22, 27, 30, 33–34, 52–54, 68, 73, 79–82, 94–95, 107, 119–124, 134, 147–148, 179–183

context, 4–8, 14–15, 18, 31–32, 37–38, 42–44, 59–66, 69–79, 83–85, 97, 117, 142–150

context-dependence, 5, 11–13, 54–55, 67–69, 98–100, 150–155

mobility, 4, 18, 53, 64, 70–72, 90
modal argument, 146–147, 157–159
mode of representation. *See* sense
models, 5, 24, 34–35, 44, 52, 84
model theory, 3, 21–33, 37–39
Mom, 172–174
Moore, George Edward, 193
Morning Star/Evening Star, 159
Mother Nature, 6, 18, 26–27, 33–34,
   41, 48, 65, 70–73, 76–77, 80, 135,
   150, 186–188
motion, 29–30, 52, 54, 66, 89, 134,
   218–219 *See also* mobility
motor pathways, 27, 34, 42, 83, 201,
   208–211, 216
movement. *See* mobility
multiple drafts, 204–205, 223

Nagel, Thomas, 8, 69–70, 114, 152,
   178
names, 146–148
natural classes, 26
natural content, 53
natural design, 203
natural language, 11–13
natural laws. *See* physical laws
natural medium. *See* media, natural
natural selection. *See* evolution
navigation, 5–7, 30, 52–56, 69, 85,
   88, 201–211, 221
network, 5, 29, 40, 50, 65, 154
   conceptual, 29, 33, 40, 47, 53, 61,
      65, 78, 104, 176–177
   inferential, 16, 79, 176–180
   representational, 25, 75, 102
nexus of information, 19, 55
Nida-Rumelin, Martine, 95, 96 n.5,
   102, 112
no-subject views, 192–198
nomological relations, 55, 130–132
   See also physical laws
normal conditions. *See* standard
   conditions
Now, 142–144, 149, 153
now-thought, 14–15

objective purport. *See* intentionality
objects, 4–5, 13–17, 21–22, 35–42, 68,
   80–81, 118
observation, 99, 107, 170
ontology, 38, 57, 121–123, 134–135, 143,
   166, 220
opacity, 80–81
ostension. *See* demonstrative
   identification

parameters, 16, 62–66, 70–73, 77,
   84–85, 115, 122
pathways. *See* causal-informational
   pathways
perception, 8, 18, 55, 69, 115, 165, 170,
   217–219
perception to action pathways, 8,
   17–18, 26, 30–33, 37, 51–56, 76,
   84, 175, 215
perceptual guidance, 52, 80
Perry, John, 8, 17–19, 21, 59, 64, 68,
   96 n.5, 99, 103, 171, 181
perspective, 52, 56, 81–82, 89, 115,
   124, 127–128, 144, 151–153,
   206–210, 216
   effective, 208–209
   meta-, 81–82
phenomenal concepts, 23, 56–57
phenomenal content, 102, 120–123,
   126, 134
phenomenal eliminativism, 125–126,
   129
phenomenal profile, 47–55, 61–67,
   72–77, 96–106, 114–116, 120,
   124–126, 150
phenomenal realism, 125–129, 135
phenomenal similarity, 56–57,
   110–115, 127
phenomenal state, 19, 41, 50, 54, 59,
   71, 79, 98, 101, 106, 127–129,
   155–159
phenomenal vocabulary, 98,
   112–114, 123
philosophy of mind, 3–4, 12,
   75, 90

representational apparatus, 53, 66, 70–71, 75, 103
representational media. *See* media, representational
representational network. *See* network, representational
representationalism, 11–20, 39
Rip Van Winkle, 14–15, 168
robotics, 19, 56, 88–89, 215
robustness, 65, 67, 80, 90, 105
Russell, Bertrand, 166

Schlick, Moritz, 193
schmausation, 25–32
self, 3–8, 83, 89–91, 145, 150–153, 163–166 *See also* unity of self
self-consciousness, 50, 217–220, 225
self-description, 45–57, 75, 79, 104–109, 112, 121, 126, 156, 216–218
self-design, 72
self-identification, 189–190, 197
self-location, 4, 29–34, 45–47, 52–56, 71–72, 84–87, 100–104, 115–116, 151–153, 186, 206–209, 215–218, 230
self-organization, 7, 55, 79, 88–89, 203–215, 221, 227
self-presentation, 46–50, 53, 79, 100, 217–219
self-reference, 30, 34, 164 *See also* self-reference
self-regulation. *See* self-organization
self-representation. *See* representation, self
self-representational loop, 52–56, 77–78, 84, 88, 90, 211, 216–219, 227
self-transformation, 81–82
Sellars, Wilfrid, 60–62, 65–66, 98, 228 n.36
semantic ascent, 29
semantic descent, 29, 46, 34, 176
semantic relations, 29–30, 33–35, 50–55, 65, 97, 107, 148, 181

sense, 12–15, 21–22, 99, 189, 194, 197
sensory information, 78–80
sensory pathways, 42, 53, 77, 204, 208–209, 216
sensory states, 4–7, 54, 73, 77, 203
sensory surfaces, 42, 49, 64, 77, 201
ship, 40–41, 52, 85, 106, 205–208
Shoemaker, Sydney, 110
signals, 4, 42, 54, 73, 76–78, 88, 182
similarity, 120–123, 178 *See also* phenomenal similarity
simple theory of perception, 52, 216 n.23 *See also* Evans
simultaneity, 123–124
singular terms, 101, 144, 149–153, 172, 197–198, 217
situated representation. *See* representation, situated
situation, 5, 17, 31, 34, 54, 60–65, 67, 68, 77, 83–85, 90, 97
social environment, 5, 44, 67, 226
sortal, 167–168, 197
space, 18, 25, 52, 54, 57, 66, 70–73, 80, 116–118, 122, 143–150, 157
of causes, 107–108, 120–121
of concepts, 120–121
of reasons, 107–108
spatial cognition, 52
spatial indexicals. *See* here-thought
spatiotemporal context, 47, 53, 66, 70, 115–116
spatiotemporal frame of reference, 52, 121–123, 222
spatiotemporal parameters, 70–73, 116, 133
spatiotemporal vocabulary, 45–46, 113, 119, 123–124, 146–148
speed, 85
standard conditions, 64, 96–101
steering. *See* navigation
storage of information, 19, 78, 84, 201–204, 214 *See also* memory
Strawson, Sir Peter, 16, 82, 166, 169, 196–197, 216–217